MW01052670

# DESISTANCE FROM SEX OFFENDING

# Desistance from Sex Offending

## *Alternatives to Throwing Away the Keys*

**D. Richard Laws**
**Tony Ward**

THE GUILFORD PRESS
*New York London*

A Division of Guilford Publications, Inc.
72 Spring Street, New York, NY 10012
www.guilford.com



Printed in the United States of America

This book is printed on acid-free paper.

Last digit is print number: 9 8 7 6 5 4 3 2 1

**Library of Congress Cataloging-in-Publication Data**

Laws, D. Richard.
Desistance from sex offending : alternatives to throwing away the keys / D. Richard Laws, Tony Ward.
p. cm.
Includes bibliographical references and index.
ISBN 978-1-60623-935-3 (hbk.: alk. paper)
1. Sex offenders—Rehabilitation. 2. Sex offenders—Services for. 3. Sex crimes—Prevention. I. Ward, Tony, 1954 Mar. 17– II. Title.
HV6556.L39 2011
365′.6672—dc22

2010027960

*To my wife, Cynthia Mills,*
*who offered encouragement and support throughout,*
*and to the late Harris B. Rubin, who introduced me*
*to the study of human sexual behavior*
*and taught me how to write like a professional*

*—D. R. L.*

*To my late father-in-law, John A. Stewart,*
*a man of integrity and compassion*

*—T. W.*

# About the Authors

**D. Richard Laws, PhD,** is Codirector of the Pacific Psychological Assessment Corporation (PPAC) and Director of Pacific Design Research, which serves as a development arm of PPAC. Dr. Laws holds appointments at Simon Fraser University (Canada) and the University of Birmingham (United Kingdom). His research interests center primarily on development of assessment procedures for offenders. He is the author of numerous journal articles, book chapters, and scholarly essays, and coeditor/coauthor of a number of books and manuals.

**Tony Ward, PhD,** is Head of School and Professor of Clinical Psychology at Victoria University of Wellington, New Zealand. His research interests include cognition in offenders, rehabilitation and reintegration processes, and ethical issues in forensic psychology. He has published extensively in these areas and has over 280 academic publications.

# Preface

Human beings are creatures of habit and tend to seek the path of least resistance when it comes to understanding the world around them and getting on with their lives. We can figure out the simple things by ourselves—what to eat, what to wear, and how to organize our finances. There are also the big questions, foundational issues about the meaning of life and other major life issues. In these matters we too easily accept the truth as it is told to us by others we acknowledge as experts or who have the assigned authority to provide advice about what to think and how to act.

The area of crime and sex offender treatment is no different. Lay people defer to political and therapeutic experts and accept their suggestions and advice concerning how to manage sex offenders. The experts tell us that these dangerous individuals must be assessed, their predilections for harmful behavior identified and scientifically treated. There is no easy way forward, they assure us; there is only the careful measurement of dispositions and behavior and the all-too-frequent verdict that such men and sometimes women are beyond hope. We therefore look to protect ourselves from sex offenders, keeping them securely locked up somewhere far away from our houses, schools, and communities. To be safe, to ensure danger does not lurk around the corner, we are told to put barriers between them and us. These barriers are legal, social, ethical, and physical.

The trouble is that in the case of offenders in general and sex offenders in particular, the experts are victims of their own myopia. They have their own blind spots that blur the truth into simple images and pat answers while hard facts and scientific evidence are overtaken by dogma, ideology, and ethical assumptions. The question of whether, in fact, sex offenders should be contained, managed, and locked away, however, remains unanswered and unaddressed.

But if we listen carefully to the whispers in the periphery of the scientific community, dissenting voices to the established viewpoint of how to treat sex offenders are now emerging. Such voices raise questions and ask us to think about what we have in common with those who hurt us. And such voices remind us that human beings share common needs, and each of us carries within us a spark of humanity, a sliver of value that means we all merit respect and a chance to belong no matter what wrong we have done.

These whispers can now be heard in every discipline but are particularly evident in criminology and its sister disciplines of law and sociology. This book seeks to listen to the messages of such scholars, and it seeks to understand just how offenders can make good by what they do to turn their lives around. This book provides a space to think differently about treatment, reintegration, reentry, rehabilitation, and punishment. It asks: What do we owe those who have harmed us? How can we help them to come back to us once they have paid their dues? It is far too easy to categorize sex offenders simply as individuals marred by deviancy and cruelty. The science of sex offender treatment needs to be broader, more flexible, and open to conversations with other disciplines.

This book represents our attempt to create a bridge between criminology, psychology, and correctional practice, and how they address the treatment of sex offenders. It is only a beginning for this much-needed discussion, however, but a beginning it is.

D. RICHARD LAWS and TONY WARD

# Acknowledgments

**D. Richard Laws:** I would like to thank a number of individuals and institutions that played critical roles in the development of my thinking and the formation of this book: Richard Packard, who first introduced me to the criminological approach to desistance and, in particular, the works of Sheldon and Eleanor Glueck and Robert Sampson and John Laub; Shadd Maruna, who generously served as a guide to the necessary portions of the criminological literature; Shawn Bushway, who provided an excellent description of trajectory analysis and a figure illustrating the results; Howard Barbaree, Robert Sampson, John Laub, and Shadd Maruna, for providing figures describing their research; Harvard University Press, Sage Publications, Springer Publications, and Wiley–Blackwell Publications, for permission to reprint figures and lengthy excerpts; Jim Nageotte of The Guilford Press, who served as our editor and guide throughout the preparation of this book; and last, but not least, my coauthor, Tony Ward, whose pioneering theoretical and practical work has changed my mind on a number of social and psychological issues.

**Tony Ward:** I would like to thank the following people for their support and intellectual companionship over the years: Tony Beech, James Bickley, Astrid Birgden, Mark Brown, Sharon Casey, Rachael Collie, Marie Connolly, Joy Creet, Andy Day, Hilary Eldridge, Dawn Fisher, Theresa Gannon, Brian Haig, the late Chris Heeney, Sonia Heeney, the late Steve Hudson, Robyn Langlands, Ruth Mann, Shadd Maruna, Bill Marshall, Mayumi Purvis, Karen Salmon, Doug Shaw, Claire Stewart, Richard

Siegert, Jim Vess, Alex Ward, Kalya Ward, Nathaniel Ward, Nick Ward, Carolyn Wilshire, and Pamela Yates. I would also like to thank Mayumi Purvis for allowing me to use Table 6 (Figure 15.1 in this book) from her PhD thesis; Taylor & Francis Group (Routledge) for giving permission to use material from Chapter 5 of my coauthored (with Shadd Maruna) book *Rehabilitation: Beyond the Risk Paradigm* (2007) in Chapter 14 of this book; and Ioan Durnescu, editor of the *European Journal of Probation*, for allowing me to use material from my article "Dignity and Human Rights in Correctional Practice," published in this journal (2009, Vol. 1, pp. 110–123), in Chapter 16 of this book. Finally, I would like to thank my coauthor, Richard Laws, for his friendship, intellectual clarity, fierce dedication to the truth, and, above all, his insistence that researchers should ask the hard questions and never settle for the easy ones.

# Contents

## IV. Reentry and Reintegration



## V. Recruitment



## VI. Desistance-Focused Intervention



## VII. Where to from Here?

Offenders differ from nonoffenders only in their tendency to offend.

—Gottfredson and Hirschi,
*A General Theory of Crime* (1990)

Damascene conversions may happen for a few, but . . . for many people, the progression is faltering, hesitant and oscillating.

—Bottoms et al., *Towards Desistance: Theoretical Underpinnings for an Empirical Study* (2004)

A study of the present that neglects the processes of change by which the present was created is necessarily superficial.

—Thernstrom, *The Other Bostonians* (1973)

Le penchant au crime, vers l'age adulte, croît assez rapidement; it atteint un maximum et décroît ensuite jusqu'aux dernières limites de la vie.

—Quételet, *Sur l'Homme et le Développement de ses Facultés, ou Essai de Physique Sociale* (1836)

# I

# GENERAL ISSUES

## Chapter 1

# Introduction

The primary subject matter of this book is encouraging and maintaining desistance from crime in sex offenders. All formal legal structures (probation, parole) and more informal structures such as treatment interventions with this clientele have desistance from future criminal activity as their goal. The book provides information from two areas of current investigation: desistance from criminal behavior and the Good Lives Model (GLM) of offender rehabilitation. The former comes to us from criminology and the latter from behavioral psychology. Although representing different social science disciplines, they are intertwined and have a theoretical resonance. Our main focus will be upon a unique and generally dreaded clientele: sexual offenders. Much of what we have to say will apply equally well to general criminal offenders.

Over 25 years ago the first author made the following observations:

> The theoretical physicist Robert Oppenheimer once said, "If you are a scientist you believe that it is a good thing to find out how the world works." Using the methods of science, we have found out a little about how the world of deviant sexuality works. . . . We believe in the power of the scientific method to throw light into some of the darker recesses of human behavior, to dispel ignorance. In those dark recesses, we will doubtless find that we resemble more than we wish those sexual outlaws whom we have scorned and labeled deviants. We will find that in matters sexual, the human being is a rather fallible and malleable organism, that in the end perhaps all of us have some capacity for loathsome acts. (Laws & Osborn, 1983, pp. 233–234)

And, indeed, that prediction has been proven accurate. The majority of apprehended first-time sex offenders are not lifetime sexual deviants and many do not have an official criminal background. A recent study of young adult *nonoffenders* (Williams, Cooper, Howell, Yuille, & Paulhus, 2009) reported that, in their sample, 95% of the respondents admitted to having at least one deviant sexual fantasy, and 74% reported engaging in at least one deviant sexual behavior. It is thus possible that deviant sexual activity is a considerably broader problem than is currently recognized. It is important to remember that sexual offending has a very low base rate (i.e., it occurs infrequently). For example, the Bureau of Justice Statistics (BJS) reported that rape and sexual assault accounted for only 1% of all violent crimes reported in 2004 (K. Bumby, personal communication, April 7, 2009). Our intent is not to minimize the societal problem, nor to suggest that some sex offenders are not very dangerous persons. "Wicked people exist," observed political scientist James Q. Wilson (1985, p. 193). "Nothing avails except to set them apart from innocent people" (p. 235). This is undeniably true but there is a considerable body of evidence indicating that they represent a tiny minority of serious criminal offenders. The majority of sex offenders are not the rampaging monsters that some politicians and the media would have us believe.

Second, the present authors have, collectively, over a half century of experience with sex offenders. We have been struck repeatedly with the realization that these offenders, with a very few exceptions, are far from extraordinary. For the most part they, like us, come from rather unexceptional backgrounds. Most of them, apart from their sexual deviance, are not criminals. They hunger for the same things that we all do: a good education, a decent job, good friends, home ownership, family ties, children, being loved by someone, and having a stable life. They are, without question, people very much like us. And given that acknowledgment, it is incumbent upon us as professionals to try to help them achieve their longed-for goals, what the second author will call "primary goods." Ward and Marshall (2007) capture this theme nicely:

> Offenders, like all other people, attempt to secure beneficial outcomes such as good relationships, a sense of mastery, and recognition from others that they matter. . . . [O]ffending can reflect the search for certain kinds of experience, namely, the attainment of specific goals or goods. Furthermore, offenders' personal strivings express their sense of who they are and what they would like to become. . . . This feature of offending renders it more intelligible and, in a sense, more human. It reminds us that effective treatment should aim to provide alternative means for achieving human goods. (p. 297)

There is a third, ethical consideration, that we think particularly relevant as well. According to the ethical universalism we embrace, all human beings possess inherent value and dignity simply because they are fellow human beings (see Chapter 16). This dignity is based on the capacity to act autonomously and to fashion a life based on individuals' personally endorsed goals. A basic implication of the inherent dignity of all human beings is that each of us has certain entitlements and obligations. Essentially these are rights to certain well-being and freedom goods, and, correspondingly, a duty to respect the entitlements of fellow members of the moral community. To hold offenders accountable to the norms of a society always implies accepting their rights to recognition and respectful treatment, and a chance to regain our trust and to reenter society once they have undergone punishment. You cannot have it both ways: if offenders are to be held accountable and punished for their actions, they should also be treated with respect when undergoing punishment and when entering treatment programs. They should not be regarded merely as objects to be manipulated for our ends. They are people like us in that they also have intrinsic value and are part of the moral community.

## Desistance

The concept of desistance has many definitions. It has been described, for example, as a self-reported complete termination of criminal behavior, a cessation of official citations for criminal behavior, a gradual slowing down of criminal behavior, and a marked decrease in the frequency, intensity, and seriousness of criminal behavior. As we shall see, there are many other definitions. The definitions we find most appealing state that desistance is not an event, but a process replete with lapses, relapses, and recoveries, quite similar to the addiction relapse prevention model originally espoused by Marlatt and Gordon (1985). In criminology we find this position echoed in the work of Maruna (2001) and Laub and Sampson (2001, 2003). Desistance research, which is primarily descriptive, seeks to understand the change processes that are associated with individuals turning away from lives of crime and becoming reintegrated into the community (McNeill, Batchelor, Burnett, & Knox, 2005).

Professionals as well as ordinary citizens have difficulty with the notion of desistance, particularly as it applies to offenders widely believed to be incorrigible and incurable. In our view, this reluctance to embrace the application of desistance ideas to sexual offenders is partly grounded in a reductionistic view of offenders as self-contained deviancy machines. That is, offenders are conceptualized as independent centers of malevolence comprising faulty structures and processes that require external management and constant surveillance. As will become evident later in the book, we believe this view is empirically unsustainable and ethically problematic. Moreover, Maruna (2001) reminds us that this belief in incorrigibility does not fit one of the best established empirical findings in criminology: sooner or later, *almost everyone participating in serious criminal activity gives it up and quits.* This is not a contemporary finding but has been observed for nearly 180 years (Gottfredson & Hirschi, 1990; Quételet, 1831/1984). In the past 70 years this declining age–crime curve has been carefully examined and found to apply to offenders of all types (Glueck & Glueck, 1950, 1968; Laub & Sampson, 2003; Sampson & Laub, 1993). The relationship between age and decreased criminal risk has been observed in sex offenders (Barbaree, 2006; Barbaree & Blanchard, 2008; Fazel, Sjöstedt, Långström, & Grann, 2006; Hanson, 2002, 2006; Thornton, 2006), although for reasons other than the study of desistance.

The most common treatment presently used with sex offenders is some form of cognitive-behavioral therapy (CBT; see, e.g., Marshall, Anderson, & Fernandez, 1999; Marshall, Fernandez, Marshall, & Serran, 2006). The conventional wisdom in the field states that treatment effects should be able to be detected 5 years after treatment completion. Meta-analyses of treatment outcome with sex offenders often report follow-ups at 5 or more years posttreatment. The problem with these "follow-ups" is that the data are most often obtained from official records (rap sheets), not from intensive interviews with treated offenders.

The problem with long-term reports, it seems to us, is the apparent underlying assumption that a treatment process that occupies, say, a couple of hours per week for 6 months to 2 years on average is going to produce such a profound intrapersonal impact that the effects can still be felt 10 years later or longer. That makes no sense to us. Something else must be happening to produce long-term effects, and it is to understand that something else that this book is directed. One possibility is that treatment equips offenders with the resources to engage with the social world and to capitalize on the opportunities to live better lives that it contains.

We might be far better off to direct our efforts to facilitating the natural processes of desistance from crime and reinforce the securing of primary goods by lawful and civil means. These statements should not be interpreted to mean that we are giving up on treatment. Far from it, as the following chapters show. However, we think it is essential to stress the idea that treatment is simply one piece of the desistance puzzle, and not necessarily the most important one.

Table 1.1 displays two rather strongly opposed views of two major paradigms for work with offenders in general (McNeill, 2004). There are two normative frameworks evident in the criminal justice system: a response to criminal behavior as opposed to the rehabilitation of offenders. Although ethical and welfare-enhancing values exist in each approach, they are weighted differently. The correctional response to crime is more grounded in ethical values (i.e., justice) and is a punishment-oriented approach. The welfarist response is more grounded in a rehabilitation approach.

One might say that the welfarist side is soft on crime while the correctional side is very tough on crime, but closer examination shows that there is considerable overlap between the categories. We find ourselves drawn to both sides of this argument. Each of the authors has long expe-

**TABLE 1.1. Welfarist versus Correctional Paradigms**

| | Welfarist rehabilitation | Correctional treatment |
|---|---|---|
| Causes of crime | Primarily structural: social and economic | Primarily individual/ familial |
| Responsibility for crime | Primarily the state's | Primarily the offender's |
| Characterization of the criminal | Unfortunate individual for whom assistance is required | One of a deficient and/ or dangerous group (classified by risk) from whom society is to be protected |
| Characterization of the practice response | Offender-oriented assistance and protection from further damage by the "system" | Public-oriented punishment, management, and treatment |
| Characterization of rehabilitation | Rights-based restoration of citizenship | Utilitarian reeducation for citizenship |
| Practice focus | Diversion from custody, practical help, advocacy, seeking opportunities | Enforcing punishment, managing risk, developing skills through (enforced) treatment |
| Intended outcomes | Reintegration of the offender | Punishment of the offender and protection of the public |

*Note.* From McNeill (2004, p. 424). Copyright 2004 by Wiley–Blackwell Publications. Reprinted by permission.

rience with dangerous offenders and we find much to support in the correctional treatment argument. However, we have also come to recognize that a strict regime such as the correctionalists propose misses much of what is essential in promoting human welfare. Therefore we strongly agree with much of the welfarist rehabilitation argument to supplement the best elements of correctional treatment.

Some readers will find our disagreement with some of the correctionalist agenda troubling. Is there something wrong in identifying dangerous people? In assessing risk? In managing that risk and enforcing public safety? The answer, of course, is no, there is nothing wrong in any of that. What troubles us is the reigning obsession with assessing risk and managing criminogenic need to the exclusion of everything else that could prove useful in rehabilitation of offenders. McNeill (2004) has spoken eloquently to this issue*:

> The methodology of the meta-analyses used to generate evidence about "what works" necessarily produce generalisations about the relationships between programme design, programme delivery and, crucially, *programme* effectiveness. . . . This produces two important problems. Firstly, though the pursuit of evidence-based principles is useful and necessary, it is an inherently homogenising approach that predictably struggles to cope with the heterogeneity of offenders to which practitioners must respond on a case-by-case basis. Secondly, at their best, "what works" studies tend only to address questions about which types of rehabilitative programmes seem to work better than others, in which contexts and with which particular target groups. While these are important questions, they conceal a flawed underlying assumption; that it is the qualities of the programme that are at the core of the pursuit of effectiveness.
>
> The research on desistance by contrast, particularly those studies that focus on ex-offenders' narratives . . . , addresses a different and broader range of questions about how and why people pursue and achieve changes in their lives. Indeed, desistance studies generally recognise that desistance itself is not an event (like being cured of a disease) but a process. Desistance is necessarily about coming to cease offending and then to refrain from further offending over an extended period. . . . Moreover, these studies suggest that this process of change, as well as being inherently individualised, is also rich and complex, sometimes ambivalent and contradictory, and not reducible to the simplicities of applying the right "treatment" at the right "dosage" to cure the assessed "criminogenic needs." For example, although desistance studies have revealed that certain life events (like securing

*McNeill quotes reprinted by permission of Wiley–Blackwell Publications.

> employment or becoming a parent) can prompt reconsideration of a criminal career, it appears that success in seizing such windows of opportunity depends on the subjective meanings that the individual concerned attaches to these life events. . . . Neither these events nor the individual's subjective interpretation of them are "programmable" in any straightforward sense. (pp. 428–429)

Harris (2005) also speaks to these issues, stating that "the emphasis on risk in the 'what works' perspective carries the potential for playing into the hands of those who pathologize or demonize people who have been convicted of crimes" (p. 321). Equally damning is Harris's observation that "we ask of a risk instrument how well it works, not whether it is just" (p. 319).

* * *

We must ask: If most offenders eventually desist, how do they do it? There are numerous possibilities. We will consider several of the major paradigms offered in a subsequent chapter. Here we will assert that our preferences are for the empirically supported theories of Sampson and Laub (1993), Laub and Sampson (2003), and Maruna (2001). These theories guide the structure of the rehabilitation program that we propose in this book. Sampson and Laub performed a reevaluation of the data published by Glueck and Glueck (1950, 1968), a longitudinal study of 500 juvenile delinquents and 500 nondelinquents from childhood to age 32. They then followed up a much smaller group to age 70, making this the longest longitudinal study in criminology ever undertaken. The result of these efforts was an age-graded theory of criminal activity and desistance across the lifespan, emphasizing the critical factors of formal and informal social controls and human agency in evaluating criminal careers.

This theory will be supplemented by the contributions of Maruna (2001), whose work focuses upon criminals undertaking a transformation of self, a redemptive, conscious, self-directed process of going straight and making good. It is our belief that this contributes additional structure to the later life stages of Sampson and Laub's theory.

## Paths to Reintegration to Society

Practitioners need rehabilitation theories, essentially conceptual maps, to help them traverse the various challenges and problems that emerge when they work with sex offenders (Ward & Maruna, 2007). Ideally, these maps will provide guidance on pressing matters such as the overall aims of intervention, what constitutes risk, what the general causes of crime are, how best to manage and work with individuals, and how to balance offender needs with the interests of the community. In recent years, strengths-based or "restorative" approaches to working with offenders have been formulated as an alternative to the very popular Risk–Need–Responsivity Model (RNR; Andrews & Bonta, 2007) of offender rehabilitation (see Burnett & Maruna, 2006; Maruna & LeBel, 2003; Ward & Gannon, 2006; Ward & Maruna, 2007).

The RNR Model is deficit-based and focuses upon three areas. First, its focus upon risk is an effort to identify those persons most in need of intensive treatment (moderate- and high-risk individuals). Second, it attempts to identify the dynamic, changeable risk factors (called "criminogenic needs") that contribute to risk and are believed to be amenable to change. Finally, it specifies that treatment must be "responsive" and be matched to the capability of the offender. Current meta-analytic evidence supports the RNR Model in that those exposed to it typically show reduced rates of recidivism. In our view there is nothing inherently wrong with this approach. The problem with the RNR Model is not what it contains but what it leaves out. The focus of treatment is almost entirely upon the identification of risk for reoffense and the management of that risk. The offender is viewed as a package of deficits, weaknesses that must be addressed by intervention. The personal needs of the offender have little or no place in the RNR Model.

On the other hand, emerging from the science of positive psychology (e.g., Seligman & Csikszentmihalyi, 2000), strengths-based approaches shift the emphasis away from dynamic risk factors (criminogenic needs) and instead ask: How can offenders lead lives that are personally meaningful and yet socially acceptable? (see Ward & Maruna, 2007). Rehabilitation theories and treatment programs that have a strengths orientation seek to build on offenders' core interests and skills by equipping them with psychological and social capabilities.

Arguably the most systematically developed rehabilitation theory in the strengths-based domain is Ward and colleagues' GLM (see Ward & Brown, 2004; Ward & Gannon, 2006; Ward, Mann, & Gannon, 2007; Ward & Maruna, 2007; Ward & Stewart, 2003). The GLM starts with the presumption that because of their normative status as human beings, offenders share similar aspirations or life goals (often referred to as "human goods") with nonoffending members of the community. We use the term *normative* to indicate that the common interests and concerns offenders share with the rest of us revolve around basic psychological needs and the values that arise from them. Individuals reflect upon the desirability or worthiness of such needs and ways they can be met. Judgments concerning the specific goals sought, and the means of achieving them, directly reflect offenders' agency status and remind clinicians of the importance of approaching their view of the world and lives from an individual rather than a purely external perspective. In his important review, Duguid (2000, p. 18) states that this type of approach allows clinicians to treat prisoners as "subjects rather than objects" and to "appreciate their complexity, treat them with respect, and demand reciprocity."

The GLM is based around two fundamental therapeutic goals that are inextricably entwined with one another: (1) to enhance the offender's ability to achieve human goods in prosocial ways, and (2) to reduce the offender's personal and environmental suite of changeable risk factors (i.e., criminogenic needs). The assumptions underlying the first point are relatively simple. By virtue of possessing the same needs and nature as the rest of us, offenders actively search for meaningful human goods such as relationships, mastery experiences, a sense of belonging, a sense of purpose, and autonomy (Deci & Ryan, 2000). However, sometimes, offenders do not possess the requisite skills or are not provided with adequate opportunities to obtain these human goods in prosocial ways. For example, a child molester may not have the competencies necessary to manage powerful emotional states and so may turn to sex with children instead to soothe himself. In terms of the second point, we argue that a focus on strengthening offenders' abilities to obtain human goods prosocially is likely to automatically eliminate (or reduce) commonly targeted dynamic risk factors (or criminogenic needs). In the above example, then, increasing the child molester's emotional competencies (internal capabilities) and providing him with social supports is more likely to reduce his emotionally driven episodes of sexual offending. By contrast, however, focusing *only* on the reduction of risk factors (as the RNR Model tends to do) is less likely to promote the full range of specific human goods necessary for longer term desistance from offending.

The key difference between the RNR Model and the GLM is the extent to which they fit with desistance concepts. The RNR Model is a rehabilitation framework built around the principles of risk, need, and responsivity (Andrews & Bonta, 2007). It was constructed from empirical analysis of the effectiveness of various *treatment programs* and is strongly based on outcome data. In other words, the theory tells us that treatment programs that exemplify RNR principles are more likely to result in lower recidivism rates than those that do not. On the other hand, the GLM is built around the concept of *good lives* and is concerned with providing offenders with the psychological and social capital to fashion ways of living that are personally endorsed and that result in reduced offending. Because of its focus on offenders' lifestyles, it naturally looks beyond the treatment setting (but still includes this important analytic focus) into the current and postrelease environments of offenders. Furthermore, the emphasis on offender agency and social embeddedness reminds clinicians to create points of connection with the broader community rather than focusing primarily on fixing internal, structural deficits. In other words, the GLM has the potential to incorporate desistance concepts and to provide correctional workers and therapists of all types with a practice framework to work effectively with sex offenders within prison, on parole, on probation orders, or serving community sentences. The fact that it focuses on identity construction, the social ecology of offending, and developmental trajectories, and that it looks beyond the offense process means that it is a natural conduit for desistance ideas to be introduced into sex offender treatment programs.

# II

# THE CRIMINOLOGICAL PERSPECTIVE

## Chapter 2

# Defining and Measuring Desistance

## Desistance Defined

We are all familiar with the word *desist*. Its formal dictionary definition is "to cease or stop doing something" (*Encarta World English Dictionary*, 1999, p. 489). We are probably most familiar with the usage of the word in an order to "cease and desist," to cease (stop) doing something and to desist (refrain) from doing it again. It is the state of stopping and staying stopped that we refer to as *desistance* (Maruna, 2001).

We stated in the previous chapter that the primary subject matter of this book is encouraging and maintaining desistance from crime in sex offenders. All formal legal structures (probation, parole) and more informal structures such as treatment interventions with this clientele have desistance from future criminal activity as their goal. Presumably probationers, parolees, and clients entering a treatment program have either stopped or curtailed their criminal behavior so the mission of these various programs is maintenance of that state of abstinence or near abstinence. How is "abstinence" defined? Bushway, Piquero, Mazerolle, Broidy, and Cauffman (2001, p. 500) define *desistance* as "the process of reduction in the rate of offending (understood as an estimate of criminality) from a nonzero level to a stable rate indistinguishable from zero."

This sounds straightforward but criminal sexual behavior, like any criminal behavior, is multifaceted and complex and cannot be approached from a single perspective. Desistance from criminal behavior is considerably more than simply stopping. As the desistance process advances, there may be intermittency, a combination of pauses, resumptions, indecisiveness, and ambivalence, all of which may finally lead to termination. Desistance is often defined as a termination point, "the last officially recorded or self-reported offense" (Kazemian, 2007, p. 9). However, it is more properly seen as a dynamic, ongoing process. This argument about whether desistance is a static or a dynamic process has bedeviled criminology for decades, although the dynamic viewpoint now seems to be emerging as the victor. Harris (2005, p. 317) has noted that

> another set of voices . . . concentrate on self-change, empowerment, and desistance . . . [with] an emphasis on the choices of people who have stopped their criminal activities. Ceasing to engage in criminal activity is not thought of as being either a distinctive event or an experience that happens to people, but a process involving a series of individual choices and actions as well as changes in self-image.

It is this perspective—self-change, empowerment, and desistance—that we wish to promote in this book.

## Desistance from Crime in Sex Offenders?

This is our goal and we acknowledge that it is a hard sell, not only to fellow professionals but importantly to policymakers, and most importantly to the general public. They simply do not wish to buy the possibility that sex offenders can reach a point at which they will not reoffend. However, the evidence from criminology that we review below argues convincingly that not only does it happen, it inevitably happens. In fairness, there is virtually no evidence of permanent desistance in sex offenders. What we have instead are treatment outcome reports that a substantial number of persons completed an intensive treatment program and, some years later, only a small percentage of these individuals recidivated. In general, the criminological literature would argue that these individuals were not followed up for a sufficient period of time, if they were followed up at all, and that they were not studied longitudinally and examined periodically to ensure that criminal behavior had stopped.

So, the bulk of our argument for the reality of desistance will come from the criminological literature. Generally speaking, criminal behavior is examined in three general areas: (1) property crime, (2) drug and alcohol crime, and (3) violent interpersonal crime, under which sexual crime would be subsumed.

## Operationalizing Desistance

To begin, let us examine how the concept of desistance has been operationalized in criminology. Kazemian (2007, p. 9) cited 11 different authors and produced the following 14 criteria and measures:

- Conviction at age 21, but not between ages 21 and 32.
- Age at the last officially recorded offense up to age 25.
- During the follow-up period, no reconviction in the previous 10 years (at least).
- Absence of new officially recorded offenses or probation violation throughout a 2-year period.
- Absence of arrest (follow-up to age 70).
- Nonoffending throughout a period of less than a year.
- Individuals who identify themselves as long-term habitual offenders, who claimed that they would not be committing offenses in the future, and who reported at least 1 year of crime-free behavior.
- Absence of reconviction after release from prison during a 10-year window.
- Last conviction having occurred before age 31 and lack of conviction or incarceration for at least 10 years.
- Individuals who reported having committed offenses in the past but who did not report any criminal income in 1979.
- Juvenile delinquents who were not arrested as adults.
- No arrests in the 36 months following release from prison.
- Behavioral desistance: Absence of self-reported illegal earnings during a 3-year follow-up period.
- Official desistance: No arrests during a 3-year follow-up period.
- Individuals who did not report having committed any offenses in the past year.

Examination of this list shows that there is no universal agreement in criminology on what constitutes desistance, although observations and recommendations abound. Maruna (personal communication, November 13, 2009) refers to Kazemian's list as "operationalizations or measures—at most, working definitions."

Note that the list above is composed entirely of information from official records of arrests, convictions, and incarcerations ("official desistance") and self-reports of the cessation of criminal activity ("behavioral desistance"). The major alternative perspective is the process, dynamic view of desistance. McNeill et al. (2005, pp. 3–4) put it this way:

- Desistance is a process which is commonly characterized by ambivalence and vacillation. It is not an event. . . .
- Desistance may be provoked by life events, depending on the meaning of these events to the offender.
- Desistance may be provoked by someone "believing in" the offender.
- Desistance . . . involves a . . . change in narrative identities (or self-stories). This suggests the need for interventions that support narrative reconstruction.
- Desistance is an active process in which agency (the ability to make choices and govern one's own life) is first discovered and then exercised.
- Desistance requires social capital (opportunities) as well as human capital (capacities).
- Desistance is about "redemption" or restoration.

McNeill et al. (2005, p. 16) supplement and expand that list with the following:

> Desistance resides somewhere in the interfaces between developing personal maturity, changing social bonds associated with certain life transitions, and the individual subjective narrative constructions which offenders build around these key events and changes. It is not just the events and changes that matter; it is what these events and changes *mean* to the people involved.

Desistance is clearly considerably more than a truncated rap sheet. Despite the rather vague and nonprogramatic nature of the statements by McNeill et al. (2005), the dynamic, process-oriented definitions of desistance are the ones that we would favor.

## Measuring Desistance

The real problem in working with the concept of desistance lies less in how the clinician or researcher defines it and more in how the phenomenon is measured, how it is determined that desistance from crime has actually occurred. Note that, of the 14 operational definitions of desistance offered by Kazemian (2007, p. 9), all but four are static definitions, that is, desistance either occurs or it does not. The four outliers accept self-report (called "unofficial desistance"), which presumably is nonstatic and modifiable.

Bushway, Thornberry, and Krohn (2003, pp. 131–133) outline the problems with a static approach. A static measure counts everyone as a desister who offends at least once before a specific cutoff point (say, age 18) but not after. Selection of the cutoff point is arbitrary and may make it impossible to determine either the onset of offending or the onset of desistance. Offenders are a heterogeneous lot. Persons who have different careers in terms of length, seriousness, and frequency are all treated as if they were members of a homogeneous group. We revisit this issue below. It is not possible to determine whether the follow-up period is long enough to know if an individual has really stopped offending.

Kazemian (2007, pp. 7–10) has described some additional problems in operationalizing and measuring desistance:

- Static definitions may mask subtle changes that are occurring in the desistance process (Bottoms, Shapland, Costello, Holmes, & Muir, 2004; Bushway et al., 2003; Laub & Sampson, 2003; Maruna, 2001).
- Sampson and Laub (2001) ask if desistance can occur after a single act of crime.
- How many years of nonoffending are required to establish with certainty that desistance has occurred (Laub & Sampson, 2001, 2003)?
- It is necessary to study desistance beyond adolescence because most adolescent offenders do not become adult offenders (Moffitt, 1993).
- Estimates of the age of termination are dependent on the length of the follow-up period (Bushway et al., 2003).
- How long does the follow-up have to be (Laub & Sampson, 2003)?
- Most longitudinal studies have followed up offenders for a limited period of the life course. Thus, "false desistance" (recording stops, but offending continues) may result in inaccurate conclusions.
- Burnett (2004, p. 169) has noted that "desistance is a process which involves reversals of decisions, indecision, compromise and lapses."
- All criminal careers are characterized by some degree of intermittency across the life course, to a lesser or greater extent. Offenders sometimes offend at high and sometimes at low rates. Termination is not likely to occur abruptly; the patterns of intermittency observed in criminal careers underline the importance

of perceiving desistance as a process as opposed to a discrete state (Kazemian, 2007).

Since there are so many existing problems in defining and measuring desistance, it is difficult to arrive at a conclusion on how to best proceed. Bushway et al. (2003, p. 130) offer that an *ideal measure* of desistance should (1) discriminate between people who stop and those who continue, (2) establish whether the change is permanent (or of long duration) or transient, and, importantly, (3) describe the transition from offending to nonoffending. Clearly, this type of measure emphasizes the dynamic, process approach.

## Static versus Dynamic Approach to Measurement

Bushway et al. (2003) argue strongly for the dynamic approach as the best way to examine desistance as a developmental process across the life course. They note that the occurrence of desistance is highly variable across individuals:

> The key defining characteristic of desistance is behavioral change, change from one state—some non-trivial level of offending—to another state—that of non-offending. . . . While desistance ultimately refers to a change in the person's pattern of behavior from involvement in crime to non-involvement in crime, the process of desistance can vary along a number of dimensions. For example, the change can be abrupt, as when someone stops "cold turkey," or it can be more gradual, as when someone slows down from a high rate of offending to lower and lower rates until they reach zero. It can begin either early or late in the person's criminal career and, independent of when it occurs in the criminal career, it can begin at younger or older ages. (p. 130)

Bushway et al. (2003) offer a convincing illustration of the preceding statement. Using data from the Rochester Youth Survey they examined the offending careers of 846 boys, seventh- and eighth-grade students from public schools, from mean age 13.5 to mean age 22. They conducted 12 waves of interviews over these years. The main instrument used to record the dependent variable was a 31-item inventory of delinquent behavior. These are self-report data, not official police data. To evaluate the data two approaches were used.

The first was the classical static measure: whether any offending occurred before or after the cutoff point of age 18. Twelve percent of the sample were identified as nonoffenders (no offenses in either period). A small group (7%) were considered late starters since they offended after 18 but not before. Fifty-four percent were identified as persisters (offended in both periods) and 28% as desisters (offended at least once before 18 but not after).

The second method produced a trajectory model that identified seven groups using Nagin and Land's (1993) semiparametric trajectory method. Several interesting features emerged from this analysis. The bulk of the sample (61%) was accounted for by two groups: very low-level and low-level offenders. Each of the remaining five groups contained less than 10% of the sample. Several points are worth noting. The developmental (dynamic) approach showed that there were different processes for different groups, an offending pattern for each sample. Only three of the groups showed desistance from offending to a zero or near zero level. These data appear to show more than they actually do. The curves are aggregate data and do not provide information on specific types of offending. That information is only available through examination of the offense profile of an individual in any group to determine who is a persister and who is a desister. The processes described are rather elegantly illustrated in Figure 3.2 in Chapter 3.

A similar investigation was undertaken by Brame, Bushway, and Paternoster (2003) to estimate the prevalence of desistance using different analytical models. Their goal was to "use several different statistical models, including the standard behavioral model, to estimate the proportion of the population who offended at least once before age 18 who can be described as 'desisters' by age 27" (p. 425). They also note that Laub and Sampson (2003) "were the first to suggest that dynamic statistical models on prospective panel data can be used to examine the process of desistance. This process places greater emphasis on modeling changes in offending over time and less emphasis on the terminating event" (p. 425). Brame et al. (2003) reevaluated data from the 1958 Philadelphia Birth Cohort. While the original sample was quite large (*N* = 13,160), Brame et al. evaluated 2,657 (20.2%) of the cases who had at least one police contact before age 18. The goal of the investigation was to examine the frequency distribution of adult police contacts from age 18 to age 27 for these individuals and estimate the prevalence of desistance using different analytic models.

The first, termed "strict behavioral desistance," defined desisters as those persons who did not offend during the follow-up period. This event count produced a "potential" estimate of 61.2%. Brame et al. (2003) considered the figure potential because apparent absence of offending did not necessarily imply that offending had actually ceased or that the propensity to offend had changed. Using a probabilistic Poisson model similar to that advanced by Nagin and Land (1993) and Bushway et al. (2003) Brame et al. divided the data into "two approximate desistance models" (p. 432). The first, termed "approximate desistance," produced three groups: low rate, medium rate, and high rate. The low-rate group was the largest (71%) and presumably contained the desisters. The second group, termed "split population desistance," contained a group of true desisters and the three groups mentioned above. This analysis revealed a rate of 36.6% for the desisters. Brame et al. (2003) concluded that "the split-population Poisson model fits the data the best and in the absence of an alternative specification that fits better, we are inclined to put the most weight on the estimate of 36.6% desistance prevalence produced by that estimator" (p. 441).

While the data produced by the Bushway et al. (2003) and the Brame et al. (2003) studies are impressive, two reservations must be kept in mind. First, Nagin and Tremblay (2005) warn against reading too much into group trajectory data. They caution that "trajectory groups, like all statistical models, are not literal depictions of reality. They are meant only as a convenient statistical approximation" (p. 882). And further:

> The trajectory group is a statistical device for creating a data summary that describes the behavior and characteristics of a set of individuals following approximately the same developmental course. . . . [N]o individual's behavioral trajectory will exactly match the group average. More subtly, it is important to recognize that the trajectory is intended to capture a long-term behavioral pattern, not short-term individual variability about that pattern. (p. 890)

Second, these two studies, like many in the desistance literature, claim to study desistance across the life course. In reality, they are studies of the life course only from adolescence to young adulthood. It has been documented since the early 19th century that, when examining aggregate data, it may be seen that crime rates peak in late adolescence or early adulthood, then steadily decline into old age (see, e.g., Gottfredson & Hirschi, 1990, pp. 124–129). The trajectory studies, then, are a window on the earlier portions of this phenomenon.

Only one series of studies (Laub & Sampson, 2003; Sampson & Laub, 1993) have actually examined virtually the entire life course from ages 10 to 70. Sampson and Laub (1993), in developing their age-graded theory of informal social control, first reevaluated the data of Sheldon and Eleanor Glueck's *Unraveling Juvenile Delinquency* (1950).

The Gluecks had developed a huge database of both official and unofficial data on two large groups of delinquent and nondelinquent boys from ages 10 to 17 in the period 1939–1948. They then performed a follow-up at two different periods, ages 25 and 32, from 1949 to 1963 (Glueck & Glueck, 1968). Sampson and Laub's (1993) reanalysis of the Glueck data showed the typical age–crime relationship (see Laub & Sampson, 2003, p. 101), peaking around age 17, then moderately trailing off to age 32. Laub and Sampson (2003) then extended their analysis, obtaining data on the surviving Glueck men and personally interviewing a small representative sample of desisters and persisters to age 70, filling in the blanks from age 32 onward. Their aggregate data show the classical age–crime curve, a left-skewed normal curve. More information on the Sampson and Laub theory and research is provided in a subsequent chapter.

Importantly for our purposes in this book, using the Nagin and Land (1993) semiparametric group-based modeling approach, Laub and Sampson (2003, pp. 104–107) not only showed distinct trajectory groups for total crime, they were also able to show trajectory groups for property crime, alcohol and drug crime, and violent crime. For the purpose of examining desistance in sex offenders, this further breakdown is important for studying the process in distinct offender groups (child molesters, rapists, exhibitionists, and other minor paraphiliacs) as one would expect them to have unique trajectories.

## Serious Follow-Up

We now have theories about the etiology and maintenance of sexual deviance (see, e.g., Laws & Marshall, 1990; Marshall & Barbaree, 1990; Ward & Beech, 2008). However, we know very little about how sexual offending careers wind down and terminate. We mentioned in Chapter 1 that there are a handful of studies that purport to have conducted long-term follow-ups, some up to 30 years. Upon examination these turn out to be examination of official records to determine who has recidivated since the last contact with the individual offender. This is not a proper follow-up as official records may mask what is truly going on in the offender's life. There is very little follow-up of sexual offenders. Typically, when probation or parole ends, monitoring ends. When a treatment program ends, the offender may be periodically followed for a period of time, then contact ends. Since probation and parole officers and treatment providers carry heavy caseloads and are not often criminological researchers, it is neither practical or possible for them to carry out decades-long follow-ups. The task thus falls to researchers who are supported by extramural funds and who can invest the necessary years to more completely understand the phenomenon of desistance in sexual offenders.

Farrington (2007) has offered some practical recommendations regarding how this could be done.*

> In investigating desistance it is desirable to measure the number of offenses committed by each individual at each age (e.g., from 10 to 70), preferably using official records and self-reports of offending. It is essential to measure events such as death, incapacity, emigration, or incarceration that will prevent offenses being recorded but possibly leave the underlying theoretical construct (e.g., antisocial propensity) unchanged. Ideally, each individual should be repeatedly interviewed and asked about offenses committed recently (e.g., within the past 3 years). It is unlikely that people could give accurate reports of offenses committed more than 10 years ago. . . . Therefore, prospective longitudinal studies are needed. Retrospective information on offending, risk factors, and life events is likely to be valuable only when contemporaneous records of these events are available. (p. 130)

Farrington recognized that it is not realistically possible to follow a sample of offenders from ages 10 to 70. Sampson and Laub were extraordinarily lucky to have had access to a huge database from ages 10 to 32 and then be able to create a second, complementary database from ages 32 to 70. This opportunity is not likely to occur again. Instead of working with a single database, Farrington recommended use of what he calls an "accelerated longitudinal design." This would involve, for example, studying six cohorts of offenders aged 10, 20, 30, 40, 50, and 60, following each for 10 years. Community samples as well as offender samples should be used. "Risk factors, life events, and offending could be measured at each age to test hypotheses about factors influencing desistance and DLC [developmental life course] theories of desistance" (p. 130). Interviews should be conducted annually or biannually if possible. All samples should be drawn from the same large city and consist of at least 500 persons (p. 131). Farrington concluded:

> There should be repeated measures of offending; individual, family, peer, school, and neighborhood risk factors; life events (e.g., marriage or cohabitation, jobs, joining or leaving gangs; substance abuse); situational or opportunity factors; cognitive or decision-making processes; and death, disability, or emigration. . . . Such an ambitious . . . proj-

*Farrington quotes reprinted by permission of Sage Publications.

> ect would be expensive. However, the expense is needed because (a) most prior longitudinal studies have focused on onset and the teenage years, (b) relatively little is known about desistance, (c) information about desistance could be of great value to sentencers, parole decision makers, and policy makers. (p. 132)

Farrington (2007, p. 131) also offered a list of key questions that he believed need to be addressed in desistance research:

- How can desistance (defined as either termination or deceleration) be measured?
- How do self-report and official measures of offending and desistance compare?
- Could there be desistance from one criminal career followed by reinitiation of another?
- Do individuals decelerate in offending before they terminate?
- What factors predict desistance (or residual career length)? Which features of the past criminal career predict the future criminal career?
- Are predictors of desistance similar to predictors of late onset and low continuity?
- Are there different predictors of early versus later desistance?
- What factors cause desistance according to analyses of within-individual changes?
- What protective factors encourage or decelerate desistance?
- What is the relative importance of later life events and earlier risk factors?
- Are life events causes or correlates of desistance?
- How accurate are predictions about desistance from DLC theories?
- Is it useful to distinguish types of individuals who differ in their probability of desistance?
- What interventions foster or accelerate desistance?
- What are the effects of criminal justice sanctions on desistance?
- Can a risk assessment instrument for desistance be developed, and would it be valuable for criminal justice decisions and reducing crime?

Each of these questions should be directed to different ages, different times and places, males versus females, different races and cultures, and different offense types and different types of antisocial behavior.

## Conclusions

Some criminological researchers would argue that a number of the questions in Farrington's list have already been addressed and partially, if not wholly, answered. Perhaps a better way of looking at that list would be to acknowledge its resemblance to any menu of things to be done in social science: there are far more questions than answers and that is as it should be. Many of today's answers will become tomorrow's questions.

## Chapter 3

# The Age–Crime Curve

## *A Brief Overview*

In the preceding chapters we alluded to the use of the age–crime curve in research without fully explaining what it is. It has prominence for two reasons. First, it is the most robust finding in criminology and has been consistently observed for nearly 180 years. Moffitt (1993, p. 675) called it "the most robust and least understood empirical observation in the field of criminology." Second, the age–crime curve is the pivot on which much of the career criminal and desistance research turns, and therefore requires our attention.

## What Is It?

The age–crime curve was first observed by Adolphe Quételet, a 19th-century Belgian astronomer, mathematician, and statistician. He is generally credited with introducing statistical procedures to sociology. Quételet used descriptive statistics to record similarities in a wide variety of human attributes (e.g., height, weight). According to Beirne (1987, p. 1151), "The average of any given scale was thought by Quételet to be more accurate, the greater the number of empirical observations. In combinations, these average values produced an image of a fictitious, statistically derived creature whom Quételet termed the average man." Part of this work was the search for regularities in criminal behavior (Quételet, 1831/1984). Quételet consulted the *Compte general de l'administration de la justice criminelle en France*, an official census of criminal acts brought before the courts. He examined the criminal statistics from the years 1826–1829 and found indisputable regularities among persons accused and convicted of crimes against persons and property. Table 3.1 shows these figures. It may be seen that while there is variation from year to year, there is also considerable consistency. Quételet also examined the backgrounds of the persons accused and convicted of crimes. Beirne (1987, pp. 1153–1155) continued:

> The disproportionate and relentless presence of certain categories in the *Compte* between 1826 and 1829 also indicated to Quételet that young males, the poor, the less educated, and those without employment or in lowly occupations had a greater propensity (*penchant*) than others to commit crimes and be convicted of them. These data seemed to enable Quételet to take issue with several conventional accounts of the factors that precipitated crime. In particular, he adduced that neither the presence of poverty nor the absence of formal education warranted the monolithic causal importance commonly claimed for them.

Further, Quételet noticed that the *Compte* data clearly indicated that age was strongly associated with criminal behavior over the life course. These data are shown in Table 3.2 and form the raw data for the first age–crime curve. Beirne (1987, pp. 1155–1156) stated that

> he tabulated crimes according to the ages of their perpetrators and divided the number of crimes by the population in the respective age groups. The results show the propensity for committing crime at various ages. This propensity is at its weakest at both extremes of life. . . . The propensity for crime is at its strongest between the ages of 21 and 25.

**TABLE 3.1. The Constancy of Crime, 1826–1829**

| Year | Accused (tried) | Convicted | Convicted from 100 accused | Accused of crimes | |
|---|---|---|---|---|---|
| | | | | Persons | Property |
| 1826 | 6,988 | 4,348 | 62 | 1,907 | 5,081 |
| 1827 | 6,929 | 4,236 | 61 | 1,911 | 5,018 |
| 1828 | 7,396 | 4,551 | 61 | 1,844 | 5,552 |
| 1829 | 7,373 | 4,475 | 61 | 1,791 | 5,582 |

*Note*. Modified from Beirne (1987); data from Quételet (1831/1984, p. 20).

**TABLE 3.2. Age and the Propensity for Crime, 1826–1829**

| Age | Crimes against persons | Crimes against property |
|---|---|---|
| Under 16 | 80 | 440 |
| 16–21 | 904 | 3,723 |
| 21–25 | 1,278 | 3,329 |
| 25–30 | 1,575 | 3,702 |
| 30–35 | 1,153 | 2,883 |
| 35–40 | 650 | 2,076 |
| 40–45 | 575 | 1,724 |
| 45–50 | 445 | 1,275 |
| 50–55 | 288 | 811 |
| 55–60 | 168 | 500 |
| 60–65 | 157 | 385 |
| 65–70 | 91 | 184 |
| 70–75 | 64 | 137 |
| 80 and over | 5 | 14 |

*Note.* Modified from Beirne (1987); data from Quételet (1831/1984, p. 56).

All of the preceding summary of Quételet's work is consistent with what is observed today and what was observed through the 19th and early 20th centuries to the present. For example, Gottfredson and Hirschi (1990, pp. 125–127) cite Neison (1957) for data from England and Wales; Goring (1913), who termed the age–crime curve "a law of nature"; McClintock and Avison (1968) for England and Wales, and Wolfgang, Figlio, and Sellin (1972) for delinquents in Philadelphia. Hirschi and Gottfredson (1983) observed that through the years 1835–1980, age–crime distributions were observed in Argentina, the United States, France, Sweden, Japan, and the United Kingdom. They stated that "the similarity between the age–crime distributions through time . . . and across place . . . is remarkable. . . . In shape or form, they are virtually identical" (p. 569).

## The Classical Curve

Figure 3.1 illustrates the age–crime curve using raw aggregate data for four categories of crime: property, violence, and drug/alcohol from ages 7 to 70 (Laub & Sampson, 2003, p. 86). These are the data from the original Glueck and Glueck studies (1950, 1968), reanalyzed by

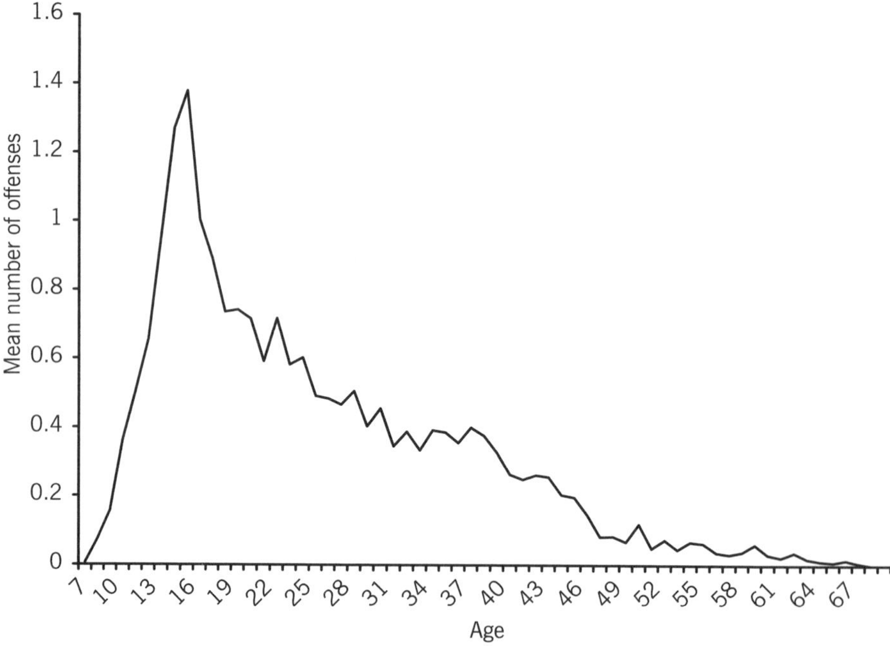


**FIGURE 3.1.** Age–crime curve, Glueck raw data, ages 7–70. Total events = 9,548. From Laub and Sampson (2003, p. 86). Copyright 2003 by Harvard University Press. Reprinted by permission.

Sampson and Laub (1993) and then followed up by Laub and Sampson (2003). While the curve is rough and somewhat irregular, note the close similarity to Quételet's data from 1831. There is a dramatic increase in criminal activity from age 7 to about age 17, then a gradual trailing off until about age 45 when it begins the final decline to zero or near zero offenses. Data highly similar to Figure 3.1 have been reported by the Gluecks (1950, 1968), although in tabular rather than graphic form, Gottfredson and Hirschi (1990), and Moffitt (1993).

The Gluecks maintained that "maturation" was the primary causal agent in the decline in criminal behavior, that offenders simply "aged out" of offending although other factors were undoubtedly at work.

A more radical position was adopted by Gottfredson and Hirschi (1990) who claimed that the age effect was "invariant," a main effect in desistance:

> An alternative interpretation of maturational reform or spontaneous desistance is that crime declines with age. . . . This . . . suggests that

> maturational reform is just that, change in behavior that comes with maturation; it suggests that spontaneous desistance is just that, change in behavior that cannot be explained and change that occurs regardless of what else happens. (p. 136)

Or, "We can distinguish between traditional 'desistance' theory and an 'age' theory of the same phenomenon. The desistance theory asserts that crime declines with age because of factors associated with age that reduce or change the criminality of the actor. The age theory asserts that crime, independent of criminality, declines with age" (p. 137).

Moffitt (1993) explained the age–crime effect with a dual taxonomy of antisocial behavior. In her view there were two tracks in criminal behavior: adolescence-limited and life-course persistent. Both groups show dramatic increases in criminal behavior in the years from childhood to late adolescence. The more properly socialized adolescence-limited group then begins to cease criminal behavior while the life-course-persistent group continues. Thus, an age–crime curve containing both groups would resemble the classical pattern that has been consistently reported.

These theories are outlined in greater detail in the following chapter.

## Trajectory Group Curves

The analysis of trajectories of offending may be difficult to understand for the statistically unsophisticated reader. Shawn Bushway (personal communication, March 24, 2009) was kind enough to provide an explanation of the procedure in language that will be accessible to most readers. That account is as follows:

> The starting point for any growth curve model is data that follows people over time for a number of years. Suppose, for example, we have the complete formal (e.g. felony conviction) criminal histories on 1000 people from age 10 to age 40. A simple first step to examining conviction over age would be to calculate the average number of convictions for each year of age from age 10 to age 40. This would give us 31 data points that would in all likelihood look like a one hump camel, peaking around age 20. This is the classic age crime pattern. A standard second step would be to fit a regression curve to this data to essentially smooth out the bumps, and create the classic "age–crime" curve or trajectory. The semi-parametric trajectory model with one group essentially fits or estimates this age crime curve/trajectory. But, sup-

pose I didn't believe that everyone followed this exact pattern—how could I explore the data to see if there are different patterns of offending in the data? This is a fundamental debate in criminology about whether the aggregate age crime curve describes the basic nature of everyone's offending (albeit with different levels) or if the aggregate age crime curve actually masks what are fundamentally different patterns of offending for the population at large.

The easiest way to ask this question would be to simply assume there are two groups—and ask a statistical model to find the two curves or trajectories that best capture the patterns available in the data. Such a model would also need to ask what proportion of the population is best described by each pattern. This is what a 2 group semi-parametric trajectory model does—it finds the two smoothed curves that best describe the data, and generates a best guess for how much the population follows each curve. Of course, if I can do that for 2 groups, I can do it for 3 groups, etc. In each case, it is important to note that, barring data limitations, the model will find the number of groups I ask for. It is the job of the researcher to choose the "best" number of groups. According to Nagin, "best" depends on what you are trying to accomplish. But, in normal usage, best means parsimonious description of the main patterns present in the data. Nagin provides a number of model selection tools for helping researchers make this assessment. Once I estimated the groups with the model, I can do a number of things:

1. I can predict for each member of my sample which group best describes their behavior.
2. I can look to see if there are factors which predict group membership, i.e., are there things that exist prior to the start of the time period in question (i.e., risk factors) that predict group membership.
3. I can try to explain or describe the shape of each trajectory using variables that vary as a person ages.

Several caveats are worth noting:

1. These statistical "groups" are not valid groups the way psychologists think about valid, qualitatively homogeneous groups or types. Even if the population is completely continuous, we will find groups—because the model approximates a continuous distribution with groups.
2. These smoothed curves are retrospective in nature, and contain no information about the degree to which these curves are predetermined. They may be predetermined—they may

not be, but the fact that I can fit retrospective trajectories that describe the basic paths apparent in the data tells me nothing about this.

3. The fact that risk factors can differentiate between groups at a better than chance rate does not say anything about the quality of the prediction. A different analysis would be necessary to evaluate the power of the prediction model.

We must remind the reader that the trajectory group analyses reported by Brame et al. (2003), Bushway et al. (2003), and Laub and Sampson (2003) show dramatically different age–crime curves. Figure 3.2 shows the data from the Bushway et al. (2003, p. 144) analysis. This analysis produced seven trajectory curves. Note that only one, termed "bell-shaped desisters," shows the classical normal distribution skewed to the left. More importantly, the classical curve represents only 8.4% of the sample.

Figure 3.3, from Laub and Sampson (2003, p. 104) shows *aggregate* data for total crime (property, violence, drug/alcohol) from ages 7 to 70. Note again that what they term the "classic desister" curve represents only 19.9% of the sample. Figure 3.4 is also from Laub and Sampson

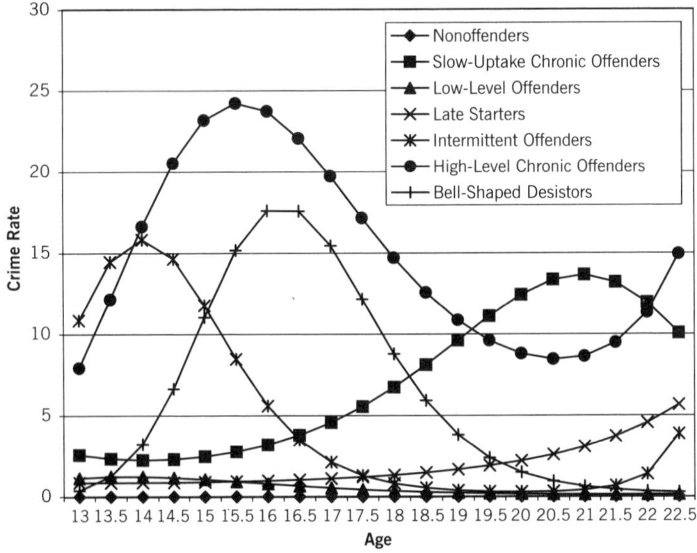


**FIGURE 3.2.** Example of seven trajectory curves. From Bushway et al. (2003, p. 144). Copyright 2003 by Springer Publications. Reprinted by permission.

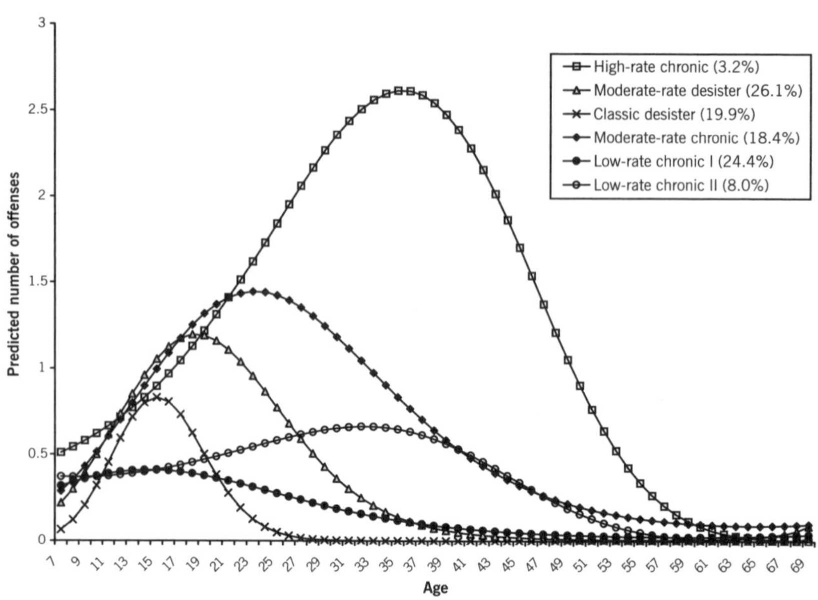


**FIGURE 3.3.** Trajectory curves for total crime. From Laub and Sampson (2003, p. 104). Copyright 2003 by Harvard University Press. Reprinted by permission.

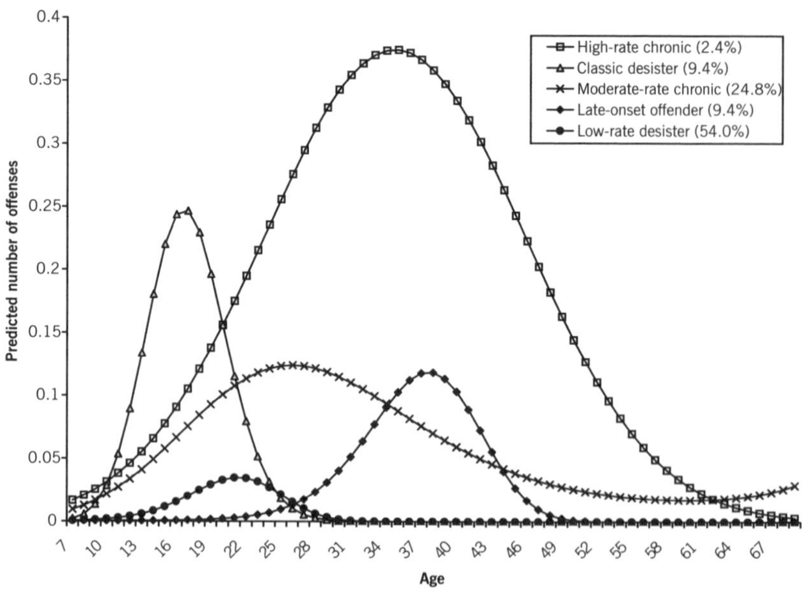


**FIGURE 3.4.** Trajectory curves for violent crime. From Laub and Sampson (2003, p. 106). Copyright 2003 by Harvard University Press. Reprinted by permission.

(2003, p. 106). This shows the offending trajectories for violent (including sexual?) crime. Note here that the "classic desister" represents only 9.4% of the sample.

## Conclusions

Curves for aggregate crimes are impressive to look at, especially when statistically smoothed. But they clearly do not tell the whole story. Acknowledging Nagin and Tremblay's (2005) admonitions not to read too much into them, the trajectory group data offer considerably more information. The main message appears to be that, just as there are many roads into crime, there are many roads out of it.

## Chapter 4

# Theoretical Perspectives on Desistance

As we stated in the preceding chapter, desistance from crime as shown in the age–crime curve has been the most robust finding in criminology for almost two centuries. It is an inexorable process variously termed "a law of nature" (Goring, 1913) as well as the "least understood empirical observation . . . in criminology" (Moffitt, 1993). It appears to happen to all offenders except a tiny proportion who continue criminal activities throughout their lives. So, we may ask, if we did not intervene in any fashion, would desistance happen anyway? The answer is certainly yes. As we will show in our treatment of some of the major theories of desistance, particularly those of Sampson and Laub and Maruna, while this process grinds on, many people live miserable and hopeless lives. Intervention, wherever possible and of whatever nature, seems an ethical and moral imperative. Age is certainly a major, perhaps *the* major, variable working to effect desistance. Many other variables, social and psychological, are also at work to produce the cessation effect. It is to a consideration of these that we now turn.

In this chapter we wish to provide descriptions of the theories of desistance that have most interested us and which have the most to contribute to the research and clinical paradigms that we will propose.

## Sheldon and Eleanor T. Glueck

The Gluecks were not theorists. In fact, they were rather antitheoretical. Sampson and Laub (1993, p. 64) noted that "the Gluecks' research sought to answer a basic, enduring, and even popular question in the study of delinquency—what factors differentiate boys reared in poor neighborhoods who become serious and persistent delinquents from boys raised in the same neighborhoods who do *not* become delinquent or antisocial?" Rather than postulate a theory of juvenile delinquency, the Gluecks amassed an enormous amount of empirical data on formal and informal influences on the boys, their families, schools, social relations, and criminal behavior and let the data speak for themselves, summarizing their findings that distinguished delinquents from nondelinquents. According to Wilson and Herrnstein (1985, p. 175), the Gluecks "conducted what was, and has remained, one of the most detailed and comprehensive longitudinal and cross-sectional studies of male delinquency." The section that follows is a synthesis of Sampson and Laub's (1993, pp. 24–63) account of the Glueck's research from 1939 to 1963.

For the *Unraveling Juvenile Delinquency* (UJD) study (1939–1949), the Gluecks selected 500 officially delinquent white boys, ages 10–17, from two correctional schools in Massachusetts. These were to be compared to 500 nondelinquents, also white males, selected from Boston public schools. These were supposedly normal youngsters who were not involved in serious persistent delinquency. These two groups were matched, case by case, on age, race/ethnicity of parents, neighborhood, and measured intelligence. Both groups resided in lower-class neighborhoods, characterized by poverty, economic dependence, and physical deterioration. Their homes were typically crowded and lacked basic necessities such as bathrooms or sufficient sleeping areas. These neighborhoods were also matched on rates of delinquency. The major issue here, obviously, was the attempt to ensure that the only major difference between the two groups was a high rate of official delinquency in the group of boys drawn from the correctional schools.

The data for UJD were collected by a small group of interviewers. The interviews were directed at the boys, their families, teachers, neighbors, and criminal justice/social welfare officials. These interviews provided a rich source of self-, parent-, and teacher-reported measures of delinquent behavior. Along with official records, these unofficial reports provided an opportunity to develop a large series of measures of delinquent and antisocial conduct. The range of data collection was enormous; Sampson and Laub (1993, p. 29) observed that "this level of detail and the range of information sources found in the Glueck study will likely never be repeated, given contemporary research standards on the protection of human subjects."

The Gluecks produced two follow-up studies, *Delinquents and Non-Delinquents in Perspective* (1968). These were conducted from 1950–1957 and from 1957–1964, when the boys were roughly 25 and 32 years of age, respectively. Criminal histories from first offense to age 32 were collected from police, court, and correctional files. Interviews and record checks were made on key life events including living arrangements as adults, marriage/divorce and children, residential changes, employment history (including work habits), military experience, continued schooling, participation in civic affairs, and, at a personal level, aspirations, companions, and use of leisure time.

At this point the Gluecks had compiled a comprehensive database for childhood, adolescence, and young adulthood. In the follow-up they were able to secure data on 88% of both groups, a success rate of 92%.

Sampson and Laub (1993, pp. 35–36) summarized the substantive findings of the two studies:

- Age of onset was a key factor in etiology and career criminals started offending early in life.
- Crime declined strongly with age. The age–crime curve, in the Gluecks' view, demonstrated "delayed maturation." Seriousness of offending also declined with age.
- Delinquent patterns showed stability over the, albeit brief, life course.
- Family variables were the most important factor that distinguished delinquents from nondelinquents.

In Sampson and Laub's (1993, p. 42) view, "the Gluecks' research on . . . key areas as age and crime, longitudinal research/criminal careers, stability of crime and antisocial behavior, and social control theory with a focus on family processes has been shown to be . . . essentially correct." As we mentioned above, the work of the Gluecks does not represent a theory of desistance. We have described it at such length because it represents a landmark study in criminal career research. More importantly, the Gluecks set the early standard for the multifactor approach to understanding delinquency. The data produced bear heavily on much subsequent theorizing and empirical research on desistance. The greatest influence has been on Sampson and Laub (1993, 2003), whose work we treat at length in a subsequent chapter.

The Gluecks' emphasis on maturation implies an intraindividual process that may neglect the importance of ecological variables (e.g., social networks, culture) that other theorists find vital. The family processes that they examined are linked to maturation and, ultimately, desistance. Family influences that foster and encourage delinquency could conceivably delay "aging out" of crime and settling down, while positive family influences will have the reverse effect.

## Michael R. Gottfredson and Travis Hirschi

*A General Theory of Crime* (1990) is distinguished by its simplicity, an almost-too-good-to-be-true simplicity that has excited considerable interest and research since it was published. The authors' position is a modification of classical social control theory.

The classical version

> proposes that people's relationships, commitments, values, norms, and beliefs encourage them not to break the law. Thus, if moral codes are internalized and individuals are tied into, and have a stake in their wider community, they will voluntarily limit their propensity to commit deviant acts. The theory seeks to understand the ways in which it is possible to reduce the likelihood of criminality developing in individuals. It does not consider motivational issues, simply stating that human beings may choose to engage in a wide range of activities, unless the range is limited by the processes of socialization and social learning. (Control theory, 2010)

Gottfredson and Hirschi's (1990) version of social control theory posits that human beings are hedonists who naturally seek pleasurable experiences and try to avoid pain. Some of those pleasures may involve the commission of crimes. For Gottfredson and Hirschi (1990, p. 89), criminal acts provide immediate gratification of desires, a "here-and-now" orientation; provide easy or simple gratification of desires—money without work, sex without courtship, revenge without delays; are exciting, risky, or thrilling; and require little skill or planning. It is equally true, they say, that crimes provide few or meager long-term benefits as they interfere with commitments to jobs, marriages, family, or friends; and crimes result in harm to victims in the sense of lost property, physical injury, or violation of privacy. They also stress (p. 90) that persons who engage in crimes will also tend to pursue immediate pleasures that are *not* necessarily criminal such as smoking, drinking, drug abuse, gambling, having illegitimate children, or engaging in illicit sex, to name a few. They refer to these as "analogous behaviors," that is, behaviors similar in nature to more outright criminal acts.

Hanson and Morton-Bourgon (2005) have noted similar characteristics in persistent sex offenders:

> Antisocial orientation refers to antisocial personality, antisocial traits (such as impulsivity, substance abuse, unemployment) and a history of rule violation. There is a strong association between rule violation and impulsive, reckless behavior, such as excessive drinking, frequent moves, fights, and unsafe work practices. (p. 1154)

Antisocial orientation, in their view, facilitates sex offending. Similarly, Lussier, Proulx, and LeBlanc (2005) agreed that "sexual offending could . . . be seen as being part of a chronic antisocial lifestyle" (p. 271).

In Gottfredson and Hirschi's view, whether or not an individual engages in criminal behavior depends upon the degree of self-control that the person possesses. They put it this way:

> The major "cause" of low self-control . . . appears to be ineffective child-rearing. . . . We think it necessary to define the conditions necessary for adequate child-rearing to occur. The minimum conditions seem to be these: in order to teach the child self-control, someone must (1) monitor the child's behavior; (2) recognize deviant behavior when it occurs; and (3) punish such behavior. This seems simple and obvious enough. All that is required to activate the system is affection for *or* investment in the child. The person who cares for the child will watch his behavior, see him doing things he should not do, and correct him. The result may be a child more capable of delaying gratification, more sensitive to the interests and desires of others, more independent, more willing to accept restraints on his activity, and more unlikely to use force or violence to attain his ends. (p. 97)

And further:

> People who develop strong self-control are unlikely to commit criminal acts throughout their lives, regardless of other personality characteristics. In this sense, self-control is the only enduring personal characteristic predictive of criminal (and related) behavior. People who do not develop strong self-control are more likely to commit criminal acts, whatever the other dimensions of their personality. As people with low self-control age, they tend less and less to commit crimes; this decline is probably not entirely due to increasing self-control, but to age as well. (p. 111)

That last statement is simply a restatement of their age invariance position—aging is something that just happens and it affects all behavior, not necessarily criminal behavior.

Arneklev, Ellis, and Medlicott (2006) also noted that

> according to Gottfredson and Hirschi . . . , low self-control comprises six dimensions: impulsivity, preference for simple tasks, risk-seeking potential, preference for physical (as opposed to mental) activities, self-centeredness, and . . . the possession of a volatile temper. . . . Low self-control . . . remains relatively stable across the life-course. Given the opportunity to do so, individuals lacking self-control will engage in a wide range of criminal and analogous behaviors. . . . People with high self-control should be successful socially, do well in school, have the potential for a good income, have strong interpersonal relationships, and have a strong marriage. Those with low self-control will have poor friendships, do poorly in school, do poorly in jobs, and have unhappy marriages. (p. 42)

Arneklev et al. (2006) tested the general theory of crime by interviewing 391 adults (18+) from a medium-sized city. They focused on (1) low self-control, (2) "imprudent" (i.e., analogous) behaviors, (3) crime, and (4) social consequences. Low self-control was assessed via a 30-item Likert scale. Regarding imprudent behavior, respondents were asked whether they smoked, drank, ate recklessly, wore a seat belt, gambled, or had seriously injured themselves in the preceding year. Arneklev et al. used Gottfredson and Hirschi's definition of crime, questioning respondents about "acts of force and fraud" done in the pursuit of self-interest as well as petty and grand theft. For social consequences they asked interviewees about quality of friendship, life satisfaction, religious attendance, marital status, educational attainment, and income. Their findings (p. 49) were straightforward:

- Behaviors that provide short-term benefits (imprudent behaviors) can be used to test Gottfredson and Hirschi's (1990) theory.
- Attitudinal measures (i.e., Grasmick, Tittle, Bursik, & Arneklev, 1993, self-control scale) can also be used to test the theory.
- The attitudinal measure was superior to the analogous behavior measure in predicting crime.
- Both indicators were equally effective in explaining social consequences.

In summary, "Regardless of the measure used, low self-control is a stronger predictor of crime than later life course influences, which is very consistent with Gottfredson and Hirschi's (1990) theory" (p. 49).

Armstrong (2005) also tested low self-control. He presented three crime scenarios to 312 male and female undergraduates. The scenarios described opportunities to (1) act aggressively, (2) commit theft, and (3) use drugs. He also administered the Grasmick et al. (1993) self-control scale. Results supported Gottfredson and Hirschi's (1990) assertion that "a single characteristic, self-control, is a strong predictor of three different types of criminal intent" (p. 17). However, Armstrong had reservations about the use of offense scenarios as well as the attitudinal measure. Neither of these is a direct measure of intent and responding to a scenario is not a measure of actual propensity to commit a crime.

Pratt and Cullen (2000) performed a meta-analysis of all published studies of the general theory of crime to that date. They noted that much of the work summarizing findings in criminology at that time were narrative reviews, which they found deficient. First, the information found in narrative reviews were based on the qualitative judgments of the persons doing the reviews. Second, narrative reviews only provided crude estimates of the degree to which theoretical variables were related to criminal behavior. Their solution was to use meta-analysis to tease out these relationships. "By treating each separate or 'independent' study as the unit of analysis, the . . . technique allows for the statistical discovery of common patterns. . . . Most salient inferences can be drawn on the basis of the 'effect size' (or predictive capacity) of variables" (p. 935).

Pratt and Cullen (2000) evaluated 21 empirical studies (17 data sets) containing 49,727 individual cases. The analysis produced 126 effect size estimates. Their purpose was fourfold (pp. 936–937):

- Assess the effect size between measures of self-control and directly criminal or analogous behaviors. Is it a predictor of criminal behavior?
- Gottfredson and Hirschi (1990) state that the interaction of opportunity and low self-control results in high levels of criminal behavior. Is there evidence for this?
- Is effect size between self-control and criminal behavior influenced by methodological factors? These would include measures used to operationalize self-control, model specifications, different research designs, and sample characteristics.
- Gottfredson and Hirschi (1990) argue that social learning is not needed for crime to occur. People with low self-control tend to

flock together creating groups that lack self-control, all members of which will tend to be delinquent.

Pratt and Cullen's (2000, pp. 951–953) data offer impressive support for the general theory of crime:

- Low self-control consistently showed an effect size greater than 0.20. This would rank self-control as one of the strongest predictors of crime. The effect size was not affected no matter how self-control was measured—attitudinal, behavioral, or scaled measure.
- The effects of self-control appeared to be general. While there were some exceptions, self-control was related to criminal behavior among men, in younger samples, and in offender samples.

On the other hand,

- "Gottfredson and Hirschi's bold contention that self-control is a stable propensity that does not work through other variables is not supported by our analysis" (p. 952).
- "Even with self-control included in a study's statistical analysis, social learning variables continued to have a strong effect" (p. 952). "Despite different views of human nature and other theoretical tensions, support exists for both the general theory and social learning theory: Low self-control and social learning variables are important predictors of crime" (p. 953).

Pratt and Cullen (2000) summarized their study as follows:

> Meta-analysis of the extant literature indicates that Gottfredson and Hirschi's core proposition that low self-control increases involvement in criminal and analogous behaviors is empirically supported. On an absolute level, therefore, it appears that low self-control must be considered an important predictor of criminal behavior and the general theory warrants a measure of acceptance. On a relative level, it is unlikely that Gottfredson and Hirschi's perspective can claim the exalted status of being the general theory of crime. (p. 953)

## Robert J. Sampson and John H. Laub

Although they have published numerous articles and reviews over the past 20 years, Sampson and Laub's basic theory appears in its most complete form in two books, *Crime in the Making: Pathways and Turning Points through Life* (Sampson & Laub, 1993) and *Shared Beginnings, Divergent Lives: Delinquent Boys to Age 70* (Laub & Sampson, 2003). They refer to their major product as an "age-graded theory of informal social control." It relies heavily on the influence of informal *and* formal social controls on behavior over the life course. It is primarily a sociological control theory, although it has more than a dash of social learning, differential association, and rational choice elements to it. We will treat this very important theory in considerable detail in a subsequent chapter so the account that appears here is necessarily brief.

Sampson and Laub's is a life-course theory in two parts. First, they reconstructed and analyzed the Glueck data from the period 1939–1963, from the time that the boys were teenagers to age 32. Second, they located the surviving delinquent members of the original Glueck study and obtained historical data on the group from age 32 to 70. Additionally they personally interviewed a small sample of the men.

Like the Gluecks (1950, 1963) and Gottfredson and Hirschi (1990), Sampson and Laub (2005, pp. 13–15) found that life-course desistance is normative for all persons and all crimes. They emphasized the importance of what they call "turning points," significant exogenous events (e.g., marriage, a good job) that may interrupt a criminal career and cause the offender to reevaluate the course of his or her life. They also emphasized the role of human agency and choice in reconstructing one's life and constructing new avenues of behavior to pursue. Also like the Gluecks and Gottfredson and Hirschi, they acknowledged the crucial role of the family, school, and social environment in the early years. Crime is more likely to occur, they said, when these social bonds are attenuated or broken. In midlife and later the social bonds are more likely to be nondeviant friends and associates, a life partner, having children, owning a home, or having a stable job with adequate income. The greater the number of these bonds, the more likely that desistance from crime will occur.

> The major objective of the life-course perspective is to link social history and social structure to the unfolding of human lives. . . . Applying the life-course framework leads to a focus on continuity and change in criminal behavior over time, especially its embeddedness in historical and other contextual features of social life. . . . [L]ife-course accounts embrace the notion that lives are often unpredictable and dynamic and that exogenously induced changes are ever present. (Laub & Sampson, 2003, pp. 33–34)

## Shadd Maruna

When Sampson and Laub (1993) published *Crime in the Making* they were taken to task by colleagues for relying a bit too much on exogenous influences and paying insufficient attention to human agency in the desistance process. Consequently, they intensely interviewed a small sample of the Glueck survivors which caused them to alter the theory somewhat (Laub & Sampson, 2003) . Maruna's theory (2001) provides a more complete supplement to the age-graded theory in his treatment of the contribution of cognitive transformation to desistance. We provide a more complete account of Maruna's theory in a subsequent chapter, so the description presented here will necessarily be brief.

In his Liverpool Desistance Study, Maruna (2001) interviewed two groups of males and females, nonrandom, targeted samples. One group, called "persisters," admitted to continuing criminal behavior. The other group, called "desisters," claimed that they had been clean for 2 or 3 years. Maruna used a life-story interview and encouraged the participants to talk about their lives as if they were writing an autobiography. One "goal was to construct a single, composite portrait of the desisting self—the identity narrative seems to best support desistance from crime" (p. 51). The other goal was to attempt to determine why some found it impossible to give up crime.

The basic finding of the Liverpool Desistance Study was that both persisters and desisters developed what Maruna called "scripts." The narrative of persisters he termed the "Condemnation Script." The persisters saw themselves as helpless, as dependent on circumstances, and as victims of society. The narrative of desisters he called the "Redemption Script." He found this to be an optimistic perception, to control one's life, to be productive and give something back to society.

Maruna's (2001) conclusions about his work do not greatly differ from Laub and Sampson's (2003) other than in his heavy reliance on cognitive transformation. Although informal social controls as outlined in the age-graded theory (marriage, stable employment, etc.) have important roles, Maruna believed that human agency is the key factor. It is the transformation of self, the generation of a new self-identity, that is the key to desistance.

## Terrie E. Moffitt

Moffitt (1993) has theorized that there are two trajectories of criminal behavior, one leading to short-term involvement (called "adolescence-limited") and one leading to lifelong involvement (called "life-course-persistent"). The age–crime curve, she noted, changes dramatically over age, with a very large burst of activity in the teenage years. Thus, the majority of criminal offenders are teenagers. From the peak in adolescence, by the early 20s the crime rate decreases by half and this decline continues into later life (p. 675).

In Moffitt's (1993) account, life-course kids were bad kids and they become bad adults, despite the fact that only a very small percentage of them would be considered psychopaths.

> Continuity is the hallmark of the small group of life-course persistent antisocial persons. Across the life-course, these individuals exhibit changing manifestations of antisocial behavior. . . . The underlying disposition remains the same, but its expression changes form as new social opportunities arise at different points in development. (p. 679)

The prospects for these individuals are poor and may include unsatisfactory employment, indebtedness, drinking, assault, unstable relationships, poor child care, and mental illness. Moffitt speculated that the origins of life-course-persistent antisocial behavior lie in neuropsychological deficits, poor family life, criminogenic environments, and personality disorder.

Adolescence-limited offenders, on the other hand, do not show continuity in their antisocial behavior. These persons

> are likely to engage in antisocial behavior in situations where such responses seem profitable to them, but they are also able to abandon antisocial behavior when prosocial styles are more rewarding. They maintain control over their antisocial responses and use antisocial behavior only in situations where it may serve an instrumental function. (p. 686)

Moffitt stated that the behavior of adolescence-limiteds represents "social mimicry" of the supposedly exciting lifestyle of the life-course-persistents. In adolescence the latter have access to forbidden goods and behavior: alcohol, drugs, easy sex, fast money. However, once adolescence has passed, and more influential social learning variables come into play (leaving the old neighborhood, university education, a good job, marriage to a prosocial person), the deviant lifestyle becomes less attractive and is given up in young adulthood. Why do they desist?: "Healthy youths respond adaptively to changing contingencies. If motivational and learning mechanisms initiate and maintain their delinquency, then, likewise, changing contingencies can extinguish it" (p. 690).

Not surprisingly, Moffitt's theory has attracted considerable research attention. Following are two examples that provide the flavor of these efforts.

White, Bates, and Buyske (2001) attempted to determine whether a group of possible risk factors could differentiate adolescence-limited from adolescence-to-adulthood persistent delinquents. They examined data from four waves of a longitudinal study of 698 males, ages 12–18 at T1 and 25–31 at T4. Risk factors included measures such as impulsivity, harm avoidance, disinhibition, socioeconomic status, family structure, and parental hostility. They were able to identify four different trajectory groups, two of which confirmed Moffitt's (1993) hypothesis. The four groups were (1) nondelinquents, (2) adolescence-limited delinquents, (3) persistent delinquents, and, unexpectedly (4) escalating delinquents. When the three delinquent groups were compared to the nondelinquents, five risk factors were significant: higher disinhibition, impulsivity, parental hostility, lower harm avoidance, and less intact family structure were related to deviant behavior (p. 607). Only one risk factor, disinhibition, distinguished adolescence-limited from persistent delinquents.

Moffitt, Caspi, Harrington, and Milne (2002) further tested and refined the taxonomy advanced by Moffitt (1993). An earlier study of young males in the Dunedin Multidisciplinary Health and Development Study from New Zealand at ages 3 and 13 years and at 15 and 18 years essentially confirmed the existence of two distinct groups: adolescence-limited (AL) and life-course-persistent (LCP) delinquents. The purpose of the Moffitt et al. (2002) research was to follow up the two types from preschool to adulthood to examine adult adjustment. In addition, Moffitt and colleagues discovered a third group who offend persistently at a high rate during childhood, then tapered off to low to moderate delinquency in adolescence. They termed them "recoveries." Moffitt and colleagues also identified a small group called "abstainers" who avoided virtually all antisocial behavior during childhood and adolescence.

The purpose of the study was to follow up these four groups at age 26 to examine adult outcomes. Moffitt et al. examined data from 79 measures in five domains: criminal offending, personality, psychopathology, personal life, and economic life for 499 males (pp. 195–200).

Fifty-one percent of this cohort were termed *unclassified* as they could not be easily assigned to one of the four groups.

The *abstainer* group (5% of the cohort), awkward and timid as youngsters, were found to be successful young adults who had the fewest number of problem behaviors of any group. They held the highest paying jobs, were likely to be married, and were college educated and financially responsible.

The *recovery* group (8% of the cohort) closely resembled low-level chronic offenders. They were prone to anxiety and depression, were often social isolates, had difficulty making friends, and were unmarried. They had hardly "recovered."

The LCP group (10% of the cohort) engaged in serious criminal offenses including violence against women and children. They had poor work histories, low-status jobs, poor educational qualifications, substance abuse problems, and conflicts at work.

The AL group (26% of the cohort) had good work histories, skilled occupations of reasonably high status, adequate educational qualifications, and, if married, they engaged in some conflict with partners. However, many of these men were still in trouble, with property and drug convictions in early adulthood.

Thus, Moffitt et al. (2002) have demonstrated the basic integrity of the 1993 theory but several of the outcomes differ rather dramatically from that theory's predictions.

## Peggy C. Giordano

Giordano, Schroeder, and Cernkovich (2007) presented a theory that is considerably different from those described above. Their view is a social interactionist perspective that "contrasts with theories of desistance that focus on the role of informal social controls and develops the view of an emotional self that flourishes somewhat independent of the major role transitions typically emphasized in . . . studies of the life course" (p. 1603). The "emotional self" refers to a concept of the self dealing with issues such as managing anger, depression, or marital/intimate partner happiness. For Giordano et al. (2007), emotions are social, have strong cognitive underpinnings, and influence long-term patterns of criminal continuity and change (p. 1604). This stance closely resembles that of Maruna (2001). Their position is opposed to a strict adherence to control theory in that it places too much weight on too few transition events (marriage, job stability, etc.) which may themselves be in a process of change. This is not to say that they discounted transition events. They focused on what they called "hooks for change" which may be a combination of cognitive transitions (or transformations) that may accompany or precede behavioral transitions.

To test their theory, Giordano et al. (2007) relied upon quantitative and qualitative data sources. They conducted three waves of structured interviews with a sample of male and female adolescent offenders as they grew into adulthood. The first interviews were conducted in 1982, then followed up in 1995 when the interviewees were an average age of

29. Life history narratives were obtained at the second wave. The third wave was conducted in 2003 when the interviewees' average age was 38. Open-ended life history narratives were again obtained to compare with the data gathered from the 1995 narratives. Self-reports identified three behavioral patterns: (1) desisters (37% of the sample), (2) persistent (31%), and (3) unstable (episodic, inconsistent) (32%) (p. 1619).

Numerous self-report scales were administered in a number of areas, including (1) problem adult outcomes (criminal involvement, perpetration of relationship violence, problem use of alcohol and drugs); (2) emotional constructs (anger, depression, marital/intimate partner happiness); and (3) background variables were also included (race, delinquency, adolescent drug and alcohol use, occupational prestige, marital status) (pp. 1618–1621).

The emergent data were hardly surprising. Giordano et al. (2007) identified three developmental changes not related to the typically cited transition events that are likely associated with declines in criminal behavior. These were (1) a decrease in negative emotions associated with crime (shame, guilt), (2) a decrease of positive emotions associated with crime (thrills and chills), and (3) development of increased skill in emotional regulation and management (p. 1649). And, even if the focus is on specific transition events (e.g., marriage), attention to emotional processes adds to the understanding of mechanisms that influence desistance. Included here are role taking, emulating emotional role models; a marriage benefit (the "respectability package"); religious conversion, and association with like-minded social network members (p. 1650). It is worth noting that the preceding are not features discovered by this research. These same features have been mentioned by a number of other theorists. On balance, Giordano et al. (2007) concluded that their theory shows that "there is more to life than transition events, and . . . there is more to transition events than is reflected in their social control potential" (p. 1648).

## Mark Warr

The position advanced here also takes issue with control theory, specifically Sampson and Laub (1993). The assertions of Sampson and Laub (1993), said Warr,

> constitute strong evidence for Sutherland's . . . classic theory of differential association, which holds that delinquency is learned from significant others in intimate groups. . . . If delinquency is indeed a consequence of peer influence, marriage takes on special significance as

> a potential cause of desistance from crime. Specifically, if delinquency stems from association with delinquent friends and accomplices, marriage ought to encourage desistance from crime. The predicted outcome—marriage leads to desistance—is of course the same under control theory or differential association/social learning theory, but the social mechanism that produces that outcome is fundamentally different. (pp. 184–185)

The purpose of the research reported by Warr (1998) concentrated on a single life transition: marriage. "The principal objective is to determine whether the effect of marriage on desistance can be attributed to any disruption or dissolution of peer relations that accompanies marriage" (p. 186).

The data for the research were obtained from the National Youth Survey, a continuing longitudinal study of delinquent behavior from a probability sample of 1,725 persons ages 11–17 in 1976. Subjects were interviewed annually and asked about events that occurred in the previous year, including illegal behavior. Warr was primarily concerned with wave 5 (when respondents were 15–21) and wave 6 (when they were 18–24). Respondents in both waves were asked how much time they spent with married and unmarried friends. Two major questions were asked. First, do changes in delinquent peer relations precede or follow marriage? The unmarried in both waves reported no changes in peer relations. Those married between the waves reported a substantial drop in peer relations. Second, does marriage lead to desistance from crime? Those respondents who were married with children reported substantially less time with delinquent friends.

Warr (1998) concluded that

> for those with a history of crime or delinquency, that transition [to marriage] is likely to reduce interaction with former friends and accomplices and thereby reduce the opportunities as well as the motivation to engage in crime. In words that Sutherland might have chosen, marriage appears to discourage crime by severing or weakening former criminal associations. (p. 209)

And further

> Criminal propensity and behavior are not stable and immutable through life, but undergo transformation in response to changing life events and circumstances. In its broadest sense, Sampson and Laub's monograph provides a logical and empirical defense of the sociogenetic school of thought. . . . The present findings join theirs . . . in support of that position. (pp. 210–211)

## Conclusions

We have presented summary information on a small number of theories of criminal behavior and desistance from crime. We wish to emphasize once again that these theories represent only a portion of those available in the criminology literature. We have chosen these specifically because they will be the ones that support the theoretical positions that we adopt in later chapters.

The main points of each of the theories and their probable influence on desistance are summarized in Table 4.1.

**TABLE 4.1. Overview of Seven Major Theories of Desistance**

| Theorist(s) | Guiding theory | Core dimensions | Major influences on desistance | Empirically validated? |
|---|---|---|---|---|
| Glueck & Glueck | None | Aging<br>Family processes | Aging | No |
| Gottfredson & Hirschi | Control | Aging<br>Self-control | Self-control<br>Social bonds | Yes |
| Sampson & Laub | Control | Desistance across the life course | Aging<br>"Turning points"<br>Social bonds | Yes |
| Maruna | Narrative | Cognitive transformation | Rescripting the life story<br>Human agency | Yes |
| Moffitt | Social learning | Two-track taxonomy | Socialization to young adulthood | Yes |
| Giordano | Social interactionism | Cognitive transformation | "Hooks for change" (cognitive and behavioral) | Yes |
| Warr | Differential association | Changing social relationships | Marriage, peer relationships | Yes |

*Chapter 5*

# Factors Influencing Desistance

Even a cursory review of the preceding chapter reveals that the various theories share a lot in common. Irrespective of the theoretical position that the authors espouse (social control, social learning, differential association, social interactionism, etc.), all of them contain similar elements although different words may be used to explain them. Desistance from crime requires behavioral change, and those changes are often facilitated by external and internal events in the life of the individual. These events are variously referred to, for example, as "turning points" (Sampson & Laub, 1993; Laub & Sampson, 2003), "hooks for change" (Giordano et al., 2007), a "change in narrative identity" (McNeill et al., 2005), or "making good" (Maruna, 2001). In order to further clarify the various theories, this chapter reviews some of these events that influence and facilitate desistance.

## Aging

Ultimately the most powerful influence on desistance, aging affects behavioral capacity across the board and will eventually serve to affect an individual's willingness to continue criminal activities. Crime may stop merely because the individual simply no longer has the energy to continue, or it may gradually decrease and then cease. Alternatively, the individual may forsake physically demanding criminal activity (mugging, stickups) for quieter and gentler pursuits such as check forgery or fraud.

## Marriage

This extremely important social event in the lives of most people can have a strong impact on criminal behavior. The important factor in marriage seems to be that, at its best, it breaks up the routine of ordinary criminal associations and activities (Warr, 1998). Marriage may take the individual out of criminogenic environments due to the responsibilities of setting up a new home. The arrival of children amplifies those responsibilities. Maruna (2001) gave credit to "the love of a good woman" and Giordano et al. (2007) cited the "respectability package" (marriage and a good job). Several of Laub and Sampson's (2003) Glueck survivors stated that marriage had saved their lives. Importantly, if the individual marries a nondeviant spouse, this opens up the possibility of gaining a circle of new, nondeviant friends who model prosocial behavior and encourage desistance.

## Work and Job Stability

It is not surprising that individuals who grow up in poverty, have indifferent or punitive parents, have many criminal companions, do poorly in school, and heavily use alcohol and drugs wind up in low-paid, unskilled occupations. That is a career path that is hard to break out of. On the other hand, work can have a very positive effect on behavior. Uggen (2000) has stated that "work is important . . . because workers are likely to experience close and frequent contact with conventional others . . . and because the informal social controls of the workplace encourage conformity" (p. 529). Sampson and Laub (1993) believed that attachment to work can serve as a turning point that can reduce crime. We have mentioned Giordano et al.'s (2007) conviction that work is one-half of the "respectability package." However, Uggen and Staff (2001) caution that only stable, high-quality work is likely to serve as a turning point.

## Military Service

Sampson and Laub (1993) and Laub and Sampson (2003) are frequently cited as promoting military service as an important factor in desistance. There are three facets to this proposition. First, the military teaches discipline and responsibility in all aspects of daily life. People who come from relatively unstructured and criminogenic environments thus learn new ways of behaving. Second, the military throws the individual into a highly heterogeneous group of people. To get along one must develop considerable tolerance for the behavior of others. Third, most of the people the individual encounters in the military will not be criminals. So, the prosocial modeling of nondeviant companions can promote desistance.

Critics of Sampson and Laub have pointed out that the Glueck men were born in the 1920s and so were just old enough to participate in World War II. The major benefit of serving in that conflict was the postwar GI Bill that permitted hundreds of thousands of people to learn skilled trades or obtain a university education. That experience almost surely served as a deterrent to further criminal activity. In the last decade, Bouffard and Laub (2004) reexamined whether military service in more recent times facilitated desistance. They examined four cohorts, three from different periods of the Vietnam War and one from the all-volunteer force. Their data suggested that military service might foster desistance in delinquents. Importantly, they also noted that military service teaches very bad behaviors: (1) it rudely interrupts social roles, (2) it promotes the use of dangerous weapons, (3) it teaches aggressive problem solving, and (4) it can produce unique stressors (e.g., posttraumatic stress disorder).

## Juvenile Detention

For many of the same reasons as service in the military, juvenile detention has been seen as an early turning point for some individuals. At its best, like the military, such an institution can teach the importance of adherence to rules, personal responsibility, and tolerance of persons unlike oneself. One of Laub and Sampson's (2003) Glueck men described his early experience in one of the Massachusetts correctional schools as one of the best things that had ever happened to him. At its worst, however, and again like the military, the juvenile correctional institution can be a school for crime and other forms of deviant behavior.

## Prison

Adult incarceration, on the other hand, may have an entirely different effect. For older offenders, particularly those who have done several prison terms, incarceration in midlife may result in a decision that "I can't take any more of this." This decision could result in an almost immediate cessation of criminal behavior. However, prison is not an environment that encourages prosocial behavior, other than to keep the peace. Individuals with strong antisocial and criminal propensities are thrown together with others having the same inclinations. While it may not necessarily be a school for crime, prison is certainly a fraternity (or sorority) of persons with strong antisocial proclivities. One may counterargue that prisons are actually operated on a military model which, in some instances, encourages self-regulation and personal responsibility, and provides educational programs and skill training. However, said Harris (2005), "The distaste for such programs is linked to a sense that these interventions involve things being 'done to' or 'prescribed for' passive recipients who are characterized as deficient, ineffectual, misguided, untrustworthy, possibly dangerous, and almost certain to get into trouble again" (p. 318). And worse, Harris (2005) continued, "It is useful to consider the degree to which prisons are structured on the basis of values that glorify aggression, control, and militarism. To that extent, prisons are criminogenic institutions, producing and reinforcing the violence and dehumanization they ostensibly attempt to control" (p. 323). It probably quite safe to say that in only in a very few isolated cases is prison a turning point toward prosocial, noncriminal behavior.

Liebling and Maruna (2005) pointed out that sociologists have long held the view that prison is damaging to people. They note, however, that a group of psychologists in the 1980s were unable to find any lasting psychological damage from incarceration. Liebling and Maruna believed that this was too narrow a view of permanent damage. They argue that, quite apart from lasting impairment, the prison experience contributes to many negative effects on communities, families, and lives that need to be better understood.

## Education

Moffitt et al. (2002), in their follow-up of adolescent delinquents to young adulthood, found that education had strongly benefited adolescence-limited delinquents in that they were able to secure good-paying jobs with reasonably high status, which in turn assisted them in maintaining stable and happy marriages and desistance from crime. Their life-course-persistent offenders, on the other hand, did poorly in school and could only secure unskilled or semiskilled occupations.

It seems superfluous to say that, for criminals and noncriminals alike, an adequate education is an important key to a stable and satisfying future life.

## Cognitive Transformation

Maruna (2001) speaks of offenders or ex-convicts creating new self-narratives in which they describe re-creating themselves as a new person, a different person, a "straight" person.

> To desist from crime, ex-offenders need to develop a coherent, prosocial identity for themselves. As such, they need to account for and understand their criminal pasts (why they did what they did), and they also need to understand why they are now "not like that anymore." Ex-offenders need a coherent and credible self-story to explain (to themselves and others) how their checkered pasts could have led to their new, reformed identities." (pp. 7–8)

This position is echoed by Ward and Marshall (2007) who said that a narrative identity of which Maruna speaks is the basic self-story.

> The rehabilitation of offenders depends crucially on the construction of a more adaptive narrative identity. . . . The view that human beings are agents who construct narrative identities and engage in person projects based on those identities indicates that they have some degree of plasticity and ability to shape their lives and circumstances. (p. 280)

Maruna (2001) took this idea a step further: "Although ex-offenders do not describe themselves as 'desisting,' they do talk about 'going straight,' 'making good,' or 'going legit.' . . . These phrases imply an ongoing work in progress. One *goes* legit. One does not talk about having *turned* legit or having *become* legit. The 'going' is the thing" (p. 26).

## The Pygmalion Effect

This is closely related to the cognitive restructuring process just described and is called "the looking-glass identity transformation." It may be summed up in a single quotation from Maruna, LeBel, Mitchell, and Naples (2009):

> In the so-called "Pygmalion Effect," the *high* expectations of others lead to greater self-belief (and subsequent performance) in an individual. . . . We argue that personal transformation . . . also contains a looking-glass element. People start to believe that they can successfully change their lives when those around them start to believe that they can. In other words, rehabilitation . . . is a construct that is negotiated through interaction between an individual and significant others. . . . Not only must a person accept conventional society in order to go straight, but conventional society must accept that the person has changed as well. (pp. 31–32)

## "Knifing Off"

This term is usually attributed to Laub and Sampson (2003) who identified four major turning points in the desistance process: marriage/spouses, military service, correctional schools, and neighborhood change. An unusual choice of words, "knifing off" refers to literally cutting one's bonds to the criminal past. The identified turning points, each in its own way, can cut off the past from the present, provide supervision and monitoring as well as opportunities for social support and growth, bring change and structure to routine activities, and provide an opportunity for identity transformation. Maruna and Roy (2007, pp. 106–109) asked, "What gets knifed off?":

- The past. This refers to moving on from the past.
- Social roles. Getting rid of old roles and their social difficulties.
- Associates. Getting rid of undesirable companions. This is similar to the differential association position (Warr, 1998).
- Disadvantage. Compensating for personal deficits (educational, social, economic).
- Stigma. A process of delabeling, either formal or personal.
- Opportunities. Eliminating old options for criminal involvement.

Maruna and Roy (2007) noted this important qualification: "In the extant literature, the phrase *knifing off the past* is rarely mentioned without the accompanying phrase *and providing scripts for the future*" (p. 118). Without a future script, knifing off would not necessarily produce behavioral or personality change.

## Spirituality

Giordano, Longmore, Schroeder, and Seffrin (2008) were interested in whether individual bonds to religion or religious institutions played a role in deterring criminal activity. They performed a three-wave study of males and females from midadolescence to midadulthood. The participants self-reported on criminal activity, social networks (romantic partners, criminal associates), adult social bonds (marital happiness, occupational prestige), and religiosity (closeness to God, church attendance) (pp. 106–110). The data indicated that "neither perceived closeness to God nor church attendance as measured . . . are associated with being in the stable desister category" (pp. 110–111) and "results consistently show . . . no association between level of religiousity and later self-reported crime" (p. 112). Undeterred by these findings, Giordano et al. (2008) concluded that "church participation potentially can provide much needed entrée to a more prosocial network and an important layer of social support" (p.122).

## Fear of Serious Assault or Death

We mentioned above that aging alone is a powerful factor influencing desistance. We should also consider that some forms of criminal behavior are highly dangerous and the threat of serious injury or death is always present. Persons who engage in armed robbery are in danger of dying in a car crash while trying to escape or being shot to death by the police. Prisons, despite their strong administrative emphasis on social control, are highly dangerous places. They are filled with rival gangs who compete and fight for access to and control of very small rewards. Getting in the way of these people, or failing to join with them in their activities, could result in serious injury or death.

## Sickness and Incapacitation

Often accompanying old age is chronic illness and incapacitation. Many persistent criminals drink and smoke heavily, with the result that some will eventually become ill or even be incapacitated by alcohol-related diseases or emphysema. The criminological literature frequently observes that at least a portion of the low end of the age–crime curve could probably be accounted for by persons dropping out of crime due to becoming too ill to continue. We would observe that that is voluntary and is still desistance.

## Conclusions

We have provided brief descriptions of 13 possible influences on desistance from crime. These are the ones that seem to us to be the most important. They do not exhaust the possibilities. We have noted above that there are many paths into crime. The described influences show that there are many paths out.

## *Chapter 6*

# Two Major Theories of Desistance

The main goal of this book is to provide a new framework for the management and rehabilitation of a single class of criminal offenders: sex offenders. We have proposed to do this by drawing inspiration from the criminological literature on the process of desistance, then providing complementary information from the forensic psychological literature to finally produce both a theoretical framework and a program to accomplish rehabilitation. We are now approaching the end of our treatment of the criminological literature. We will now sharpen our focus to concentrate on two theoretical positions that we believe best express what we hope to accomplish. These are the theories of Sampson and Laub (1993), Laub and Sampson (2003), and Maruna (2001). These three statements best express the theoretical stance of these authors.

## Sampson and Laub's Age-Graded Theory of Informal Social Control

In Chapter 4 we provided an overview of the landmark research by the Gluecks, the *Unraveling Juvenile Delinquency* (1950) study, and its follow-up, *Delinquents and Non-Delinquents in Perspective* (1968). This very large database formed the foundation for Sampson and Laub's initial work, *Crime in the Making: Pathways and Turning Points through Life* (1993). The reanalysis of the Glueck data forms the bedrock on which the age-graded theory rests.

The Glueck data were a rich resource. Sampson and Laub noted that many criminological studies do not have many serious, persistent offenders. The Glueck delinquents were responsible for 6,300 arrests to age 32. Also, about 20% of the nondelinquent group were arrested as adults. These data were central to the *Crime in the Making* analysis (Sampson & Laub, 1993) since they were "well suited to the explication of factors that distinguish serious and persistent delinquents from non-delinquents. Moreover, the Gluecks' longitudinal data can be used to assess both between-group and within-group variation in criminal and deviant behavior over the life course" (p. 38).

The *Unraveling* and follow-up data were stored at the Harvard Law School where Sheldon Glueck had been a faculty member. The reanalysis required coding, recoding, and computerizing the original data. Those data were stored in old-style punch cards and handwritten accounts and had to be reconstructed to run in a modern computer. Sampson and Laub read over 15,000 cards and developed a range of data containing 2,600 variables. They found a very high level of agreement between raw data found in handwritten accounts and coded data (98% for 2,600 variables). Data were available from self-, parent, and teacher reports plus official records of criminal behavior. They created a composite measure of total unofficial delinquency and a summary measure of the unofficial reports for each particular offense. Interviews with the boys began in 1939; the authors noted that this was probably the earliest self-report study of this kind. In the end, Sampson and Laub reconstructed and validated a data set of complete criminal histories for 480 (of 500) of the original delinquents from first arrest to age 32. This file was composed of 60 different offense types and more than 20 different legal dispositions. For purposes of analysis they used broad crime categories (violent, property, robbery, burglary, etc.). The age–crime curve was very evident in the data. Sampson and Laub (1993) were able to obtain supplementary court information on the Glueck men from ages 32 to 45. For that period, they were able to code only the number and type of offenses (pp. 47–63, *passim*).

The theoretical rationale of the *Crime in the Making* analysis is as follows:

> Consistent with the theory of informal social control and crime and deviance over the life course, the general organizing principle is that the probability of deviance increases when an individual's bond to society is weak or broken. . . . In other words, when the social ties (that is, attachment, commitment) that bind an individual to key societal institutions (such as the family, school, work) are loosened, the risk of crime and delinquency is heightened. The specific feature of our model

> involves a two-step hypothesis: structural context [residential mobility, parental criminality] influences dimensions of informal social controls by the family [parental rejection, harsh discipline], which in turn explains variations in delinquency. (Sampson & Laub, p. 65)

The model of which they speak may be seen in Figure 6.1, which illustrates the hypothesized relationship between structural factors, family processes, and delinquency. The balance of *Crime in the Making* is concerned with multiple statistical analyses, primarily linear and logistical regression, of these relationships. The emergent data, for the most part, confirmed the hypothetical assertions. This is a very complex study with a multitude of interrelated variables and requires close reading to gain its full impact.

The empirical findings of the *Crime in the Making* analysis (Sampson & Laub, 1993) can be summarized in two parts: causes of delinquency and stability and change in criminal behavior over the life course (pp. 247–257, *passim*).

### Causes of Delinquency

- "The strongest and most consistent effects on both official and unofficial delinquency flow from the social processes of family, school, and peers."
- "Low levels of parental supervision, erratic, threatening, and harsh discipline, and weak parental attachment were strongly and directly related to delinquency."
- "School attachment had large negative effects on delinquency independent of family processes."
- "Attachment to delinquent peers had a significant positive effect on delinquency regardless of family and school process."
- "Family and school processes appear most important in the causal chain."
- "Structural background factors have little direct effect . . . , but instead are mediated by intervening sources of informal social control."

### Stability and Change in Criminal Behavior over the Life Course

- "Delinquency and other forms of antisocial conduct in childhood were strongly related to troublesome adult behavior across a variety of life's domains (crime, economic dependence, marital discord)."
- "Our qualitative and quantitative findings suggest that social

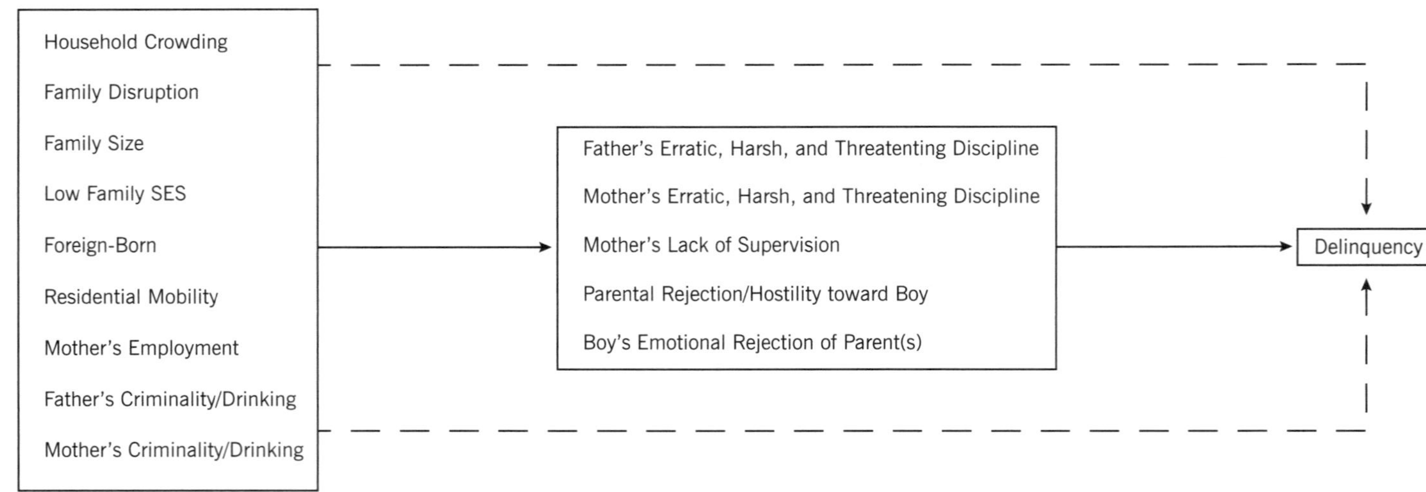


**FIGURE 6.1.** Theoretical model of Glueck data: Structural background factors, family process, and delinquency. From Sampson and Laub (1993, p. 66). Copyright 1993 by Harvard University Press. Reprinted by permission.

> ties embedded in adult transitions (for example, marital attachment, job stability) explain variations in crime unaccounted for by childhood propensities."

Sampson and Laub (1993) also performed a limited qualitative analysis of selected data. The Glueck data contained detailed handwritten interviews that had been conducted by their research team. These were supplemented by miscellaneous notes, correspondence, employment histories, and the like. Keeping in mind that their theory emphasizes the importance of marriage and stable employment as turning points, Sampson and Laub (1993) wished to examine different relationships of these two variables with criminal history. Using the qualitative interview data, they examined, for example, relationships such as weak marital attachment, weak job stability, and persistent offending, as opposed to strong marital attachment, strong job stability, and desistance. Seventy reconstructed life histories were examined. Sampson and Laub concluded that

> through an analysis of the qualitative data found in the Glueck case files, we found that poor job stability and weak attachment to one's spouse increase the likelihood of criminal activity and deviant behavior. Conversely, these case records affirmed that strong job stability and marital attachment reduce the likelihood of involvement in criminal and deviant behavior. (p. 240)

*Crime in the Making* (1993) is the basic opening statement of the age-graded theory of social control. The basic theoretical structure appears in Figure 6.1 above. Unfortunate structural background factors do not necessarily produce a delinquent child. For example, although living in a crowded, disruptive home; in a poor, economically depressed neighborhood; with drunken, drugged, or criminal parents, represent an unlikely beginning, these features may not have a significant effect. Rather it is the family processes of lack of supervision, harsh and threatening parental discipline, and hostility and rejection of the child that are more influential. Association with delinquent peers and poor school performance will accentuate these effects. These features, which foster delinquency, are likely to extend into adult life. Given all that, Sampson and Laub say, strong social bonds developed in early adult life, such as marriage and achieving stability in a good job, can interrupt the course of deviant and criminal behavior and result in desistance.

*Shared Beginnings, Divergent Lives: Delinquent Boys to Age 70* (Laub & Sampson, 2003) represents the follow-up to *Crime in the Making* and is the final statement of the age-graded theory. The follow-up was conducted as a result of some unresolved questions raised by colleagues. Moffitt (1993) had earlier stated that life-course persisters are unlikely to change in adulthood (Could this mean that turning points are irrelevant?). Nagin and Land (1993) had previously recommended use of the trajectory analysis described in Chapter 3 to examine stability and change over the life course. Longitudinal models such as those used in *Crime in the Making* might fail to capture the progression of change. Modell (1994) argued that the combination of variable-based and the qualitative person-based analysis used in *Crime in the Making* were not adequate. The authors needed to be more "adept at discerning (or portraying) the inner logic of lives" (p. 1391) as revealed in qualitative data. He argued that the authors treated their small qualitative sample as a quantitative test of their hypotheses. "Reflecting on this critique," replied Laub and Sampson (2003, p. 8), "we are compelled by the evidence to agree."

The authors proceeded as follows (2003, p. 9):

- "We . . . revise our age-graded theory of informal social control by bringing into account the interplay of human agency and choice, situational influences, routine activities, and historical context."
- They conducted national death record and criminal history searches for all 500 men in the delinquent sample to age 70.
- They tracked, located, and conducted detailed life-history interviews with 52 men from the original delinquent group as they approached age 70. These men had not been contacted in 35 years.
- Cases were selected on the basis of their trajectories of juvenile and adult offending (labeled "persisters," "desisters," and "intermittent") as derived from official records.
- The 52 life-history interviews were combined with the collection of criminal histories and death records for all 500 former delinquents to age 70.
- Integrating these diverse data illuminated age, crime, and human development using both quantitative and qualitative methods.
- The bulk of *Shared Beginnings* rests on these life-history narratives.

Finding the surviving Glueck men was not easy. When Laub and Sampson (2003) began the follow-up in 1993, the oldest subject was 69, the youngest 61. Data were collected for 483 (88%) of the original sample for all three time periods (childhood, adolescence, adulthood). The Glueck men had last been contacted between 1957 and 1964. The last addresses available for them were 35 years old and few had telephone numbers in their files. Only one in 20 had a Social Security number. An additional problem was that persisters would likely not wish to be contacted. And the families, employers, and significant others of the desisters might not be aware of the subject's former criminal life (p. 62).

- *Criminal records search.* In Massachusetts Laub and Sampson (2003) found criminal records for 475 men. The histories from age 31 (the last Glueck analysis) were updated. Arrest charges were coded as violent, property, alcohol/drug, or other. FBI rap sheets were more complete and they supplemented the Massachusetts records (pp. 63–64).
- *Death records search.* Twenty-five men had died during the Glueck research. A death record search from age 32 for the remaining 475 was performed in Massachusetts. Additional deaths were found in the National Death Index. Obituaries in the *Boston Globe* were scanned daily (p. 65).
- *Other means of locating people.* The research team also searched telephone books (paper and electronic), web-based search engines, motor vehicle records, and voter lists.

The multiple search strategies found that sufficient records were available for 455 of the original sample. Two hundred twenty-five men had died (49%). Two hundred thirty were thought to be alive but 40 could not be located. Of this remaining sample, 52 men were selected for intensive interviewing.

### *Life History Narratives*

Dependent upon their criminal histories, Laub and Sampson (2003) formed five categories for the 52 men:

- Persistent violent or predatory offenders (*N* = 14).
- Nonviolent juvenile offenders who desisted in adulthood (*N* = 15).
- Violent juvenile offenders who desisted in adulthood (*N* = 4).
- Intermittent (or sporadic) offenders who had an onset of violence in later adulthood (*N* = 5).
- Intermittent offenders with an onset of violence in young adulthood and desistance in middle age *or* those showing an erratic offending pattern over the entire life course (*N* = 14).

Sampson and Laub (2005) commented on the composition of this group:

> The sample of men to interview was strategically selected to ensure variability in trajectories of adult crime. . . . The combined data represent a roughly 50 year window from which to update the Glueck men's lives at the close of the twentieth century and connect them to life experiences all the way back to early childhood. We believe these data represent the longest longitudinal study to date in criminology of the same men. (pp. 16–17)

The authors developed a *Life History Calendar*, shown in Figure 6.2. The abscissa of the figure shows the years from age 30 to 70 and the ordinate the various categories that form the basis of the life-history interview: marriages, children, housemates, family, education, employment, residences, arrests, and convictions. Such a calendar permits a recording of a large number of crucial life events and their timing, sequence, and duration.

The authors (Laub & Sampson, 2003) also used an open-ended interview schedule that focused on retrospective views of the life course. It contained questions such as: Is life improving or worsening (since childhood, adolescence, and adulthood)? It requested a self-evaluation of turning points and their relationship to criminal activity. This was followed by questions on the influence of these life-course transitions (marriage, divorce, employment, military service, residence changes, etc.). The aim was to combine these life-course narratives with the obtained institutional records and data from the Glueck archives. The interviews were conducted in a variety of settings, although the subject's home was preferred. It is interesting that a majority of the interviewees had no memory of participating in the Glueck study. No one knew, or cared, who the Gluecks were (Laub & Sampson, 2003, pp. 66–70 *passim*).

Reflecting on this experience, Laub and Sampson (2003) later said that

> tracing, locating, and interviewing the men for this study turned out to be an incredible experience. These men revealed life stories that were often filled with sadness and tragedy. The men . . . spoke of loved ones lost, missed opportunities and regrets, and personal tragedies that they had experienced and somehow survived. It was not unusual for tears to accompany their life-history narratives. (p. 79)

### *Long-Term Trajectories of Crime*

Laub and Sampson (2003) state that there are four major criminal career positions (p. 81):

| Subject: | | | | | | | | | | | | | | | | | | | | | | | | | | | | | | | | | | | | | | | | | | |
|---|---|---|---|---|---|---|---|---|---|---|---|---|---|---|---|---|---|---|---|---|---|---|---|---|---|---|---|---|---|---|---|---|---|---|---|---|---|---|---|---|---|---|
| Reference years—> | | | | | | | | | | | | | | | | | | | | | | | | | | | | | | | | | | | | | | | | | | |
| Birthday: | | 30 | 31 | 32 | 33 | 34 | 35 | 36 | 37 | 38 | 39 | 40 | 41 | 42 | 43 | 44 | 45 | 46 | 47 | 48 | 49 | 50 | 51 | 52 | 53 | 54 | 55 | 56 | 57 | 58 | 59 | 60 | 61 | 62 | 63 | 64 | 65 | 66 | 67 | 68 | 69 | 70 |
| **MARRIAGES** | # | | | | | | | | | | | | | | | | | | | | | | | | | | | | | | | | | | | | | | | | | |
| MARITAL EVENTS | | | | | | | | | | | | | | | | | | | | | | | | | | | | | | | | | | | | | | | | | | |
| LIVING W/ SPOUSE | | | | | | | | | | | | | | | | | | | | | | | | | | | | | | | | | | | | | | | | | | |
| PARTNER EVENTS | | | | | | | | | | | | | | | | | | | | | | | | | | | | | | | | | | | | | | | | | | |
| LIVING W/ PARTNER | | | | | | | | | | | | | | | | | | | | | | | | | | | | | | | | | | | | | | | | | | |
| **CHILDREN** | # | | | | | | | | | | | | | | | | | | | | | | | | | | | | | | | | | | | | | | | | | |
| BIRTHS/DEATHS | | | | | | | | | | | | | | | | | | | | | | | | | | | | | | | | | | | | | | | | | | |
| **HOUSEMATES** | | (if ever lived without spouse/partner) | | | | | | | | | | | | | | | | | | | | | | | | | | | | | | | | | | | | | | | | |
| LIVING W/ RELATIVES | | | | | | | | | | | | | | | | | | | | | | | | | | | | | | | | | | | | | | | | | | |
| LIVING W/ FRIENDS | | | | | | | | | | | | | | | | | | | | | | | | | | | | | | | | | | | | | | | | | | |
| **FAMILY** | | | | | | | | | | | | | | | | | | | | | | | | | | | | | | | | | | | | | | | | | | |
| PARENT DEATH | | | | | | | | | | | | | | | | | | | | | | | | | | | | | | | | | | | | | | | | | | |
| OTHER DEATH | | | | | | | | | | | | | | | | | | | | | | | | | | | | | | | | | | | | | | | | | | |
| OTHER—MISC. | | | | | | | | | | | | | | | | | | | | | | | | | | | | | | | | | | | | | | | | | | |
| **EDUCATION** | Y / N | | | | | | | | | | | | | | | | | | | | | | | | | | | | | | | | | | | | | | | | | |
| FULL-TIME | | | | | | | | | | | | | | | | | | | | | | | | | | | | | | | | | | | | | | | | | | |
| PART-TIME | | | | | | | | | | | | | | | | | | | | | | | | | | | | | | | | | | | | | | | | | | |
| **EMPLOYMENT** | # | | | | | | | | | | | | | | | | | | | | | | | | | | | | | | | | | | | | | | | | | |
| FULL-TIME | | | | | | | | | | | | | | | | | | | | | | | | | | | | | | | | | | | | | | | | | | |
| PART-TIME | | | | | | | | | | | | | | | | | | | | | | | | | | | | | | | | | | | | | | | | | | |
| SPOUSE WORK | | | | | | | | | | | | | | | | | | | | | | | | | | | | | | | | | | | | | | | | | | |
| UNEMPLOYED | | | | | | | | | | | | | | | | | | | | | | | | | | | | | | | | | | | | | | | | | | |
| DEPENDENT | | | | | | | | | | | | | | | | | | | | | | | | | | | | | | | | | | | | | | | | | | |
| **RESIDENCES** | # | | | | | | | | | | | | | | | | | | | | | | | | | | | | | | | | | | | | | | | | | |
| IN BOSTON | | | | | | | | | | | | | | | | | | | | | | | | | | | | | | | | | | | | | | | | | | |
| IN MASS. | | | | | | | | | | | | | | | | | | | | | | | | | | | | | | | | | | | | | | | | | | |
| OUTSIDE MASS. | | | | | | | | | | | | | | | | | | | | | | | | | | | | | | | | | | | | | | | | | | |
| INSTITUTION | | | | | | | | | | | | | | | | | | | | | | | | | | | | | | | | | | | | | | | | | | |
| **ARRESTS** | # | | | | | | | | | | | | | | | | | | | | | | | | | | | | | | | | | | | | | | | | | |
| **CONVICTION** | # | | | | | | | | | | | | | | | | | | | | | | | | | | | | | | | | | | | | | | | | | |
| VIOLENT | | | | | | | | | | | | | | | | | | | | | | | | | | | | | | | | | | | | | | | | | | |
| PROPERTY | | | | | | | | | | | | | | | | | | | | | | | | | | | | | | | | | | | | | | | | | | |
| DRUG/ALCOHOL | | | | | | | | | | | | | | | | | | | | | | | | | | | | | | | | | | | | | | | | | | |
| OTHER | | | | | | | | | | | | | | | | | | | | | | | | | | | | | | | | | | | | | | | | | | |

**FIGURE 6.2.** Life History Calendar for follow-up of Glueck delinquents at age 70. From Laub and Sampson (2003, p. 68). Copyright 2003 by Harvard University Press. Reprinted by permission.

- Persons who are chronic offenders at an early age do not stop offending as they grow older (Wolfgang et al., 1972).
- Moffitt (1993) agreed that there is a subset of life-course-persistent offenders who continue to offend as they grow older.
- Gottfredson and Hirschi (1990) asserted that the age effect is invariant. All offenders will commit fewer crimes as they grow older.
- There are discrete groups of offenders who have varying propensities for criminal activity, that is, there are different age–crime curves for different groups of offenders (Nagin & Land, 1993).

Laub and Sampson (2003) set out to examine these theoretical/empirical positions using the trajectory analysis method advanced by Nagin and Land (1993) and described in Chapter 3 by Bushway (personal communication, March 24, 2009). We stated above that the authors divided the recoded arrest charges into four categories: violence, property, and alcohol/drug. Figure 6.3 shows the data for total crime disaggregated by offense category. It is clear that only property offenses display the classic age–crime curve.

As previous researchers have done (and answering Nagin's objection to the *Crime in the Making* analysis) the authors asked, Are there latent (unobserved) classes of offenders as defined by trajectories of crime over the life course? Said another way, are all criminals exhibiting essentially the same behavior or are there subgroups reflecting different trajectories of criminal activity and desistance?

Figure 6.4 shows the offending trajectories for total crime. The analysis revealed seven classes of offenders, only one of which shows the classic desister pattern (19.9% of the sample). These data permitted some conclusions regarding the above-stated theoretical/empirical positions on career criminality. "The ultimate conclusion to be derived from these figures is that the age–crime relationship is *not* invariant for all offenders and offense types. Moreover, the data firmly reject the typology of two offender groups" (Laub & Sampson, 2003, p. 104). The data disagree with the basic positions of Gottfredson and Hirschi (1990) and Moffitt (1993). However, we mentioned above that Moffitt et al. (2002) have now identified groups in addition to the original dual taxonomy but not by the trajectory model analysis. Of the chronic offenders identified in Figure 6.4, only the high-rate chronics (3.2% of the sample) appear to resemble the famous 6% identified in the Wolfgang et al. (1972) research.

Since our interest in this book is violent crime, specifically sexual crime, we need to see what the trajectory analysis produced for that offense category tells us. Figure 6.5 shows that the latent class anal-

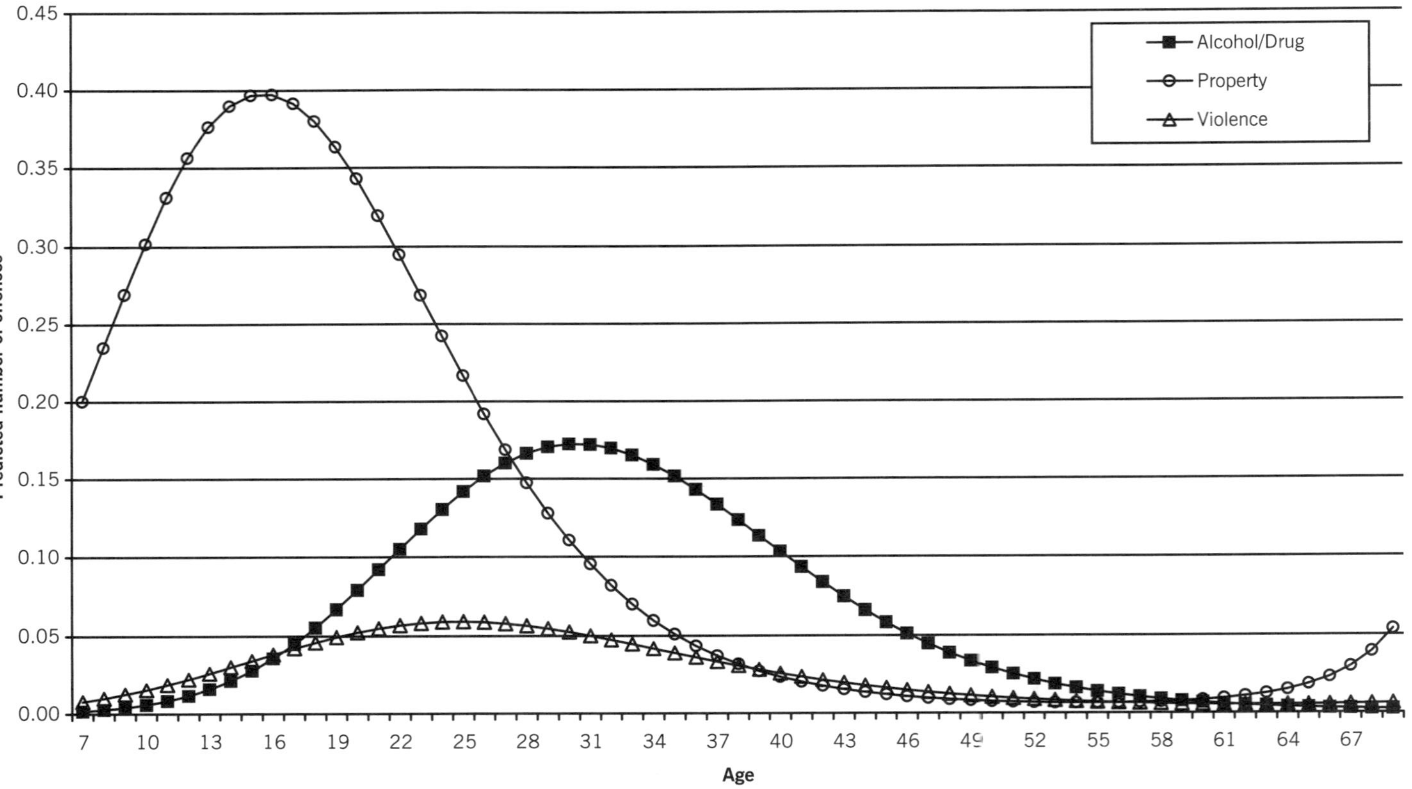


**FIGURE 6.3.** Trajectories of total crime × offense categories. From Laub and Sampson (2003, p. 89). Copyright 2003 by Harvard University Press. Reprinted by permission.

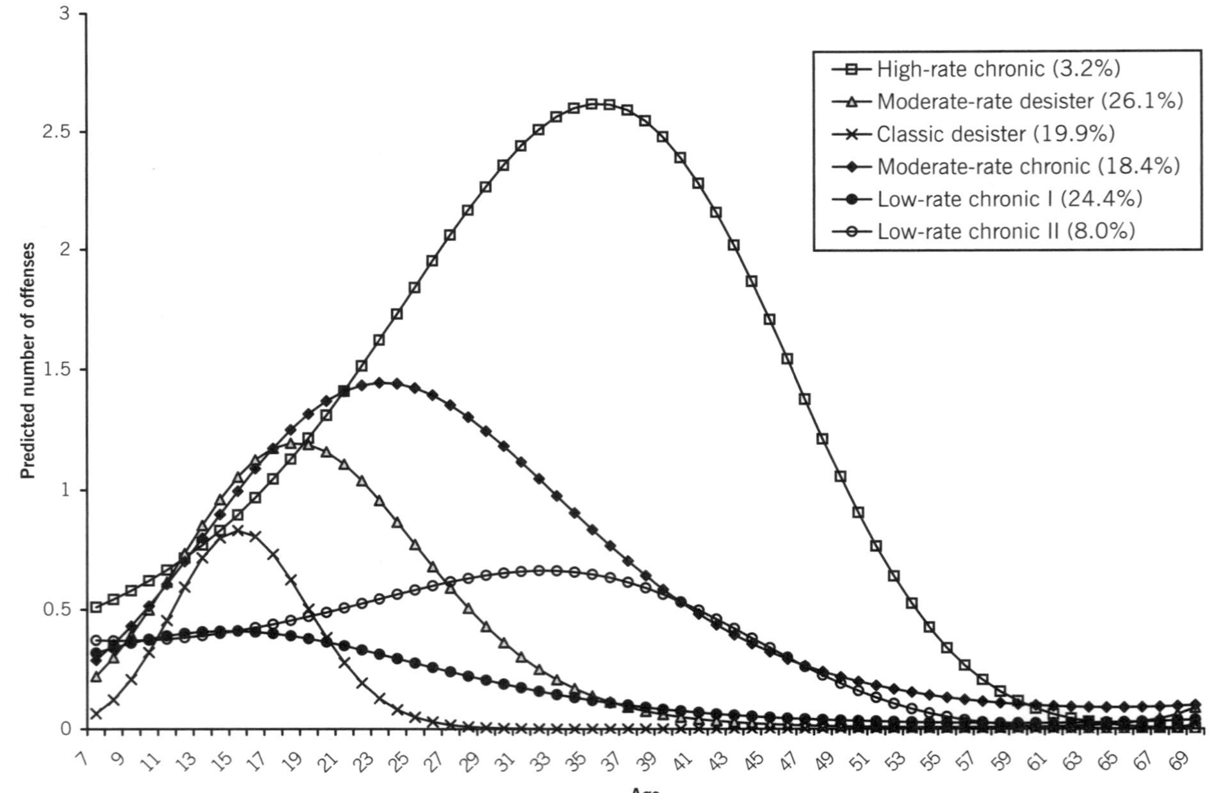


**FIGURE 6.4.** Total crime × class of offender. From Laub and Sampson (2003, p. 104). Copyright 2003 by Harvard University Press. Reprinted by permission.

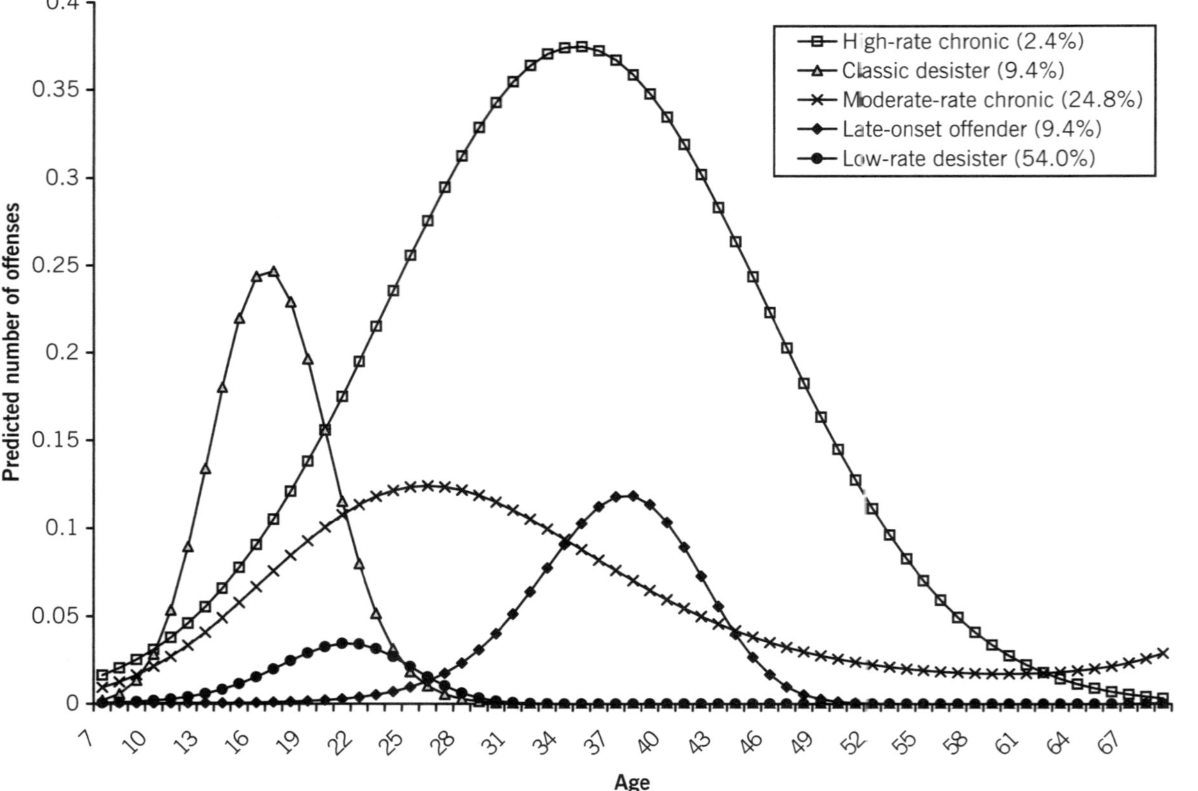


**FIGURE 6.5.** Trajectories of violent crime. From Laub and Sampson (2003, p. 106). Copyright 2003 by Harvard University Press. Reprinted by permission.

ysis identified five groups. Once again, the classic desister is a small portion of the sample (9.4%). Two features of this figure are important. First, low-rate desisters (54%) represent more than half of the sample. Second, moderate-rate chronics (24.8%) offend at fairly low rates, then gradually trail off across the life course. These data pose an interesting question. Nearly 80% of the total sample engaged in a fairly modest amount of criminal behavior and, more importantly, 54% appeared to be not very dangerous at all. We suspect that, if the sample was composed exclusively of sex offenders, much the same data would emerge.

The data obtained from the trajectory analyses caused Laub and Sampson (2003) to modify some of the conclusions from the *Crime in the Making* analysis. "The main conclusion from these analyses is that . . . individual differences and childhood characteristics defined by risk rather than by crime itself do not do a good job of distinguishing different offending trajectories over the long haul" (p. 107). Further, "although latent classes of offenders appear to yield distinct trajectories of offending, supporting Nagin and Land (1993), group membership is not easily, if at all, predictable from individual, childhood, and adolescent risk factors" (p. 110).

### *Life History Narrative Analysis*

Laub and Sampson (2003) emphasized that their approach in *Shared Beginnings* is a blending of quantitative and qualitative data.

> The life histories . . . are informed not only by the trajectory analyses . . . but by further quantitative data on criminal histories . . . and social data . . . for the 52 men in the follow-up. . . . This quantitative analysis is informed, in turn, by the narrative data. In the end, our approach represents a blending of diverse methods of data collection and analysis that could not be achieved by exclusive reliance on a single mode of research. (p. 114)

### *Desistance from Crime*

Laub and Sampson (2003, pp. 114–149 *passim*) found:

> four major self-described turning points implicated in the desistance process: marriage/spouses, the military, reform school, and neighborhood change. Each of these creates new situations that (1) knife off the past from the present; (2) provide not only supervision and monitor-

ing but opportunities for social support and growth; (3) bring change and structure to routine activities; and (4) provide an opportunity for identity transformation. (pp. 148–149).

### Marriage

Desisters had stable marriages with few divorces and separations. The state of marriage was acknowledged by the men as a time to become serious and responsible. The authors emphasize that marriage restructures routine, daily activities and provides direct social control, as in limiting or eliminating contact with deviant associates. A residential change accompanying marriage allows the individual to get away from bad family and peer relationships. The arrival of children will also function to restructure routine activities, with more time spent in family-oriented pursuits. The authors noted that the changes that occur are likely to be gradual and the effects of desistance will be cumulative.

### Military Service

The effect of military service on the Glueck men may have been partially an historical artifact. They were born in the 1920s, raised in the Great Depression, and served in the military in World War II. For these poor and disadvantaged young men, the military offered a new life, a new beginning, a home better than the one from which they came. As we noted in the previous chapter, military service instills discipline, imposes order on one's life, and forces tolerance of individual differences. These features and the availability of the postwar GI Bill constituted turning points for some of the desisters.

### Correctional School

Recall that the delinquent boys in the Glueck study were recruited from two correctional schools in Massachusetts. One of the Glueck men stated that his stretch in reform school taught him to "respect the things that count in life" and that life in the institution was "the best thing that ever happened" because he was subjected to "firm authority and close supervision" (in Laub & Sampson, 2003, p. 128). Another said that "I learned how to be away from home and how to get along with other people" (in Laub & Sampson, 2003, p. 130). Yet another did not have fond memories, "I didn't learn anything up there, except not to go back. That's about it" (in Laub & Sampson, 2003, p. 131). Nonetheless, the reform school, like the military, imposed order and discipline upon young men's lives. The authors note that it was also a place where one could perform a task and be rewarded for it, unlike what occurred in their family and school experiences.

### *Employment*

The desisters showed stability in their work lives. Work, like spouses, can provide direct social control and can change one's sense of identity. If an individual is drawing a paycheck on a regular basis, then he could conclude that he was stable and responsible. Many of the men who desisted, say the authors, worked extensively. If their spouses also worked, that provided even more structure to routine activities. One of the interviewees summed up the influence of work as "being able to work, being able to get a pay check. . . . Being able to go to the store and buy something and not have to steal it. That's important in life . . . what changed my life is work" (in Laub & Sampson, 2003, p. 139).

### *Human Agency*

Although Laub and Sampson's theory is one that emphasizes the (mostly external) influence of formal and informal social controls, they provide some space for personal interventions. In their words, "What is most striking in the narratives . . . is the role of human agency, or choice, in desistance from crime and deviance. The men who desisted are 'active' players in the desistance process" (2003, p. 141). Citing another author they go on to say that "a subjective reconstruction of the self is especially likely at times of transition" (p. 141) but do not provide further comment on the issue.

### *Persistence in Crime*

Laub and Sampson (2003) defined persistence as "being arrested at multiple phases of the life course. This . . . seems consistent with the idea of persistent offending as enduring, repetitious, and tenacious" (p.150). They examined two types of persistent offenders (pp. 150–195, *passim*). One group was men who were arrested as juveniles, young adults, and older adults for crimes of violence. The second group consisted of men arrested as juveniles, young adults, and older adults, including arrests for violence in at least two of the three categories. Unlike the desisting group, the persisters spent less time married, working, and in the military over their lives.

### *Lifestyles*

The persisters had chaotic lifestyles. Few of them were in a position to take advantage of opportunities to quit criminal behavior early because many of them had spent their young adulthood in prison. Unstable home life was typical and some changed residences frequently. Almost none of them held a steady job or had a trade. If they entered the military they had difficulty by disobeying orders, going AWOL, and the like. Many could not join the military because they had a criminal record. Some had histories of marital instability and most were divorced or had never married at the time of interview.

### *Turning Points*

The critical turning points for desisters were mostly absent in the lives of persisters. Some of the life events that they experienced could be characterized as turning points that led to persistence in crime rather than the opposite. Included here are things such as hatred of society's rules and regulations or the perception that the individual was a victim of society. Turning points in this sense could also be missed opportunities. For example, one man said, "I feel I could have made something out of myself real big, if I got the education. . . . And then I kind of realized, I says, well you ain't got the education, you are what you are. Don't look for nothing in life, just be satisfied with what you got now" (in Laub & Sampson, 2003, p. 176).

### *The Excitement of Crime*

Many persistent offenders said that, from an early age, they had a strong desire for action and adventure. One said that he "enjoyed delinquency" when he was 12. They did not think about getting caught and were not afraid of the criminal justice system. Laub and Sampson (2003) stated that

> in their adulthood as well as in their youth, these men didn't seem to care about anything or anybody. This lack of caring can be viewed as a form of alienation and seems quite different from bumbling insensitivity or lack of self-control. The men had an "edge" about them that seemed to indicate that because they had nothing, they had nothing to lose. (p. 182)

### *Resistance to Authority*

"Persistent offenders have a difficult time with all types of authority, rules, and structure" (Laub & Sampson, 2003, p. 182). The men expressed defiance of authority and the authors noted that this did not seem to decrease as they got older. In their contacts with the criminal justice system, many felt that they had been harassed and poorly treated and that the system itself was unjust and corrupt. The Glueck men came from poor neighborhoods and much of their resentment appeared to be based on their lower-class position in their early years.

### *Alcohol Abuse*

The Glueck men did not grow up in an era where the use of hard drugs like heroin or crack cocaine were freely available. Rather, they grew up in a culture where alcohol was freely available and people drank a lot. For these men drinking in bars often led to fighting in bars which led to repeated contacts with the police. The authors stated that the men started drinking early in life and when interviewed in their later years referred to themselves as alcoholics. Not surprisingly, alcohol abuse interfered with job stability and caused conflicts in marriages and relationships.

### *Prison Experience*

Unlike some of the desisters, the persistent offenders did not see a stretch in prison as a turning point in their lives. Prison industries are often devoted to jobs such as making license plates or furniture for state offices and are not skill building. As a result, most of the men returned to their home communities and easily lapsed into the criminal and deviant lives they had led previously. They noted prison brutality inflicted both by guards and by fellow inmates. Long prison terms could result in institutionalization. One man said that "I've been in jail most of my life . . . I'm sort of like a half cripple" (in Laub & Sampson, 2003, p. 190).

### *Conclusions on the Age-Graded Theory of Informal Social Control*

We have provided a rather lengthy account of Sampson and Laub's theorizing and empirical work. It is apparent to us that they are staunch behaviorists, although they would probably not characterize themselves as such. Rather they characterize themselves as "modified" social control theorists. However, over and over again we see that the bulk of the social controls invoked to account for behavioral change are exogenous variables.

In response to Modell's (1994) critique of the empirical work in *Crime in the Making* (1993), Laub and Sampson (2003) intensively interviewed a small sample of the Glueck survivors. Those interviews revealed a wealth of information on cognitive changes that the men experienced from age 32 to 70, far too much to ignore or fail to incorporate into the theory. However, they managed to do so. Following are some summary comments by Laub and Sampson (2003):

> Our stance on the desistance process contrasts with emerging theories of desistance that emphasize cognitive transformations or identity shifts as necessary for desistance to occur. . . . We believe that most offenders desist in response to structural turning points that serve as the catalyst for long-term behavioral change. The image of "desistance by default" best fits the desistance process we found in our data. Desistance for our subjects was not necessarily a conscious or deliberate process, but rather the consequence of . . . "side bets." . . . Many men made a commitment to go straight without even realizing it. Before they knew it, they had invested so much in a marriage or a job that they did not want to risk losing their investment. . . . We agree that offenders' own perspectives and words need to be brought into the understanding of desistance, and we believe we have done so. However, offenders can and do desist without a conscious decision to "make good" . . . and offenders can and do desist without a "cognitive transformation." (pp. 278–279)

We doubt that Modell would be satisfied with that summary. We are not entirely satisfied either. It is our position that Sampson and Laub's theory of informal social control can indeed be usefully supplemented by Maruna's theory, to which we now turn.

## Maruna's Narrative Theory of Desistance

Maruna's theory, while not in opposition to Sampson and Laub's, is quite unlike theirs in that it places primary emphasis on cognitive transformations that precede and accompany the process of desistance. In Maruna's view, desistance involves changes in a person's narrative identity, a re-storying of one's life in order that the enormous changes involved in abandoning a life of crime make sense to the person. The theory takes issue with the concept of the turning point so central to Sampson and Laub's theory. The value of the turning point, said Maruna, has probably been overstated and overrated. To be sure, exogenous events (e.g., marriage or divorce, achieving or losing job stability, developing nondeviant relationships or maintaining procriminal relationships) occur in the lives of offenders. Some are planned and some occur unexpectedly. However, one of these events may serve to turn one individual toward desistance from crime, while the same event may propel another toward deeper involvement in criminal activity. The theory argues that it is not the external event that matters most, but rather the psychological import of the event, what it means to the individual, and its implications for the present as well as the future. Laub and Sampson's (2003) analysis of their 52 life-history narratives do make mention of cognitive transformations and these are acknowledged as important, but not important enough to be incorporated into the theory because these are not phenomena that fit the definition of informal social control variables. Cognitive transformations and cognitive events in general are phenomena that can be measured and therefore may be accommodated in a theory of somewhat harder science.

Arguing for the inclusion of subjective data in criminological theory, Maruna (2001) put it this way:

> Subjective aspects of human life (emotions, thoughts, motivations, and goals) have largely been neglected in the study of crime, because the data are presumed to be either unscientific or too unwieldy for empirical analysis. . . . Although we know that individuals respond to situations differently on the basis of their interpretations and outlooks . . . , these individual differences have not received the same attention as the more easily measured structural factors influencing criminal behavior. Narrative research methodology makes it possible to empirically examine the cognitive mediators between these environmental influences and individual behavior. (p. 8)

The "narrative research methodology" of which Maruna speaks forms the empirical foundation of his theory. The data that undergird the theory are found in the Liverpool Desistance Study (LDS).

### *Liverpool Desistance Study*

Maruna (2001) stated the goals of the LDS as follows: "Using narrative methodology, the life stories of these ex-offenders were content analyzed and compared quantitatively and qualitatively for the systematic differences between the two groups that might hold the clues to understanding desistance as a psychological process" (pp. 10–11).

The sample, composed of 50 males and females, was handpicked to maximize the chances of obtaining two groups, desisters and persisters, who markedly differed from each other. When actively involved in crime, all participants had offended on at least a weekly basis for at least 2 years. The persisters admitted that they were carrying on with criminal behavior; the desisters estimated that they had been clean for about 2 or 3 years. There were three criteria for admission to the study. Participants were required to identify themselves as long-term habitual offenders, identify themselves as either going straight or actively persisting, and be known to probation officers, reintegration workers, friends, or associates as a person who was either desisting or persisting (Maruna, 2001, pp. 44–48). Table 6.1 provides a description of the LDS sample. Note that these individuals did not differ very much, except in age, from the Glueck men in Laub and Sampson's (2003) *Shared Beginnings*. They came from impoverished backgrounds and had experienced physical and emotional abuse. They had long criminal histories that began in early adolescence. They had long-term histories of alcohol and drug abuse. They were people who preferred adventure and excitement over routine tasks and taking responsibility. Finally, they resided in areas of Liverpool known for poor economic opportunities (Maruna, 2001,

**TABLE 6.1. The Liverpool Desistance Study Samples (Maruna, 2001)**

| | Characteristics of the sample | |
|---|---|---|
| | Active group ($N$ = 20), Mean ($SD$) | Desisting group ($N$ = 30), Mean ($SD$) |
| Age at time of interview | 30 (4.8) | 31 (6.9) |
| Age at first arrest | 14 (2.8) | 15 (4.4) |
| Age at first jail term | 20 (6.0) | 20 (4.7) |
| Years spent in prison | 4.0 (4.3) | 3.8 (3.6) |
| Left school at 16 | 70% | 63% |
| Raised in "bad" neighborhood | 75% | 80% |
| Raised in single-parent household | 55% | 63% |
| Abused, neglected as a child | 45% | 37% |

p. 11). Despite their unfortunate status, two-thirds of the sample identified themselves as desisters. The sample was composed of young, working-class, street offenders who engaged in "relatively 'ordinary' crimes such as burglary, theft, and drug sales . . . petty thieves, vandals, and punks" (Maruna, 2001, p. 13). They were selected because their histories represent the common societal image of the persistent irredeemable criminal. "Their transition away from criminal behavior . . . was deemed the most interesting conversion to explore in this study of self-change" (Maruna, 2001, p. 13). And, importantly, "the focus here is not on the transition or change, but rather on the maintenance of crime-free behavior in the face of life's obstacles and frustrations" (Maruna, 2001, p. 26). And, departing from Sampson and Laub's mantra of "continuity and change," Maruna counters by suggesting that "the study of desistance might best be construed as the study of *continuity* rather than change—the continuity of nondeviant behaviors" (2001, p. 27).

Maruna referred to the LDS as an example of "phenomenological criminology," an examination of what the offender was seeking in criminal behavior, what meaning the individual was assigning to the behavior, what Katz (1988) called the "foreground of crime," "what it means, feels, tastes, or looks like to commit a particular crime" (Maruna, 2001, p. 3). Broadly speaking, then, the LDS was (Maruna, 2001, p. 38):

- An empirical analysis of the phenomenological or sociocognitive aspects of desistance.
- A systematic comparison of the self-narratives of desisting ex-offenders with a matched sample of persisting offenders.
- An attempt to specify the cognitive adaptations and self-schemas that may help ex-offenders make good and stay that way.

The LDS is a qualitative analysis of these self-narratives that serve a variety of purposes.

> The narrative identity can be understood as an active information-processing structure, a cognitive schema, or a construct system that is both shaped by and later mediates social interaction. Essentially, people construct stories to account for what they do and why they did it. These narratives impose an order on people's actions and explain people's behavior with a sequence of events that connect up to explanatory goals, motivations, and feelings. These self-narratives then act to shape and guide future behavior, as people act in ways that agree with the stories or myths that they have created about themselves. (Maruna, 2001, p. 40)

### The LDS Procedure

In addition to the interview the participants were administered a personality trait questionnaire, a criminal behavior checklist, and a social background survey. The interview was conducted using a modified version of the *Life Story Interview* (McAdams, 1995, Ch. 12, this volume). This was supplemented by open-ended questions about crime and experiences in correctional institutions. In the interview participants were asked to describe their lives as if they were writing an autobiography. They were also encouraged to describe their own theories of rehabilitation and reform (Maruna, 2001, p. 50). "The goal was to construct a single, composite portrait of the desisting self—the narrative identity that seems to best support desistance from crime" (Maruna, 2001, p. 51).

Following the interviews Maruna conducted what he called "18 months of ethnographic field observations in a variety of rehabilitation and resettlement programs in the Liverpool area" (p. 50). This time provided a rich resource of background information on the lives of the study participants. The field research included discussions on the possibility of offender reform with police officers, social workers, prison staff, and probation officers. Maruna met individuals at all stages of the reintegration process and was able to observe one-to-one interactions as well as group counseling sessions. He stayed in touch with the study participants and met their families, partners, and children. Information gained in these offender follow-ups did not alter the original interview data. Finally, to obtain the flavor of the reintegration process himself, Maruna lived for a month in an inner-city men's hostel (Maruna, 2001, pp. 50–51).

### The LDS Outcome Data

An analysis of self-narratives of individuals' lives in a phenomenological study of two disparate groups such as this could be expected to produce fairly distinct self-schemas. And that was the result. The basic findings of the LDS were that persisters and desisters developed what Maruna called "scripts."

#### *The "Condemnation Script" (the Narrative of Persistent Offenders)*

That some persisters would develop a self-condemnatory script is not surprising. Maruna commented that "making an honest living is not easy for a poorly educated, poorly connected, working-class ex-convict with a massive criminal record, weak family ties, and no savings" (Maruna, 2001, p. 51). Sampson and Laub would certainly agree with that assessment.

Persisters believed that their life script had been written a long time ago, that they were "condemned" to the life of crime that they led. When asked about turning points, most could not think of any beyond childhood. They expressed ever-present feelings of helplessness, that their life outcomes were largely dependent on circumstances and chance events. They saw themselves as pushed around, victims of society, repelled by authority, regulation, and external control (Maruna, 2001, pp. 75–77).

### *The "Redemption Script" (the Narrative of Desisting Offenders)*

The redemption script, on the other hand, is markedly upbeat and optimistic. In Maruna's view, ex-offenders need a credible story about why they are going straight to convince themselves that what is happening is a real change. That change "tends to involve incremental internally consistent shifts rather than a wholesale overthrow of the previous self-story. . . . The life stories of desisting narrators . . . maintain this equilibrium by connecting past experiences to the present in such a way that the present good seems an almost inevitable outcome" (Maruna, 2001, pp. 86–87).

Maruna (2001) identified three themes in the redemption script: "(1) an establishment of the core beliefs that characterize the person's 'true self,' (2) an optimistic perception . . . of personal control over one's destiny, and (3) the desire to be productive and give something back to society" (p. 88). Maruna seemed surprised at the optimism shown by the desisters who

> displayed an exaggerated sense of control over the future and an inflated, almost missionary sense of purpose in life. They recast their criminal pasts not as the shameful failings that they are but instead as the necessary prelude to some newfound calling. In general, the highly positive accounts bore almost no resemblance to the ugly realities of the ex-offenders' lives. . . . These distortions were made by the ex-convicts who were going straight—the "reformed" ex-cons—not those who were still committing crime. (p. 9)

And further:

> I describe this process of willful, cognitive distortion as "making good." To make good is to find reason and purpose in the bleakest of life histories. . . . By "making good," not only is the desisting ex-offender "changed," but he or she is also reconstituted. (pp. 9–10)

### *Conclusions on the LDS*

Maruna's conclusions on the LDS do not differ greatly from Laub and Sampson's (2003) conclusions other than the strong reliance on cognitive transformation. Although expressed in somewhat different language, neither do they differ greatly from Giordano et al.'s (2002) conclusions on the role of cognitive change and the inclusion of the "respectability package." Maruna acknowledges that informal social control factors (a good marriage, stable employment, good family and social relations, residential stability) may play important roles, but argued that human agency, making the choice to change, is the key factor. Above all, it is the transformation of the self, the generation of a new self-identity, that is the key to desistance.

## Conclusions

The style and tone of the writings of Sampson and Laub and Maruna are markedly different and, at first glance, the two theories appear to be quite divergent. Simply stated, Sampson and Laub's theory focuses for the most part upon the external conditions of desistance while Maruna's stresses the internal conditions. Both are needed and they are interlinked. Each contains elements of the other and, taken together, they can be seen as quite complementary. Sampson and Laub, while adhering closely to their modified control theory, do acknowledge the role of human agency and cognitive transformation in the process of desistance across the life course. Of particular interest to us are not only the various turning points that they have identified, but the attention that they give to a wide variety of events and influences working during the transit across the life course. Here their indebtedness to the Gluecks is obvious. A number of the 52 men that they interviewed clearly indicated that they had experienced cognitive changes (if not transformations) over the years but this thread was not pursued by Sampson and Laub. Maruna, on the other hand, exploits this deficit. He acknowledges the important influence of many of the formal and informal social variables that Sampson and Laub emphasize but states that many of them are probably overrated. Maruna, in our view, supplies what Sampson and Laub's theory lacks: the detailed examination of narrative identity changes, the transformation of self, the re-storying of offenders' lives. This, we feel, supplies a richness that is not to be found in a strict reading of control theory, modified or not. In summary, we believe that the two theories reinforce each other nicely and can be comfortably merged into a single theoretical and practical framework.

# III

# THE FORENSIC PSYCHOLOGICAL PERSPECTIVE

## Chapter 7

# Do Sex Offenders Desist?

Similar to the accounts in the criminological literature regarding the onset of criminal behavior and tracking of criminal careers, the authors of this book have contributed to the psychological literature regarding the etiology and subsequent maintenance of sexually deviant behavior (Laws & Marshall, 1990; Ward & Beech, 2008). These psychological theoretical accounts imply lifelong commitment to deviant behavior and do not consider either tapering off or desistance. The fact that desistance was not considered contributes to the widely held belief by practitioners in the sexual deviance field that deviant behavior can be expected to continue across the life course. A similar popular belief is continually fueled and presented by the mainstream media. However, as the following review illustrates, in forensic psychology at this writing, the study of desistance per se is nonexistent. Although there is considerable evidence in obtained data for desistance in sex offenders, forensic psychologists do not emphasize the fact.

Hanson and Bussière (1998) performed a meta-analysis of 61 studies representing over 23,000 sex offenders. They identified antisocial behavior and deviant sexual interest as strong predictors of recidivism. Age was found to lead to reductions in deviant behavior, with young offenders recidivating at a higher rate.

Hanson, Steffy, and Gautier (1993) and Prentky, Lee, Knight, and Cerce (1997) considered recidivism 25 years or longer after release. Long-term recidivism rates were not high, but for some people deviant sexual behavior persists into late life. Barbaree and Blanchard (2008) observed that "if . . . the average sex offender is released sometime after age 35, recidivism 25 years later would indicate persistence to age 60, at least" (p. 38). Consider here that several of the criminological studies that we reviewed previously showed that very small groups (usually called "high-rate chronics") offended into late life. The fact that a handful of chronic sex offenders persisted into old age is hardly surprising.

Barbaree and Blanchard (2008) considered the development of actuarial risk assessment "the most significant advance" in evaluating sex offender recidivism in the past 20 years. They went on to outline the main limitation of these instruments: they are based on unchangeable risk factors and are not amenable to adjusting risk for older offenders (or, we might add, those who are gradually desisting from crime). Change is in the wind, however. Thornton, coauthor of the widely used Static-99 (Hanson & Thornton, 1999) has informed us (David Thornton, personal communication, March 12, 2009) that "overall, the sexual recidivism rate at all Static-99 scores, but especially the higher scores, is now lower than it used to be. . . . There are debates over the reason for the change . . . (population becoming more risk-adverse; obesity; diabetes; older; worst cases removed by civil commitment; better treatment; better or more aggressive supervision, etc.)." There are other instruments that evaluate dynamic as well as static risk factors such as Sexual Violence Risk-20 (SVR-20; Boer, Hart, Kropp, & Webster, 1997) and the Risk for Sexual Violence Protocol (RSVP; Hart et al., 2003). These instruments can evaluate change over time and suggest, if not establish, desistance.

The preceding paragraphs reveal the status of the study of desistance in forensic psychology. The study of desistance per se is nonexistent. The list of reasons for modifying the Static-99 provided by Thornton show only two that would fit the definitions of desistance that we provided in earlier chapters: "population becoming more risk-adverse" (i.e., avoiding risk) and aging. The goal here is to make actuarial risk assessment instruments more effective, not to examine potential avenues to desistance. The literature in this area is very limited, it is devoted to the effects of aging on recidivism, and, while it is not discussed, it shows the same pattern of decreasing involvement in sexual crime that we have seen in the criminological literature. Following are a sample of those studies.

Thornton (2006) acknowledged Hanson and Bussière's (1998) finding of a negative correlation between age and sexual recidivism. Thornton's study examined the relationship between age at release from prisons in England and Wales and reconviction over a 10-year period in a large sample ($N = 752$). He found that the odds of being reconvicted declined by 0.02 with each year of increasing age. The percentage of reconvictions varied by different age bands as follows: (1) 18–24 = 80%;

(2) 25–59 = < 50%; and (3) > 60 = no reconvictions. Of course, these are official data and, as we have seen, may not tell the whole story. However, they are exactly the sort of data one might find in the general criminological literature.

Doren (2006) came close to recognizing the need to study desistance when he noted that there were no currently available longitudinal empirical studies of the effect of aging on recidivism. He examined the findings of four studies in this area in an attempt to integrate the empirical results and found more conflict than agreement. For example, there are many variables involved in the assessment and management of sex offenders, for instance, treatment or no treatment, risk assessment used, type of sex offender, or jurisdiction. "Age" in these studies may simply mean the passage of time associated with a wide variety of correlated variables: physical vitality, sexual arousability, emotional maturity, or degree of impulsivity, to name a few. To date, Doren concluded, research relevant to the effect of age on recidivism is defined in only one way, probability.

Fazel et al. (2006) performed an average 8.9-year follow-up of reconviction for all sex offenders released from prison in Sweden between 1993 and 1997 ($N$ = 1,303). They examined the rates of repeat offending for four age bands. The data revealed a decrease in the older age bands: < 25 = 10/103; 25–39 = 47/498; 40–54 = 30/539; 55+ = 10/163. To be sure there is a dramatic decrease in the older age bands. What is remarkable about these data is the fact that the overall reconviction rate at 9 years was only 3%. The authors stated that their data agree with findings from the United States, the United Kingdom, Canada and that this may indicate that there is some generalizability of results in Western countries.

Hanson (2006) examined reoffense risk in eight international samples ($N$= 3,425). He found that older offenders had lower Static-99 scores than young offenders. Moreover, the older offenders had lower sexual recidivism rates than would be expected based only on their Static-99 scores. Hanson cautioned forensic evaluators to consider advanced age in their risk estimates.

Harris and Rice (2007) conducted three studies of age and recidivism on groups of mentally ill and highly dangerous offenders. In one of the studies they found that age at release and the passage of time made no independent contribution to the actuarial risk assessment prediction of violent recidivism. They noted that this result was in contrast to a large body of longitudinal research (i.e., criminological) that showed that as men aged they committed fewer antisocial acts. They attributed this result to the fact that their sample consisted only of adult offenders and therefore excluded the majority of all offenders: the adolescence-limited (Moffitt, 1993). Harris and Rice (2007) believe that the greatest risk lies in a subgroup of offenders whose violent crime is age-invariant but who represent a very small percentage of the total offender population: the life-course-persistent (Moffitt, 1993). They mention that when Laub and Sampson (2003) examined aggregate data for the Glueck survivors, they could not identify any subgroup that did not show the typical age-related decline in crime. However, when Laub and Sampson reexamined the data using trajectory analyses, they found a subgroup that they labeled *high-rate chronic* offenders. This group contained only 3.2% of the total sample and showed a midlife peak of violent offending. Their rate of offending then dropped by 50% at age 50 and essentially to zero by age 70. Thus, Harris and Rice (2007) caution, so long as such a life-course-persistent group exists, forensic evaluators must be extremely careful in attempting to adjust risk assessments downward.

Portions of these data are more similar to the criminological data when shown graphically. Hanson (2002) performed a follow-up from 4,673 sex offenders in 10 international samples. Figure 7.1 shows what amounts to an age–crime curve for sex offenders from this large group. When number of offenders is plotted against age, we can see that these curves bear close resemblance to those from criminological studies on general crime. The three curves of Figure 7.1 show the classical desister shape. The rapists peak earliest, between 25 and 29 and are approaching zero around age 50. They are followed by the extrafamilial child molesters, peaking around age 32 and approaching zero by age 60. Late onset is shown by the incest offenders, who peak in the late 30s and are near

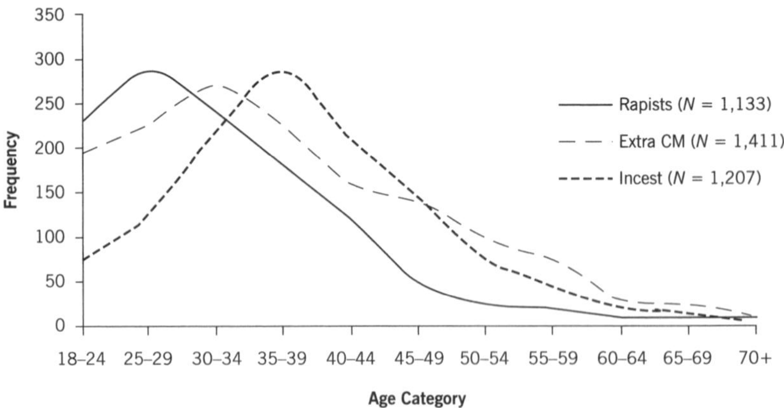


**FIGURE 7.1.** Age–crime for sex offenders. From Hanson (2002, p. 1053). Copyright 2002 by Sage Publications. Reprinted by permission.

zero by age 60. These data support our earlier statement that there is no reason to suppose that the classical age–crime curve does not apply to sex offenders. However, Hanson (2002) was not a desistance study and this matter was not discussed.

In keeping with the data that we have been discussing, Figure 7.2 shows the recidivism rates for this sample by age categories. These data are consistent with the observed fact that recidivism declines with age. Note that it declines very slowly, with all groups essentially at zero by age 60. A somewhat contrary finding was offered by Barbaree, Langton, Blanchard, and Cantor (2009). They state that their data "support the idea that the shape of the age–recidivism curve is linear and best described as a straight line decrease from the mid-20s to old age" (pp. 462–463).

Some psychophysiological data support the contention that age can have a powerful effect on sexual offending. Blanchard and Barbaree (2005) evaluated phallometric measures on 2,028 males, ages 13–79, who were referred to Toronto's Centre for Addiction and Mental Health for assessment of "criminal or otherwise disturbing sexual behavior" (p. 441). These persons were pedophiles, hebephiles (attracted to adolescents), or teleiophiles (attracted to mature adults). Figure 7.3 shows the data for all participants from this evaluation. Sexual arousal measures were obtained by use of the Freund volumetric transducer (Freund, Sedlacek, & Knob, 1965). The ordinate of Figure 7.3 shows the mean of the three largest responses (cc) and the abscissa the ages of the participants. The bars show the mean recorded blood volume increase.

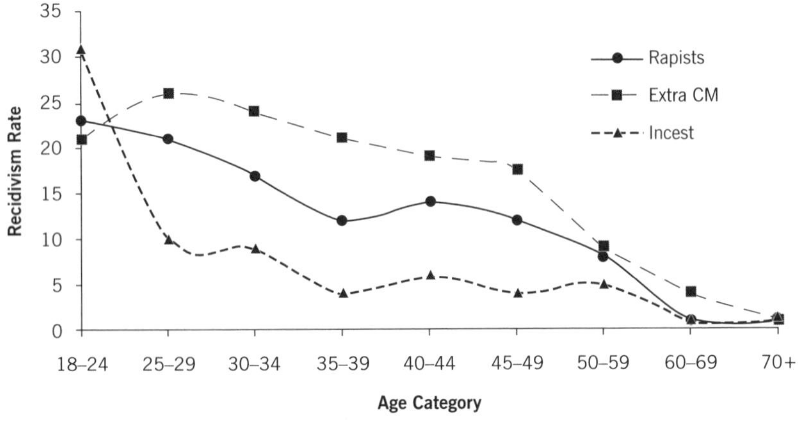


**FIGURE 7.2.** Decline in sex crime × age. From Hanson (2002, p. 1054). Copyright 2002 by Sage Publications. Reprinted by permission.

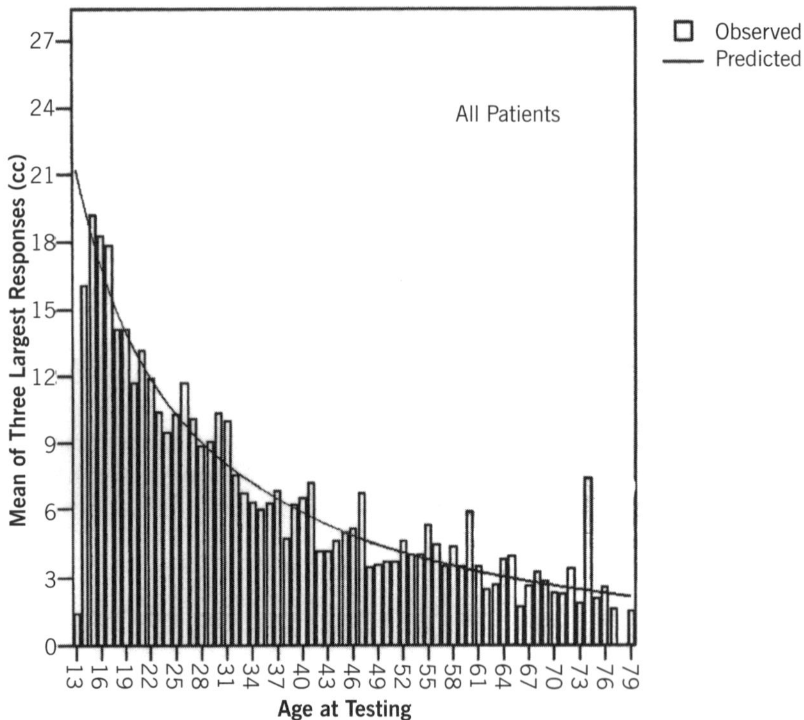


**FIGURE 7.3.** Decline in sexual arousal × age. From Blanchard and Barbaree (2005, p. 448). Copyright 2005 by Sage Publications. Reprinted by permission.

The curved function is the line of best fit for the data. This figure shows very clearly that increasing age has a dramatic suppressive effect on sexual arousal. Viewing such a striking figure, one is tempted to conclude that this should have an effect on the commission of sexual offenses. That is a highly problematic assertion. An erect penis is not required for the commission of many sex offenses. What the figure shows is that age has a debilitating effect on bodily function and that age affects behavior across the board (Gottfredson & Hirschi, 1990).

What has forensic psychology contributed to the study of desistance in sex offenders? The short answer is: not very much. A more considerate answer would be that some researchers and clinicians have touched upon the issue of desistance for other reasons. The focus has been to consider aging as a factor that might affect assessment of risk for recidivism. In the studies cited, only that of Hanson (2002) presents data similar to what we have illustrated in previous chapters from the criminological literature. That study showed the functional equivalent of three classical age–crime curves.

Taken together, the information presented thus far strongly suggests that sex offenders, to varying degrees, show the same desistance effect across the life course. Some preliminary data from the criminological literature has now offered substantiation of this assertion. Lussier, Tzoumakis, Cale, and Amirault (2010) examined trajectories of offending in 393 adult sex offenders spanning the ages of 12 to 35. They used the group-based method for analysis of developmental trajectories offered by Nagin and Land (1993). This analysis revealed four groups: "very low-rate" (56% of the sample), "late-bloomers" (10%), "low-rate desisters" (26%), and "high-rate chronics" (8%). These data are highly similar to those seen in the criminological literature for general criminal offenders. Displayed graphically, the very low-rate group showed very little offending over 23 years; the low-rate desisters and the high-rate chronics showed the classical age–crime curve, peaking in the early 20s; and the late-bloomers showed onset of offending in the mid- to late 20s.

These data provide some confirmation of the position that we have taken throughout this book. They mean that there is nothing special about sex offenders. They are just another kind of criminal. However, it seems to us that forensic psychology's current emphasis on actuarial risk assessment and close attention to criminogenic variables is obscuring the need to look beyond these issues to variables that may promote the desistance process. Subsequent chapters are devoted to exactly that task.

## Conclusions

Forensic psychology has contributed very little to the study of desistance in sex offenders. Studies continue to emerge that clearly show the age–crime effect in sex offenders that has been observed in criminological investigations for decades. These data are not seen as markers of desistance from crime. Rather, they are used to modify assessment of risk for reoffense. A recent study from criminology has clearly shown different offending trajectories of in sex offenders, data that match what we have seen in general criminal offenders. We may hope that this heralds a change of focus in future forensic psychological studies.

*Chapter 8*

# Sex Offender Treatment and Desistance

## Some General Issues

According to Barbaree (2006), generic cognitive-behavioral therapy (CBT) is widely recognized as an effective therapeutic approach to the modification of problem behaviors and the reduction of undesirable symptoms. He stated that CBT had been used with reported beneficial effects in medical, mental health, educational, and correctional settings. Our observation has been that CBT has been used in sex offender treatment, with positive results typically reported, since about 1975.

The public as a whole does not share this view. Constantly bombarded by mainstream media accounts of heinous crimes, citizens typically hold a low view of sex offenders and are not optimistic about their chances for rehabilitation. For example, Chasen-Taber and Tabachnick (1999) reported on a pilot program in Vermont to make an "assessment of public attitudes and beliefs" (p. 280). Laws (2008, p. 623) summarized an initial phase of the project:

> Information was initially gathered by a telephone survey. . . . The researchers asked the participants whether they were familiar with the term "child sexual abuse," what they thought it was, and whether they could identify characteristics or warning signs of sexually abusive behavior. The results indicated that most adults were familiar with the term; however, only about half could define it. Two-thirds of the

> respondents believed that sex offenders lived in their communities, but were unsure of what signs might indicate who was an abuser. Slightly fewer than half believed that abusers could stop their behavior.

Uncertainty about the rehabilitation of sex offenders was not limited to the public at large. As late as 1989, nearly 15 years after the introduction of CBT to sex offender treatment, a crucial and highly critical review of sex offender treatment was published by Furby, Weinrott, and Blackshaw (1989) in the *Psychological Bulletin.* This review examined the early efforts to treat this population and concluded that it could not be determined if a program was successful due to poor methodology and outcome evaluation. This information was not presented in an alarmist fashion, but many professionals as well as those opposed to treating sex offenders at all concluded that this review indicated that sex offender treatment did not work. The review is often misinterpreted despite the fact that its conclusions are quite straightforward. Furby et al. (1989) offered specific suggestions for improving clinical intervention and outcome evaluation, many of which have been adopted in the ensuing years (Laws, 2008, p. 616).

## Who Gets Treatment?

Let us assume that CBT interventions with sex offenders provide a measure of success in preventing reoffense (see the summary of several meta-analyses below). We must ask: Who is likely to receive these benefits? What follows is our assessment of this effort. It is based on official data. The following data refers to rape and sexual assault in general (Kurt Bumby, personal communication, April 7, 2009).

- In 2004 the Bureau of Justice Statistics compiled information on incidence-based victimization reports, arrest/clearance data, prosecution and conviction data, and sentencing data for serious crimes.
- Some representative figures on incidence included:

  1. All crimes—22,879,700
  2. Violent crimes—5,177,100
  3. Rape/sexual assault—248,300 (1% of all crimes)

- Approximately 40% of rapes/sexual assaults are reported to the police (99,320).
- 42% of these reports are cleared by arrest (41,713).

- 62% result in conviction (mostly by guilty plea rather than a trial) (25,862).
- 11% of felony sentences explicitly included a treatment mandate but the type of treatment was not specified (2,845).
- The 11% mandated to treatment represented 3% of all reported rapes and sexual assaults.

A large number of that 11% will never complete treatment, and some may never enter treatment. As the following paragraphs explain, some major correctional programs in prison allow offenders to decline treatment with no consequences. If the offender is placed on probation, he may not live in an area where treatment is offered or is otherwise inaccessible. The inescapable conclusion is that only a tiny number of sex offenders ever receive treatment.

We queried two of our colleagues regarding participation in two of the strongest sex offender programs in the world: HM Prison Service in the United Kingdom, and Correctional Service of Canada. We asked several questions. First, was participation expected? Second, what happened if the inmate refused to participate? Third, what happened if he participated and then dropped out? We received the following replies:

**HM Prison Service**

> If he refuses to participate, he doesn't participate. It's a voluntary programme. He may get offered it several times to see if he has changed his mind. The most common reason for refusing . . . is denial of the offence. We don't currently have any treatment options for deniers. If he drops out, he drops out. However, our drop out rate is pretty low. Under 5%. . . . Probation programmes are ordered by the sentence so are not voluntary, although there would usually be an assessment of suitability for treatment before the sentence is passed. The drop out rate is higher in the community, as you would expect. (Ruth Mann, personal communication, April 3, 2009)

**Correctional Service of Canada**

> Participation is voluntary. That said, there is (or is perceived to be) an unwritten expectation that all sexual offenders receive treatment. Thus, participation rates are relatively high—not as high as one might expect, but higher than typical. If an offender refuses to participate, or participates and then drops out, he is placed back on the waiting list. The national standards and policy indicate that he will be offered the opportunity to participate again, though sometimes practice var-

ies at individual sites. (Pamela Yates, personal communication, April 3, 2009)

Thus we see that two of the strongest treatment regimes in the world do not enforce mandatory participation in sex offender treatment. The exception is probation-supervised community programs in the United Kingdom where dropout is high.

## Sex Offender Treatment

### *Current Treatment Practice*

Our aim in this section is to give a brief description of current best practice rather than a detailed account of the assessment and treatment of sex offenders (for a comprehensive review, see Laws & O'Donohue, 2008; Marshall et al., 2006). In Chapters 13, 14, and 15 we will argue for a strengths-based approach to treatment and rehabilitation that is a significant departure from the contemporary preoccupation with risk assessment and management.

The treatment of sex offenders has evolved considerably over the last 30 years and now consists of multiple components, each targeting a different problem domain and primarily delivered in a group format. While there are some minor variations in the specifics of treatment programs across the world, any credible program will typically have the following structure, orientation, and elements. Following a comprehensive assessment period where static and dynamic risk factors are assessed and an overall level of risk determined, offenders are allocated into a treatment stream. The default etiological assumption appears to be that sexual offending is a product of faulty social learning and individuals commit sexual offenses because they have a number of skill deficits that make it difficult for them to seek reinforcement in socially acceptable ways. Thus the primary mechanisms underpinning sexual offending are thought to be social and psychological, although it is acknowledged that some individuals' sexually abusive actions are partly caused by dysfunctional biological mechanisms such as abnormal hormonal functioning (Laws & O'Donohue, 2008; Marshall et al., 2006). Furthermore, treatment is typically based around an analysis of individuals' offending patterns and takes a cognitive-behavioral/relapse-prevention perspective. The major goal is to teach sex offenders the skills to change the way they think, feel, and act and to use this knowledge to avoid or escape from future high-risk situations. There are usually discrete treatment modules devoted to the following problem areas: cognitive distortions, deviant sexual interests, social skill deficits, impaired problem solving, empathy deficits, intimacy deficits, emotional regulation difficulties, impulsivity, lifestyle imbalance, and postoffense adjustment or relapse prevention (Laws, 1989; Marshall et al., 2006; Ward, Yates, & Long, 2006; Yates, 2003). There are specialized programs for adolescent, intellectually disabled, female sex offenders, and younger children who act out sexually although they are strongly influenced by the above structure and program content (Laws & O'Donohue, 2008). The length of programs vary but for a medium-risk or higher offender will likely be at least 9 months in duration and frequently quite a bit longer (Marshall, Fernandez, Hudson, & Ward, 1998).

### *Treatment Effectiveness*

In this section we examine the question of how effective treatment for sex offenders actually is. In this necessarily brief discussion our focus will be on the methodologically most robust recent papers on treatment outcome, all using meta-analysis, a statistical technique for combining the findings from a number of independent studies (Crombie & Davis, 2009; Rosenthal & DiMatteo, 2001; Shelby & Vaske, 2008). Before outlining the key findings of the meta-analytic reviews by Hanson et al., (2002), Lösel and Schmucker, (2005), Robertson, Beech, and Freemantle (in press), and Hanson, Bourgon, Helmus, and Hodgson (2009), we will summarize the key features of meta-analysis and consider its strengths and weaknesses. This will hopefully provide a platform for our interpretation of the findings from treatment outcome research and allow us to reflect on their significance for desistance theory.

#### *Meta-Analysis: Key Features*

According to Shelby and Vaske (2008), "Meta-analysis is a quantitative technique that uses specific measures (e.g., an effect size) to indicate the strength of variable relationships for the studies included in the analysis. The technique emphasizes results across multiple studies as opposed to results from a single investigation" (p. 96). In other words, meta-analysis allows researchers to combine results from different studies in a summary statistic such as an effect size in a way that allows for more precise estimation of treatment effects. For example, a meta-analysis of the effectiveness of psychological therapy in the treatment of depression would combine the results from multiple, independent studies and hopefully give clinicians a better idea of just how useful such an approach actually is. In contrast to narrative reviews of the literature, meta-analysis is able to avoid bias due to selective inclusion of studies and the subjective interpretations of authors. Its transparency means that any errors made are easily spotted and can be rectified or taken into account in subsequent decisions concerning treatment policy and so on. A good meta-analysis can also overcome problems such as low statistical power by combining the treatment effects from independent studies, thus enabling practitioners to benefit from effective interventions. A methodologically sound meta-analysis should exhibit the following features (Crombie & Davis, 2009; Rosenthal & DiMatteo, 2001; Shelby & Vaske, 2008):

- It should clearly and explicitly define the criterion variable (e.g., recidivism) and carefully state the criteria used to identify target papers (e.g., design, use of a comparison or control group, age, gender, location of program, type of interventions).
- It should be based on a comprehensive search strategy of the available studies using a wide range of databases.
- Efforts should be made to include both published and unpublished studies to avoid the *file drawer* problem (where studies with negative effects are not published). This refers to the issue of publication bias.
- The quality of the individual studies used should be evaluated using rating criteria that are explicit, reliably administered, and valid. Only studies that meet an acceptable level of quality should be used in the meta-analysis. The adage *garbage in, garbage out* is clearly relevant and the validity of the conclusion of a review crucially depends on the quality of the studies utilized in the analysis.
- The combined effect size should be calculated using an appropriate statistical method.
- The heterogeneity between the studies should be assessed and taken into account in the selection of the statistical model used (e.g., fixed effects or random effects models). Studies may vary with respect to variables such as risk level, duration, intervention used, therapist characteristics, and so on. The greater the degree of heterogeneity, the greater the danger that differences between the studies could influence the effects of treatment. This could make it harder to discern significant results.

There are a number of controversies in the meta-analysis literature over such issues as its definition, whether it is a methodological approach or a statistical technique, the use of effect sizes, or what constitutes the most appropriate unit of analysis (e.g., experiments vs. data sets). They need not concern us here. What most researchers involved in critical reviews of literature agree on is that meta-analysis is a useful technique for analyzing data from multiple studies. Its advantages are that it is rigorous and provides a broad picture of a domain of interest and can be practically extremely useful (Rosenthal & DiMatteo, 2001). Most of the disadvantages revolve around potential problems in combining different studies: care needs to be taken to ensure that inattention to study selection and quality does not render any conclusions invalid.

### *Efficacy of Sex Offender Treatment*

A controversial and unresolved issue in the sexual offending treatment outcome field concerns the question of what constitutes an acceptable research design. Most of the interest has focused on the merits of randomized control trials (RCTs; in essence, where offenders are randomly assigned to either treatment or nontreatment groups) versus incidental assignment designs where there are good reasons to believe that preexisting differences that might confound any findings have been controlled for through matching techniques. It is now commonly accepted that it is not appropriate to use designs that compare treatment groups with dropouts or people who refuse treatment (Hanson et al., 2009; Robertson et al., in press). How to control for subtle, preexisting differences between treated and untreated groups in non-RCTs that might bias treatment outcome research remains a serious methodological concern for researchers and practitioners who are looking to ground their treatment of sex offenders on solid empirical evidence.

In an important outcome study Hanson et al. (2002) conducted a thorough review of studies up until the year 2000 and subjected their findings to a meta-analysis. This study utilized criteria arrived at by the Collaborative Outcome Data Committee, a group set up in 1997, when selecting studies to be included in the review. A total of 43 published and unpublished studies ($N$ = 9,454) were selected to be included in the meta-analysis and their results analyzed to ascertain, among other things, whether treatment was effective in terms of its impact on both sexual and general offending and what type of programs were most effective (e.g., CBT, systemic). Hanson et al. found that treated sexual offenders sexually reoffended at lower rates (12.3%) than untreated sex offenders (16.8%). Furthermore, treatment significantly reduced general offending as well, 27.9% for treated versus 39.2% for untreated sexual offenders.

Evaluating the quality of Hanson et al. (2002) study against the features of a good meta-analysis, it fares well. The authors systematically sought out appropriate studies using well-defined criteria and ensured that they included both published and unpublished ones too. They assessed the quality of each of the studies using a valid set of criteria and were at pains to explicitly explain and justify their use of the odds ratio as an effect size indicator. However, a notable omission was that they did not explicitly discuss whether a fixed effects or random effects method of analysis was followed. In view of the large amount of variance between the various studies, one can assume it was the latter. The authors concluded that the overall result of the various studies provided evidence for the utility of treatment. They did point out that the strongest support for the effectiveness of sexual offending treatment came from studies with an incidental assignment design, and therefore it was not possible to rule out the possibility that preexisting differences between the treatment and comparison groups may explain the contrasting recidivism rates.

In their meta-analytic review of sex offender treatment, Lösel and Schmucker (2005) set out to improve on previous reviews by broadening the scope of studies included and increasing the size of the sample pool. They finally incorporated 69 studies ($N$ = 22,181) up until 2003 into their meta-analysis, a third of which came from countries outside North America. The results supported the efficacy of treatment, with sex offenders reoffending at a significantly lower rate (11.1%) than the various comparison groups (17.5%). Furthermore, similar results were evident for general offending and also suggested that CBT was more effective than other types of treatment.

The Lösel and Schmucker (2005) review is impressive in its rigor and attention to the requirements for a good meta-analysis. The authors defined the criteria required for studies to be included carefully and assessed the quality of each study using a detailed coding manual. Furthermore, they explicitly defended their use of a random effects method of analysis due to the heterogeneity of the studies recruited. Lösel and Schmucker concluded with a recommendation that methodological issues concerning moderators (context, duration, location, etc.) and sample sizes should be addressed by further research, and the need for examining the role of offender subtypes and treatment was flagged.

In a recent review Hanson et al. (2009) investigated whether the principles of effective intervention—those of risk, need, and responsivity (RNR)—for general offenders (Andrews & Bonta, 2007) also applied to sex offenders. In brief, the *risk* principle specifies that the treatment of offenders ought to be organized according to the level of risk they pose to society. The *need* principle states that the most effective and ethical approach to the treatment of offenders is to target *dynamic risk factors* (i.e., criminogenic needs) that are causally related to criminal behavior. Finally, the *responsivity* principle is primarily concerned with the problem of matching the delivery of correctional interventions to certain characteristics of participants (e.g., motivation, learning style, and ethnic identity). Hanson et al. included 23 studies in their meta-analysis ($N$ = 6,746). The results confirmed the findings of the above studies that sexual offending treatment can reduce recidivism rates in treated offenders. More specifically, the authors found that treated sex offenders had lower reoffending rates (10.9%) than members of the comparison groups (19.2%). Furthermore, treatment also reduced the rates of general offending in those individuals who participated in specialized sexual offending programs (31.8% vs. 48.3%). Programs that adhered to the principles of risk, need, and responsivity produced better outcomes than those that did not.

The Hanson et al. (2009) study is meticulous in its adherence to the criteria for a sound meta-analysis. It includes clear and explicit descriptions of standards to be used to recruit and code studies and the rationale for using both fixed effect and random effects methods for calculating the summary statistics is convincing. The authors conclude that practitioners should use the RNR principles to guide their practice. While they recommend that criminogenic needs ought to be primary treatment targets, they do acknowledge the important role of noncriminogenic needs such as denial or self-efficacy in the treatment process (see Chapter 14). An important observation by Hanson et al. is that while there is (arguably) modest evidence that treatment results in lowered recidivism, we know comparatively little about the *process* of treatment change. They end their paper with a note of caution, stating that the best evidence for treatment comes from relatively weak designs and that a skeptic could "reasonably conclude that there is no evidence that treatment reduces sexual offense recidivism" (p. 881).

Finally, Robertson et al. (in press) recently undertook a meta-analysis of 61 sexual offender treatment studies ($N$= 15,931). The studies used a variety of treatment designs ranging from RCT to assignment based on need and a random effects meta-analysis model was used in the calculation of the effect size. Their results were reported in terms of odds ratios (ORs) and indicated a positive effect of treatment on both sexual (OR = .49, 95% confidence interval = .39 to .62, $p < .0001$) and general reoffending (OR = .54, 95% confidence interval = .44 to .66, $p < .0001$). Essentially, these results indicate that for every 100 nontreated sex offenders who reoffend sexually, 49 treated offenders will reoffend, and for every 100 nontreated sex offenders who commit nonsexual offenses, 54 sex offenders will reoffend generally.

The Robertson et al. (in press) study is methodologically sound and follows the guidelines for good meta-analytic research. We have no concerns about their design but note that they concluded that the RCT studies provided no evidence for the effectiveness of treatment, while studies that used incidental assignment did. This finding is consistent with the above reviews and does raise questions concerning the possibility of subtle biases in sexual offender treatment research.

### *Implications for Desistance*

What do the above reviews tell us about the effectiveness of sexual offending treatment programs? In our view, their combined results provide reasonable, although not totally compelling, evidence for the efficacy of contemporary best practice treatment programs. However, we would like to sidestep the methodological debates over matters such as the dangers of not using RCT, and consider the relevance of the outcome literature for the desistance process and offender rehabilitation. There are two points we would like to make. First, even if one accepts the idea that treatment is effective, at best the results are modest. It may be that adopting a rehabilitation model that incorporates desistance research and ideas, and that is more constructive in nature, could improve the effectiveness of current practice (see Chapters 13, 14, and 15). Second, while outcome studies tell us that treated sex offenders recidivate at a lower rate than untreated ones, we do not know why this is the case. That is, it is far from clear how treatment works, what mechanisms are operating to facilitate successful reintegration (see below). A problem is that offenders are not followed up for long enough or in their natural (personal, unique) environments. What is evident to us is that desistance research will be able to shed some light on the social and psychological mechanisms involved in crime cessation. We return to this issue in the conclusion to this chapter.

## Outcome Evaluation

Posttreatment follow-up of sex offenders has historically been the weakest link in the process. With the exception of extramurally funded programs where it might find support for a brief period, say 1 year, serious follow-up for the most part does not occur. Barbaree (2006) referred to current models of treatment evaluation as "suboptimal." He noted that the currently accepted model of treatment efficacy would require that treatment effects be detected at least 5 years after treatment had been completed. The ideal model would look something like this:

Pretreatment Posttreatment Follow-up

Assessment → Treatment → Assessment → Follow-up → Assessment

"Ideal" is the correct word because such a model is obviously extensive, not to mention expensive.

Barbaree (2006) conducted a small but provocative survey of a highly selective portion of the outcome literature. The obtained results call into question the durability of CBT treatment effects. PsychArticles was searched using the key words CBT, meta-analyses, and treatment target (depression, anxiety, substance abuse, aggression, etc.). All articles for the preceding 10 years were examined for follow-up results. The search revealed nine meta-analyses published in high-quality journals such as *Journal of Consulting and Clinical Psychology* or *Psychological Bulletin*. There were five analyses with adults and four with children. Each reported analyses of a reasonably large number of outcome studies with a large aggregate *N*. Only outcomes for adults are considered here.

The meta-analyses fell into two categories: (1) no follow-up mentioned, and (2) follow-up described. All found strong treatment effects for CBT based on *immediate posttreatment assessment*. However, no follow-up was reported for behavioral martial therapy, bibliotherapy for depression, generalized anxiety disorder, or irritable bowel syndrome. Follow-ups ranging from 6 to 18 months were reported for depression, panic disorder, generalized anxiety disorder, and smoking cessation. Of these, the only CBT treatment effect that persisted was for panic disorder, follow-up of 12–18 months.

## Implications for Sex Offender Treatment

The preceding are not encouraging results. The treatment interventions evaluated in the reported meta-analyses were performed on a fairly wide range of predominantly mental health problems commonly seen in adults. They hardly exhaust the possibilities for CBT intervention. Nor is the full range of possible publications considered. However, the meta-analyses appeared in high-quality journals with rigorous standards for publication. They thus represent top-of-the-line research and the disappointing results should give us pause.

As noted by Barbaree (2006), in the sex offender assessment and treatment field the conventional wisdom states that treatment effects should be evident at 5 years posttreatment for an intervention to be judged credible. Most follow-ups in the sex offender treatment literature (in the form of recidivism checks) rarely go beyond 5 years. As we have shown earlier in this chapter, the reoffense rate differentials that are found in these follow-ups are not particularly impressive and those results might be explained in other ways.

### Sex Offender Follow-Up

This is not to say that no reports exist of treatment effects for sex offenders persisting. There are a few reports—very few—that attest to long-term effects. For example, Aylwin and Studer (2008) claimed a 9.2% recidivism rate in a sample of 576 offenders with a mean time at risk of 122 months (10 years) ($R$ = 6–215 months). Takacs (2008) reported similar data from the same treatment program. Swinburne Romine, Dwyer, Mathiowetz, and Thomas (2008) reported follow-ups of over 700 offenders seen for periods ranging from 10 to 30 years. Recidivism rates varied from 9 to 14%. Except for brief periods following cessation of treatment, as Barbaree (2006) reported, these are very unlikely to have been long-term follow-up studies. Posttreatment, offenders were not periodically seen for periods of 10, 20, or 30 years. Rather, official records were consulted to determine reoffense. As we have seen in the criminological data, undetected offenses could have been occurring throughout these periods until the first official contact.

A major clinical concern in these programs is the extent to which participants actually incorporate what they have learned and, hopefully, use that information to change their behavior. A study by Sawyer and Pettman (2006) offers some encouragement in this area. They conducted interviews and consulted official records to assess posttreatment functioning and reoffense rates of 153 men in an outpatient program. They performed 555 interviews with 134 men at regular intervals for 5 years following discharge from the program. The interviews posed questions in these areas:

- Precursors to offending and coping strategies.
- Status of partner and family relationships.
- Substance use and abuse.
- Work adjustment.
- Contact with law enforcement.

The authors reported that the interview results showed positive posttreatment adjustment. The former participants could name precursors and describe the coping mechanisms that would occur early in the reoffense cycle. There is some discussion of family relationships but nothing about work adjustment or substance abuse.

There was an official records review at 67 months posttreatment. The following reoffense rates were found:

*Treated group (N* = 153)
12.4% overall criminal reoffense rate.

- 2.6% were sex-related.
- 9.8% were non-sex-related.

*Comparison group (N* = 113)
32.7% overall criminal reoffense rate.

- 4.4% sex-related.
- 28.3% non-sex-related.

The comparison group was composed of men (presumably sex offenders) referred to the same agency for evaluation but who were not admitted to treatment following evaluation.

The authors noted some limitations of their study. They acknowledge that official records are not the best index of reoffense because undetected offenses could have been occurring in those 67 months posttreatment. More importantly, the interviews were conducted by the main treating clinician. This introduces the possibility of positive response bias in the data. Limitations notwithstanding, this is an interesting study in a very important area that receives almost no attention.

## Conclusions

Research evidence indicates that treatment programs for sexual offenders can result in modest reductions in both sexual and general offending. Programs that are implemented according to principles of risk, need, and responsivity appear to be particularly effective, but even they do not cut dramatically into reoffending rates. While researchers and clinicians accept that treatment programs can lessen offenders' chances for committing further crimes, why or how this occurs is somewhat of a mystery. One possibility is that treatment programs work by providing offenders with the internal and external resources to capitalize on social and personal opportunities more effectively. In effect, therapy may assist the natural desistance process and artificially compensate for what happens during normal socialization. Psychological and social capital is supplied during structured intervention programs that usually are imparted to children by parents, teachers, siblings, friends, employers, and other members of the community. Arguably it is the possession of basic adaptive skills that enables individuals and offenders who do not receive therapy to independently resolve their various problems in personally satisfying and socially acceptable ways. From this standpoint, it may be a mistake to concentrate our therapeutic and rehabilitation resources just on creating more intensive and powerful programs and techniques. Perhaps we should also look outwards toward the edges of the correctional practice arena where individuals seek to establish meaningful and fulfilling lives. In other words, the delivery of treatment is not enough. We need also to be seeking to strengthen offenders' social networks and their relationship to the world beyond the therapy room. We return to this point in Chapters 13, 14, and 15.

# IV

# REENTRY AND REINTEGRATION

## *Chapter 9*

# Barriers to Reentry and Reintegration

It is initially important to understand that the bulk of the literature on barriers to reintegration is devoted to parolees, not probationers. There are three reasons for this situation. First, in the eyes of the law, the persons called "parolees" have been convicted of the most serious crimes, have served time in federal or state prisons, and have been released (paroled) to community supervision under strict conditions. Second, the laws that impose considerable barriers to reentry and reintegration are primarily directed at parolees. Third, the states and federal governments publish detailed statutes and regulations governing the behavior of parolees and maintain extensive statistics on their movements in and out of custody. Thus, the most complete picture of the barriers to reentry and reintegration to society is available from parolees. Many of the conditions imposed upon parolees are also applicable to probationers (e.g., avoid criminal associates, refrain from alcohol), but the restrictions on their behavior are not as confining.

Readers should note that, in this chapter and to a lesser extent in Chapter 10, we have relied heavily upon two works for general background. These are Joan Petersilia's (2003) *When Prisoners Come Home: Parole and Prisoner Reentry* and Jeremy Travis's (2005) *But They All Come Back: Facing the Challenges of Prisoner Reentry*. Of course, we are aware of other works in this area, such as Jeff Manza and Christopher Uggen's (2006) *Locked Out: Felon Disenfranchisement and American Democracy*, Shawn Bushway, Michael Stoll, and David Weiman's (2007) *Barriers to Reentry?: The Labor Market for Released Prisoners in Post-Industrial America*,

Anthony Thompson's (2008) *Releasing Prisoners, Redeeming Communities: Reentry, Race, and Politics*, and Todd Clear's (2009) *Imprisoning Communities: How Mass Incarceration Makes Disadvantaged Neighborhoods Worse.* In the interest of comprehensive coverage of the entire area of reentry and reintegration, we judged the Petersilia and Travis works as the best choices.

## The U.S. Prison System

Most citizens have no conception of the magnitude of the U.S. penal system, a Western-style Gulag Archipelago of jails, prison, and community surveillance.

> The U.S. has the world's highest incarceration rate. With only 5% of the world's population, the U.S. now has 25% (2.3 million) of the world's reported prisoners. The U.S. currently incarcerates 756 inmates per 100,000, a rate five times the world-wide average of 158 inmates per 100,000. Also, in the U.S., more than five million more people who recently left prison, remain under correctional supervision including parole, probation, and other community sanctions. Today, one out of every 31 adults in the U.S. is in prison, in jail, or on supervised release. (*The Correctional Psychologist*, 2009, p. 19)

### *Pictures of the Ex-Prisoner*

The picture is bleak. One of the major works on reentry and reintegration states that

> just as the rate of incarceration in America has increased fourfold, the number of people leaving prison each year has also quadrupled. In 2002, more than 630,000 individuals (1,700 per day) left federal and state prisons—compared with 150,000 who made a similar journey 30 years ago. . . . Except for those few individuals who die in custody, every person we send to prison returns to live with us. (Travis, 2005, p. xvii)

Travis has recently stated that the number leaving prisons in 2009 will be 700,000 (Fader, 2009). Petersilia (2003, p. 3) noted that, in 2002, there were 1.4 million persons in prison in the United States. Seven percent of those were serving death or life sentences. Only about 3,000 will die in prison each year. Ninety-three percent of all inmates will eventually be released.

What do these returnees look like? Petersilia (2003, p. 21) provides the following description:

> Ex-prisoners are . . . mostly male, minority, and unskilled. . . . Today's inmate is likely to have been in custody several times before, has a lengthy history of alcohol and drug abuse, is more likely to be involved in gang activities and drug dealing, has probably experienced significant periods of unemployment and homelessness, and may have a physical or mental disease. . . . A significant number of inmates will have spent weeks, if not months, in solitary confinement or supermax prisons, devoid of human contact and prison program participation.

It would be comforting to think that the preceding snapshot is representative of only a small proportion of the American population. Far from it. In 2000, 13 million Americans were ex-convicts. That figure represented 6.5% of the entire adult population, 11% of the adult male population. In 2000, more than 59 million Americans had a criminal record on file. In that year 29% of the entire adult population had a criminal background of one degree or another.

The overall gloomy picture becomes even more bleak when broken down into some of its essential components (Petersilia, 2003, pp. 21–51, *passim*).

### *Age*

At the close of the 20th century the average age of state prisoners released to parole was 34. As sentence lengths have increased over the past 20 years, so has the average age of parolees. It is more expensive to keep older offenders in prison.

### *Gender*

Most prisoners and parolees are male, but females are a growing population.

### *Race*

One third of ex-prisoners entering parole are white, 47% are black, and 16% are Hispanic. About two-thirds of returnees are racial minorities. The picture is especially bleak for blacks. In 1991, a black male had a 29% chance of being incarcerated at least once in his lifetime, a percentage six times higher than that for a white male. Twenty percent of black males will be imprisoned before reaching the age of 35. The chance for white males is less than 3%.

### *Education*

Poorly educated, barely literate persons are disproportionately represented in prisons. In state prisons, 19% of prisoners are completely illiterate and 40% are functionally illiterate. In 1999, 49% of state prisoners entering parole had a high school diploma or some college, compared to 85% of the general population.

### *Health*

Many prisoners come from disadvantaged environments and bring health problems with them to prison, which itself is not a healthy environment. In 2001 the Bureau of Justice Statistics reported that one-third of state inmates and 25% of federal inmates self-reported a physical impairment or mental condition. Thirteen percent of the prison population had *both* a substance abuse and a mental health problem.

### *HIV/AIDS and Infectious Diseases*

Many individuals enter prison with a history of itinerant living conditions, prior IV drug use, and high substance abuse—all conducive to contraction of infectious diseases. Two to three percent are HIV-positive or have AIDS, a percentage five times greater than that of the general population. Eighteen percent are infected with hepatitis C, which is nine to ten times the rate in the general population. The rate of infection by tuberculosis among inmates is six times greater than that of the general population. How seriously is this health situation taken? Petersilia (2003, p. 50) observed that courts have held that "the Constitution does not require that the medical care provided to prisoners be perfect, the best obtainable, or even very good. The courts have supported the principle of least eligibility and said that prison conditions . . . must be a step below those of the working class and people on welfare."

### *Drug and Alcohol Abuse*

Alcohol abuse is more closely linked with violent crime than drugs are. Continued criminality is related to substance use and abuse. More than 40% of first-time offenders have a history of drug use. This already very high percentage increases to more than 80% with five or more prior convictions.

#### *Employment*

In 1997, 31% of state prisoners and 27% of federal prisoners reported that they were unemployed in the month before their arrest. At that time only 7% of Americans over the age of 18 were unemployed. Eight percent of state prisoners and 3% of federal prisoners had *never* been employed.

#### *Marital and Family Relationships*

A large percentage of prisoners are unmarried. Only 17% of state prisoners and 30% of federal prisoners are married. This compares with 61% of the general population. Petersilia (2003, pp. 41–42) reported two consistent findings regarding marriage and family ties. Male prisoners who maintain strong family ties during imprisonment have higher rates of postrelease success, as do men who assume husband and parenting roles upon release. These findings are consistent with Laub and Sampson's (2003) observations concerning their interviewees.

### *Conclusion on Demographics*

The descriptions of problems common to returning ex-prisoners do not encourage optimism regarding their amenability to or enthusiasm for interventions to assist them in multiple realms. Further, their disadvantaged status presents problems in overcoming obstacles that militate against successful reentry and reintegration to society. However, before we proceed to examine those obstacles, it is necessary to provide some history on the development and evolution of the concept of parole over the past 150 years. The period from about 1980 to the present is crucial because it was during that era that dramatic changes occurred in the institution of parole that today pose enormous obstacles to reentry.

## A Brief History of Parole

Prisons, although never pleasant residences, were not initially intended to be places where severe punishment was meted out, where prisoners were unable to work, unable to be educated, and isolated from their fellow beings, often in solitary confinement for 23 hours a day. Travis (2005, p. 7) has noted that in the 18th century

> Quaker reformers sought to replace such barbaric forms of punishment as pillories, gallows, and branding irons with more humane pun-

> ishments, such as hard labor, fines, and forfeiture. The cornerstone of these reforms was the workhouse. . . . [F]elons would be separated from minor offenders, separated from each other, and forbidden to speak to the other prisoners. The Quakers hoped that this form of isolation would give the felons an opportunity to reflect on their sins, repent, and return to free society less likely to violate communal norms. For this reason, these institutions were called "penitentiaries," or places where penitents could realize the error of their ways. This experiment laid the foundation for the belief that prisons should be places where criminals can be reformed.

Rothman (2002) has described how variations of the basic idea of convict reformation were tried throughout the 19th and early 20th centuries, and then progressively abandoned in favor of mere confinement and control. However, in the midst of these changes the idea of parole emerged. The basic constituents of that idea persist in one form or another to the present day. Early 19th-century sentences were what we would today call "determinate," that is, a set period of time had to be served before release was obtained. Then, in midcentury, the notion of "good time" emerged.

In 1840 Alexander Maconochie, often called the "Father of Parole," was in charge of a penal colony at Norfolk Island, New Zealand. He developed what came to be called the "mark system." In this system prisoners progressed through five stages: (1) imprisonment, (2) chain gangs, (3) freedom in a limited area, (4) ticket of leave on parole (conditional pardon), and (5) full restoration of liberty. The basic idea was a gradual, conditional release to full freedom. The sentence was always indeterminate and progression through the stages was dependent upon the inmate's work and behavior (Petersilia, 2003, p. 6).

Also appearing at midcentury was the "Irish system" proposed by Sir Walter Crofton. The Irish system was based on Maconochie's mark system. Tickets of leave were awarded to prisoners who showed achievement and attitude change. What made this approach different, and very similar to parole as it was eventually applied in the United States, was that parolees had to submit monthly reports to the police. A civilian inspector helped parolees find jobs, visited them, and supervised their activities (Petersilia, 2003, p. 57). Importantly,

> Sir Walter Crofton's Irish system first embodied the two critical elements of the modern system of indeterminate sentencing: (1) a prisoner could earn his freedom through work and good behavior, and (2) he could be released fully if he maintained good behavior while on conditional release. (Travis, 2005, p. 10)

In 1870, Enoch Wines convened the National Congress on Penitentiary and Reformatory Discipline in Cincinnati. The conference produced a declaration of principles that had two major points:

- There should be a progressive classification of prisoners. This would be based on Maconochie's mark system where a person could work his way out of prison, serving a portion of his sentence in the community.
- Determinate sentences should be replaced by ones of indeterminate length.

These recommendations formed the birth of the parole system in the United States (Travis, 2005, pp. 10–11).

In 1876, Zebulon Brockway initiated the first parole system in the United States at the Elmira Reformatory in New York. His was a two-component system: indeterminate sentencing followed by parole supervision. "His ideas reflected the tenor of the times: the beliefs that criminals could be reformed and that every prisoner's treatment should be individualized" (Petersilia, 2003, p. 58). New York was the first state to adopt a full parole system. Forty-five states had parole systems by 1927; all states and the federal government had one by 1942.

Although parole as a system of personal reformation has never been taken seriously by correctional administrators or the general public, the rehabilitation ideal persisted into the 1960s. "The rehabilitation ideal . . . affected all of corrections well into the 1960s and gained acceptance for the belief that the purpose of incarceration and parole was to change the offender's behavior rather than simply to punish" (Petersilia, 2003, p. 61).

## What Works?

Then the axe fell. In 1974, Martinson published his famous "nothing works" meta-analysis.

> This paper is commonly credited with expediting the demise of human service and ideals of rehabilitation. . . . Martinson (1974) reviewed 231 studies of prison rehabilitative programmes. On the basis of his analysis he concluded that offender treatment was largely ineffective. For example, "education . . . or psychotherapy at its best, cannot overcome, or even appreciably reduce, the powerful tendency for offenders to continue in criminal behaviour. (Anstiss, 2003, p. 84)

Anstiss notes that subsequent work by Lipton, Martinson, and Wilks (1975) and by Brody (1976) further bolstered this argument that there was little evidence that treatment could be relied upon to reduce recidivism. Although Martinson (1979) eventually published a partial recantation, the damage was done. The "nothing works" doctrine fit the temper of the times and was warmly greeted by political ideologues. There followed a shift away from funding rehabilitation programs and toward funding primary crime prevention and deterrence programs.

According to Anstiss (2003), subsequent meta-analyses (e.g., Andrews, 1995; Andrews et al., 1990; Dowden & Andrews, 1999, 2000: Izzo & Ross, 1990; Lipsey, 1992; Lipsey, Chapman, & Landenberger, 2001; Lösel, 1995; McGuire & Priestly, 1995; Wexler, Falkin, & Lipton, 1990; Whitehead & Lab, 1989) appeared to demonstrate that some types of correctional programs did in fact work. However, these studies arrived 20–25 years too late to stem the tide away from indeterminate sentencing and toward mandatory sentencing. The reader should note that the cited meta-analyses were concerned with the treatment of criminal offenders, not sex offenders. Research devoted to that population is detailed in the preceding chapter.

Robinson (2008) has offered the proposition that the ideal of rehabilitation is not dead but has rebranded itself and adopted a new penal strategy. The argument here is that rehabilitation programs, now called "risk management," are actually good for us in that they have the potential of preventing future victims. The work of Andrews and Bonta (2007) represents an exquisite expression of this theme from a psychological perspective. Administratively the rebranding of rehabilitation as a protective enterprise finds expression in the United Kingdom in the National Offender Management Service (NOMS) which unites prison and probation services under a single umbrella (Raynor & Robinson, 2006).

### *The Demise of Indeterminate Sentencing*

The "what works/nothing works" debate essentially put an end to the rehabilitation ideal in corrections. Several arguments were raised against indeterminate sentencing (Travis, 2005, p. 17):

- Assigning sentencing responsibilities to the judicial branch was seen as an inappropriate exercise of unchecked, unguided, and unreviewable power.
- Reliance on the discretion of judges, corrections administrators, parole boards, and parole officers was seen as arbitrary, racially discriminatory, and fundamentally unfair.

- A belief in the individualization of justice, the potential for redemption, and the goal of rehabilitation was seen as coddling criminals.
- Concern for offenders' reintegration was seen as the idealistic view of social engineers who minimized the offenders' potential for doing harm.

What was needed instead, it was argued, was a regime that applied punishment (i.e., imprisonment) in proportion to the seriousness of the crime. This is often referred to as the "just desserts" or "truth in sentencing" option. Under the previous regime of discretionary parole release, many observers felt, offenders were given sentences that were too brief, they did not serve a sufficient period of time in prison, they were let out too early, and were thus free to commit additional crimes that did not need to happen. Many offenders obligingly fulfilled this prophecy. Petersilia (2003, pp. 69–71) has argued that the determinate position is mistaken:

- The length of time spent in prison is actually greater under indeterminate sentencing. Violent offenders serve long terms.
- Prisoners released by a parole board actually had higher success rates than those released after serving a full term.
- Discretionary release ultimately leads to greater public safety because it encourages both inmates and prison officials to focus more intensely on reintegration programs.

Travis (2005, p. 13) has provided an outline of what indeterminate sentencing looks like in operation:

- The state sets broad ranges of possible sentences for criminal offenses.
- In sentencing, a judge determines a "range within the range," a sentence with upper and lower limits.
- If the offender receives a prison sentence, a parole board later reviews the prisoner's progress toward rehabilitation and assesses his or her readiness to return to society.
- If these conditions are met, the board may release him or her from confinement.
- The prisoner then serves the remainder of his or her sentence in the community.
- The prisoner can be returned to prison if the conditions of parole are violated.

### *Determinate Sentencing*

"A mandatory sentence is a . . . court decision where judicial discretion is limited by law. Typically, people convicted of certain crimes must be punished with at least a minimum number of years in prison" (Mandatory sentencing, 2010). In the mandatory system the exact term of imprisonment is set at the time of sentencing. The prisoner must be released when the term expires. However, many offenders are now required to serve a specific term of "supervised release" upon release from prison (Petersilia, 2003, p. 65). Parole boards have not been entirely abolished, but their authority has been severely limited.

## Parole Supervision

Historically, the parole officer (PO) was seen as a sort of social worker. Originally the PO was seen as a "friend" who could provide counseling, assist with housing and job searches, and the like. In more recent times, given the negative political and social climate against offenders, POs have become more control- and surveillance-oriented. Drug testing, house arrest, and electronic monitoring are now common parole supervision procedures.

> While rehabilitation remains in parole's rhetoric, as a practical matter, parole services are almost entirely focused on control-oriented activities. Agents have constructed an image of the prototypical parolee as someone who chooses to maintain an involvement with crime, who needs no more than an attitude adjustment to get on the "right track," and who does not need the agent to provide intervention and services to facilitate reform. (Petersilia, 2003, p. 80)

Cullen, Myer, and Latessa (2009) echo this assessment in their statement that parole officers and correctional administrators are likely to adopt a perspective that says if the threat, discipline, or pain is strong enough, that should be sufficient to straighten out offenders.

Standard conditions of parole applicable to most offenders include the following (Petersilia, 2003, p. 82):

- Report to the parole agent within 24 hours of release.
- Do not carry weapons.
- Report changes of address and employment.
- Do not travel more than 50 miles from home nor leave the coun-

try for more than 48 hours without prior approval of the parole agent.
- Obey all parole agent instructions.
- Seek and maintain employment and/or participate in education or work training.
- Do not commit crimes.
- Submit to search by the police and parole officers.

A particularly egregious example of a parole condition has been described by Crosner (2007–2008). Section 3067 of the California Penal Code requires every prisoner eligible for parole to agree in writing "to be subject to search and seizure by a parole officer or other peace officer at any time of the day or night, with or without a search warrant and *with or without cause*" (p. 413). Crosner states that this requirement is "the nation's first codification of a *suspicionless* search condition . . ., making it arguably the most severe legislative intrusion on parolees' . . . [constitutional] . . . rights in United States legal history" (p. 414).

Parole can be revoked for two reasons: (1) commission of a new crime or (2) disobeying any condition of parole (e.g., failing a drug test, failing to maintain employment, moving without permission) (Travis, 2005, pp. 48–49). Travis (2005) finds parole revocation and reimprisonment a particularly unfair process that he calls "back end sentencing": "We deprive hundreds of thousands of citizens of their liberty with a minimum of due process, and imprison them for significant amounts of time, often for minor infractions of administrative rules or for low-level criminal conduct" (p. 51).

So, is intensive supervision a good or bad thing? Unfortunately, it is a bit of both. Travis (2005) puts it this way:

> Viewed from a public safety perspective . . . we will not reduce crime much, if at all, simply by increasing the intensity of supervision. Viewed from a corrections management perspective, more supervision sends more people back to prison, mostly for technical violations. Viewed from a reintegration perspective, more supervision increases participation in programs that place offenders in jobs, helps offenders with addictions to alcohol and drugs, and facilitates restitution to victims. (p. 111)

Whether an ex-prisoner is on probation or parole, on supervised release, or under no conditions at all, he or she faces an enormous set of obstacles in an attempt to reenter and reintegrate into society. We now turn to a consideration of some of these barriers.

## Obstacles to Reentry and Reintegration

The problems that will beset ex-prisoners begin during the prison term and in the immediate period following release. The following sections describe some of these persistent problems.

### *"Invisible Punishments"*

These barriers are called "invisible" because they do not appear in sentencing orders or in orders of supervision. Taken together they form a veritable wall that is sometimes unbreachable. The term is attributed to Travis (2005), who had this to say about them:

> Beginning in the 1980s . . . as the nation embarked on a steady buildup of prisons and extended the reach of criminal justice supervision, America's new punitive attitude also led to an expansion in the network of invisible punishment. Taken together, the laws enacted by the states and Congress during this resurgence of collateral sanctions constructed substantial barriers to participation in American society. These laws became instruments of the "social exclusion" of people with criminal convictions. (p. 66)

And further:

> Punishment for the original offense is no longer enough: one's debt to society is never paid. . . . In the modern welfare state, these restrictions on the universe of social and welfare rights amount to a kind of "civil death," in which the offender is deemed unworthy of societal benefits and is excluded from the social compact. (p. 73)

We treat some of these invisible punishments in subsequent pages. For the moment, the following examples provide a flavor of the pernicious effects of these sanctions (Travis, 2005, p. 63; Petersilia, 2003, p. 105).

Typically they include (1) ineligibility for public assistance, education loans, public housing, or food stamps; (2) prohibition of voting, holding public office, or service on a jury; and (3) possible grounds for divorce, termination of parental rights, lifetime registration with the police, or deportation.

### *Work*

Two of the major publications on parole and reentry (Petersilia, 2003; Travis, 2005) both stress the importance of meaningful jobs within the institution. This ideal is almost never met. For example, according to the California Department of Corrections and Rehabilitation (2009), the California Men's Colony (CMC) in San Luis Obispo, a minimum–medium security facility, offers a wide variety of inmate programs that include:

- Prison Industry Authority (PIA): Glove factory, jacket line, knitting mill, laundry, shoe factory, silk screening, T-shirt line, specialty printing plant, textile products, firefighting clothing, maintenance. *The PIA manufactures and services are for state use.*
- Vocational: Auto body repair, auto mechanics, dry cleaning, electronics, landscaping, machine shop, small engine repair, welding, office technology, building maintenance. *Again, these activities mainly serve state use. They provide marginal skills for use in the outside world.*
- Academic: Adult Basic Education, High School/GED, English as a Second Language, Literacy Program, Computer Assisted Education, Pre-Release. *These programs are obviously useful to educationally disadvantaged persons.*
- Other: Community service crews (firefighting, beach cleanup), Religious, Arts in Corrections, Victim Awareness, Drug and Alcohol Treatment/Diversion, Alternatives to Violence, Anger Management, Hospice, Criminal and Gangs Anonymous, Personal Growth Seminar. *Programs such as these are typical of large correctional institutions. How the effectiveness of these programs is assessed is unknown.*

While this array of activities is far larger and varied than what may be found in many, if not most prisons, with few exceptions they have very little to do with work in the real world and very little to do with documented effective treatment of real problems. However, they look good on paper. Cullen et al. (2009) have noted that politicians and correctional administrators are quick to welcome programs that make the system look good. Some critics would argue that *any* activity that keeps idle hands and scheming minds busy is a good thing.

Travis (2005, pp. 160–162) has offered a bleak general summary on this problem.

> Theoretically, a prison could be a full-employment economy—anyone who wanted and was capable of performing a job could work, if prison management embraced this goal. . . . All in all, America's prisons fall far short of a full-employment economy and exhibit a high level of idleness. To the extent that prisoners do work, the goods and services that

> they produce are overwhelmingly consumed by the prison community or by state governments. Most important . . . prisons represent a massive failure to prepare prisoners for their return to the world of work. By failing to achieve full employment and failing to prepare prisoners for a return to work, our current prison policies damage the . . . economy, one prisoner at a time. Moreover, these negative effects are not evenly distributed. They are concentrated in impoverished communities that already experience high rates of unemployment and social disadvantage.

### *Employment*

Postrelease supervision orders always contain a requirement that the ex-prisoner seek and maintain gainful employment. The very fact of having served time in prison as well as the failure of the institution to prepare the prisoner to enter a free market has a direct and negative effect on postprison employment. Petersilia (2003, pp. 112–119, *passim*) cites a meta-analysis of 400 studies by Lipsey (1995) who determined that employment was the single most important factor in reducing reoffending. Petersilia also noted (p. 113) a number of potentially irremediable barriers to employment: very low levels of education and previous work experience; substance abuse and mental health problems; residing in poor inner-city neighborhoods with weak connections to stable employment opportunities; and lack of motivation for and attitudes of distrust and alienation from traditional work.

Lucken and Ponte (2008, pp. 47–48) provided a similar picture of offenders leaving prison. One-third will have received vocational or educational training; one-quarter will have participated in substance abuse programming; fewer than 10% will have participated in a pre- or postrelease program; and two-thirds will remain unemployed for up to 3 years after release.

Some types of jobs (e.g., child care, education, security) have legal prohibitions against ex-prisoners. Some unions will not admit ex-convicts because they are unable to be bonded. It is difficult to obtain some basic forms of identification such as driver's licenses (needed to establish identity), social insurance cards, or birth certificates. Potential employers can gain access to criminal records on the Internet. They will almost always ask about any criminal history and failure to disclose can result in failure to hire or dismissal. When questioned, employers will often say that they would "probably not" or "definitely not" hire an ex-prisoner, mainly because they have concerns about trustworthiness. When they are hired, ex-prisoners tend to earn 20–30% less than similar employees with no criminal record. Lucken and Ponte (2008) state that "while employers are more likely to hire ex-offenders in manufacturing and construction positions, as opposed to service and retail positions, such jobs constitute 15 percent of all employment" (p. 50).

Lucken and Ponte (2008) offer this assessment of barriers to employment:

> It is . . . reasonable to assert that given the real and symbolic importance of work in both the penal system and in the ethos of American society, the statutory and regulatory barriers facing ex-offenders in the job market seem antithetical to expectations of good citizenship, familial responsibility, and meaningful (re)integration into community life. (p. 49)

### Housing and Homelessness

Coupled with employment, housing is an essential component for successful reentry and reintegration. Petersilia (2003, p. 121) cited Bradly, Oliver, Richardson, and Slayter (2001, p. 7): "Housing is the linchpin that holds the reintegration process together. Without a stable residence, continuity in substance abuse and mental health treatment is compromised. Employment is often contingent upon a fixed living arrangement." Travis (2005, pp. 220–240, *passim*) has vividly described the housing problems facing ex-prisoners.

Most ex-prisoners return to live with their families, who may or may not want them back. If rejected, they may turn to other relatives or friends, some of whom may have criminal records or be criminally active.

Poor people such as most ex-prisoners are often unable to muster a deposit for private housing. Landlords may require credit references, information about current and prior jobs, or information on a prior rental. Some communities simply want to keep probationers and parolees out of their neighborhoods. There has always been community resistance to group homes.

The U.S. Public Housing Administration (PHA) can deny "applicants whose habits and practices reasonably may be expected to have a detrimental effect on the residents or the project environment. . . . [A] history of criminal activity . . . would adversely affect the health, safety or welfare of other tenants" (Travis, 2005, p. 229). Therefore, if the ex-prisoner formerly lived with his family in public housing, he would be ineligible to return. The PHA can terminate leases for criminal behavior "carried out by a household member, guest, or 'other person under the tenant's control' " (Travis, 2005, p. 231). The PHA can evict a tenant when any household member's use of alcohol or drugs affects the rights of other tenants. The PHA's powers of eviction are broad: a conviction is not required, there need not be an arrest, the incident need not be recent, and the incident can occur on or off the premises.

There are hundreds of thousands of people homeless in the United States. Of these, about 25% have done time in prison. Ten to twenty-five percent of released prisoners will be homeless within a year. "All of the variables are present for an equation that produces homelessness—diminished social ties, significant legal barriers, and social stigma" (Travis, 2005, p. 240). Ex-prisoners are "a subpopulation that experiences two revolving doors—one that leads in and out of prison, and one that leads in and out of homeless shelters" (Travis, 2005, p. 240).

### *Communities*

Ex-prisoners often return to communities that are impoverished and broken. These are called "core counties," areas that contain the central city of a metropolitan area (Travis, 2005, p. 281). These are places of dire economic and social disadvantage.

> In the era of mass incarceration, several building blocks of civil society have been weakened in communities of concentrated return. Families are weaker and marriage is undermined. Voting rights are restricted, political participation is diminished, and political representation is diluted. The economic viability of neighborhoods already struggling with economic disadvantage has been harmed. These communities suffer a new brand of stigma as places that send high percentages of residents to prison. Finally, the very legitimacy of the criminal justice system—in the agencies of government directed to enforce the policies that result in mass incarceration—has been undermined, leading to a cycle of distrust, cynicism, and further noncompliance with society's laws. (Travis, 2005, p. 294)

When Clear (2009) speaks of "imprisoning communities," he refers to poor urban areas such as those described above where literally millions of dollars are spent to incarcerate residents. The absence of these people from the neighborhood causes social disruption, breaking up families and depriving them of support, and threatening the economic structure of the area. Thompson (2008) focuses upon the disproportionate racial dimension of this problem.

### *Voting Rights*

In 2005, only two very small U.S. states permitted incarcerated persons to vote. Thirty-one states disenfranchised prisoners, probationers, and parolees. In 11 states, many ex-felons faced a lifetime ban on voting. Thus approximately one in 50 adults is currently or permanently prohibited from voting. Due to their disproportionate representation in prisons and as ex-felons, this has a similar disproportionate effect on blacks and Hispanics (Travis, 2005, pp. 255–257). Manza and Uggen (2006) present evidence that ex-convicts who vote are less likely to reoffend.

### Public Access to Records

It is possible, using the Internet, for any citizen to gain access to at least some supposedly confidential information on ex-prisoners. Such information can be used in a variety of ways to create barriers to reentry and reintegration. Petersilia (2003, pp. 108–109) notes that "some of the criminal record information in the FBI and state registries has been shown to be inaccurate, and yet it is shared with landlords, financial institutions, and employers as if it were valid." As an example she points out that anyone can search the Illinois Department of Corrections (DOC) website by entering an inmate's name, date of birth, or DOC number. The screen that then appears will show:

- A current picture of the inmate (or parolee)
- The inmate's current status
- Residence location (if paroled)
- Date of birth
- Height and weight
- Race
- Color of hair and eyes
- Any scars or tattoos
- Security classification
- County of commitment (and release)
- Discharge date
- Crime for which convicted
- Number of counts
- Sentence imposed

In other states, notes Petersilia, Internet sites may contain information on modus operandi, cars driven, home address, gang affiliation, and substance abuse history. To say that this is an outrageous invasion of privacy is an understatement.

Blumstein and Nakamura (2009) have noted that in 2006, over 81 million criminal history records were in state archives. A large number of these records were acquired many years ago. An individual could have been crime free since that time but that evidence could remain in the archive. The problem for people who believe that they are legitimately consulting these records (e.g., employers, bankers) is: How can one know that the individual has been rehabilitated? Blumstein and Nakamura note the lack of empirical evidence that criminal activity has ceased or, put another way, how long a period of time away from crime is sufficient to consider the person to be going straight or "redeemed"?

### *Health Concerns*

We mentioned above that prisoners are in very poor health compared to the general population, particularly with respect to HIV/AIDS infections, TB, hepatitis C, and mental illness. Histories of alcohol and substance abuse are much greater than that seen in the general population. Travis (2005) described the problems as follows: "The prisoner population reflects the communities from which the inmates came—typically low income with limited access to high quality health care and substantially greater health concerns than the general population" (p. 193).

According to Travis (2005, p. 186), more than 15,000 HIV-positive prisoners, 2,500 inmates with AIDS, and 200,000 prisoners with hepatitis C leave prison and reenter society every year.

Within the prison itself (Travis, 2005, pp. 194–203, *passim*) we find the following. The HIV rate was five to seven times higher than that of the general population. The confirmed AIDS cases were five times greater. Consensual sex provides a ready avenue to disease transmission but American prisons do not provide condoms to inmates. In 2000, the Bureau of Justice Statistics (BJS) estimated that 16% of state inmates had a mental disorder. Human Rights Watch estimated that only inmates suffering from a major mental disorder (e.g., schizophrenia, bipolar disorder) received treatment in prison. In 1997 about 80% of state prison populations reported a history of drug and/or alcohol abuse. According to the U.S. Department of Health and Human Services, those needing drug and alcohol treatment do not get it. In 1997, 45% of state prisons offered no treatment at all.

## Barriers Specific to Sex Offenders

Depending upon the individual's criminal offense patterns and past history, many of the regulations, conditions, and deprivations imposed upon criminal offenders will apply to sex offenders as well. However, in the public and particularly in the legalistic, retributivistic mind, they are seen as something special—very special in that they are believed to be extremely dangerous, high-rate offenders, who prey on strangers, and who are highly likely to reoffend. These beliefs are aggravated by a persistent media focus on rare and highly sensational cases. All of these assumptions are false. As we showed in preceding chapters, only a tiny minority of criminal offenders would meet the criteria of persistent, life-course criminals. The same is true of sex offenders. Indeed, criminologists would consider them to be just another type of criminal and nothing special.

Laws (2009) has provided a selective review of restrictions placed on sex offenders and punitive measures enacted over the years. As with our preceding consideration of restrictions on criminal offenders, we will be concerned here with restrictions on sex offenders in the community. While historically relevant, consideration of the sexual psychopath laws from the 1930s to the 1980s and the current trend toward civil commitment of "sexually violent predators" is outside the limits of this discussion.

Sex offenders under supervision in the community, whether released from prison or placed on probation, are typically under the same standard reporting conditions as criminal offenders. Additional conditions have emerged since the early 1990s.

### Sex Offender Registries

In 1994 the Jacob Wetterling Act (Megan's Law) was enacted. This provided for a state registry of sex offenders. It was later amended to include community notification of an offender's presence and lifetime registration for recidivists. In 2005 Jessica's Law increased minimum sentences, increased registration requirements, and increased monitoring requirements. For the first time, residency restrictions were introduced. The most sweeping registration law is the Adam Walsh Child Protection and Safety Act of 2006. This act created a national sex offender registry in three "tiers." Tier 3 contains the most dangerous offenders who are subject to lifetime registration and must update their whereabouts every 3 months. Tier 2 are the moderately dangerous, who are subject to 25 years registration and must update their whereabouts every 6 months. Tier 1 are the least dangerous, who are subject to 15 years registration and must update their whereabouts every year. It is obvious that setting up such a system state by state would be enormously complex and expensive. The *Washington Times* (July 7, 2009) reported that no state has complied with this law (the deadline is July 2010). States that fail to comply will lose 10% of their federal criminal justice grant, which supports crime control and prevention, victim services, and public defenders. The *Washington Times* stated that some states have concluded that they would be better off to lose the money than meet the requirements of the law. Whether the Adam Walsh Act registry is ever realized, the extant registration laws provide a stigma that the offender could conceivably carry for the rest of his life. The "sex offender" stigma is far more pernicious and far reaching than the "burglar" or "car thief" stigma.

### *Residency Restrictions*

These are the second set of requirements that pose the greatest hazard to community reentry and reintegration. The restrictions are the direct result of the "stranger danger" myth, that is, that sex offenders are roaming around looking for strange children to molest. Stranger danger crimes are, in fact, relatively rare. Some 93% of sexual offenses against children are committed by acquaintances and relatives. Nonetheless, residency restrictions prohibit sex offenders from living near places where children are known to congregate: playgrounds, schools, swimming pools, school bus stops, and the like.

Craun and Theriot (2009) examined this common misperception through a self-administered mail survey. They found that "in neighborhoods where registered sex offenders reside, awareness of a local sex offender significantly increases the likelihood that a respondent is more worried about a stranger sexually abusing a child" (p. 2057). Such findings, say these authors, may demonstrate an unintended consequence of sex offender registries.

Duwe, Donnay, and Tewksbury (2008) examined the reoffense patterns of 224 sex offenders released from prison between 1990 and 2002. A few offenders contacted victims within close proximity to their residences. None did so near schools, parks, playgrounds, or other locations specified in these laws.

A very striking study was performed by Chajewski and Mercado (2009). Using GIS mapping software they plotted the residences of sex offenders and the location of schools in a rural, a suburban, and an urban area of New Jersey. The maps showed the schools ringed by buffer zones of 1,000 or 2,500 feet. In the rural area and to a lesser extent in the suburban area there was room for sex offender residences with buffer zones of 1,000 feet. In the suburban area and, dramatically, in the urban area the buffer zone of 2,500 feet took up virtually all of the space, leaving the offender no place to go. Since these are the community areas where offenders will most likely access services, this is an unfortunate result. The California Coalition on Sexual Offending (Delson, Kokish, & Abbott, 2008) published a position paper on residency restrictions. They concluded that available research shows no relationship whatsoever between where a registered sex offender lives and the pattern of any new sex crimes he or she commits. They concluded that the policies appear to result in significant increases in the number of homeless and transient sex offenders, thereby increasing risk.

### *Additions to Sex Offender Laws*

Communities have made some highly creative additions to the existing laws which greatly increase the misery of the sex offender in the community. Following are some examples:

- Georgia, 2006. No exemption from residency restrictions for persons living in a nursing home or hospice care facility.
- Iowa, 2006. Residency restrictions cause sex offenders to change addresses without notification or new location, register false addresses, or just disappear.
- Iowa, 2006. Physically or mentally disabled sex offenders are prohibited from living with family members who see to their daily needs.
- Florida, 2008. A person designated a sexual predator may not possess a prescription drug for erectile dysfunction.
- Florida, 2008. A court may sentence a sex offender to be treated with medroxy-progesterone acetate (Depo-Provera) if convicted of sexual battery or, with consent, physical castration.
- Nebraska, 2008. Communities tried to develop restrictions that would essentially ban sex offenders from the community.
- Florida, 2008. During a hurricane, sex offenders must go to a "designated shelter." Going to other shelters (e.g., with family) would violate supervision requirements.
- Florida, 2008. CNN reports that homeless sex offenders are sleeping under bridges. The local probation office responded: "At least we know where they are."

It is becoming increasingly clear, and excruciatingly clear in the case of sex offenders, that crime control, rather than crime itself, may be the real danger for the future. In the name of simple, common humanity, this cannot be allowed to continue.

## Conclusions

What we have described in this chapter represents only a part of the picture of the barriers that ex-prisoners face in attempting to reenter society. Travis (2005, p. 87) puts forth the case very succinctly:

> The odds against successful reentry are daunting. According to the Bureau of Justice Statistics . . ., two-thirds of released prisoners will be rearrested for one or more crimes, including felonies and serious misdemeanors, within three years after they get out of prison. Nearly half will be convicted of a new crime. One-quarter will be returned to prison for these new convictions. . . . [U]nder current conditions, most prisoners will fail to lead law-abiding lives when they return home.

The rush to enact ever more punitive laws and regulations, the tightening of restrictions on ex-prisoners, the seemingly inexorable tide toward ever more and longer incarcerations, is taking a heavy toll on former prisoners and, one might argue, on the quality of our society as well. Consider the following:

> Society does not readily set a place at the communal table for those who have violated the law. We deny ex-felons access to jobs, housing, health care, welfare benefits, voting rights, and other privileges and rights of citizenship through a vast network of invisible punishments. On a more fundamental level, we create a symbolic distance between mainstream society and ex-felons by attaching a powerful, seemingly indelible stigma to those who have violated society's laws. Society shuns ex-felons, while simultaneously expecting them to work, support their children, respect the law, and observe their release conditions. (Travis, 2005, p. 250)

## Chapter 10

# Overcoming Barriers to Reentry and Reintegration

There are two voices, two ways of looking at the reentry problem. On the one hand, we have what Robinson (2008) has called the "late modern" penal narrative of "expressive rehabilitation." This is an example of the rebranding of rehabilitation that we mentioned in the preceding chapter, the risk management option. In this narrative the expressive nature of words is changed. For example, the old terms such as "throughcare" or "aftercare," which have a rather psychotherapeutic flavor to them, are replaced with words such as "reentry" or "resettlement" (p. 436). As she puts it, the pure rehabilitative (i.e., psychotherapeutic) notion is extinct. "In the context of the 'what works' movement . . . the 'technical superiority' (i.e., empirical demonstrations of effectiveness) [also called "evidence-based"] of the new interventions has played a significant role in the re-legitimation of rehabilitation" (p. 437). This, it seems to us, is simply a renaming and repackaging of the repressive practices we described in the preceding chapter. "Rehabilitation" of offenders in this sense is good for all of us because its sole aim is the assessment and management of risk.

It is no surprise that the other voice is a humanistic one, a voice that does not deny the need to punish crime, but leans more strongly toward the original ideal of rehabilitation. O'Hear (2007) has outlined this position quite eloquently:

> If reentry initiatives are not understood as primarily recidivism measures, but as the fulfillment of an ethical obligation to some of the most socially marginalized and disadvantaged members of our communities, then the reentry movement may be better able to live up to its humanizing potential. Thus, the greater ethical question for reentry-based reform is who are we doing it for: Us or Them, those outside the prison walls or those within? Are we doing it for Us, because we are afraid of Them? Or are we doing it for Them, because we recognize in Them a common spark of humanity (however revolting some of their misdeeds) and genuinely wish for Them to rejoin and enrich our communities, to rebuild their lives, and to atone in some way (not merely to suffer) for the harm they have done. (pp. 9–10)

The practical side of that argument may be seen in the work of the Re-Entry Policy Council.

*The Report of the Re-Entry Policy Council: Charting the Safe and Successful Return of Prisoners to the Community* (Re-Entry Policy Council, 2005) proposes the broadest agenda yet seen for overcoming the barriers facing ex-prisoners. The sponsoring organization, the Council of State Governments (CSG), founded in 1933, is a nonpartisan, nonprofit organization serving state legislatures, state courts, and executive branch officials and agencies. The CSG's mission, as stated on their website (*www.csg.org*), is to use their committees and task forces, supported by policy and research specialists, to make recommendations to states on matters of public policy.

*The Report of the Re-Entry Policy Council* was coordinated by the Justice Center of the CSG. Partner organizations included, for example, the American Probation and Parole Association, the National Association of Housing and Redevelopment Officials, the National Association of State Alcohol and Drug Abuse Directors, and the National Association of State Mental Health Directors. Funding was provided by the U.S. Departments of Justice, Health and Human Services, and Labor, with additional funds provided by six private foundations.

The Re-Entry Policy Council was convened in 2001. One hundred experts in various areas worked in committees to produce their recommendations. The reentry process was divided into five major sections: admission to the facility, prison and jail, release, transition, and community supervision.

The substantive issue areas to be considered were:

- Assessments
- Children, families, and communities
- Education and employment

- Federal benefits
- Housing
- Mental health
- Physical health
- Substance abuse
- Victims
- Community and faith-based organizations

The 658-page *Report* addresses all of the issues outlined in the preceding chapter. Its recommendations are broad and sweeping, but it is not boilerplate. Having said that, it must also be acknowledged that the remedies proposed are extremely complex and expensive. Much of the *Report* must be considered aspirational. To illustrate this point, consider the following excerpts from the Executive Summary:

> **Development of Programming Plan**
>
> Develop, for each person incarcerated, an individualized plan that, based upon information obtained from the assessments, explains what programming should be provided during the period of incarceration to ensure that his or her return to the community is safe and successful. (p. xxi)
>
> **Educational and Vocational Training**
>
> Teach inmates functional, educational, and vocational competencies based on employment market demand and public safety requirements. (p. xxii)
>
> **Housing**
>
> Facilitate a person's access to stable housing upon his or her re-entry to the community. (p. xxii)

The *Report* is, without question, a remarkable document. What is most remarkable is that a highly diverse group of scholars, practitioners, and administrators could agree upon such a broad set of recommendations. Many of these recommendations have been made by criminologists and other criminal justice professionals for years. Of course the question remains: How much of this is practicable and can be implemented under current social, legal, and policy conditions? Nothing as broadly based as the *Report*'s agenda is presently available or on the horizon. However, there have been some encouraging developments in recent years, and it is to a consideration of these that we now turn.

## The Second Chance Act

There are actually two Second Chance Acts. First, in his State of the Union address in 2004 President Bush proposed a $300 million prisoner reentry initiative (O'Hear, 2007). This was proposed in the U.S. Congress as the Second Chance Act of 2007 (H.R. 1593). The purpose of the act was "to reauthorize the grant program for reentry of offenders into the community in the Omnibus Crime Control and Safe Streets Act of 1968, to improve reentry planning and implementation, and for other purposes." It is thus an amendment to the Omnibus Act to "reauthorize, rewrite, and expand provisions for adult and juvenile offender state and local reentry *demonstration projects* [emphasis added] to provide expanded services to offenders and their families for reentry into society" (Second Chance Act, 2009, pp. 1–2). This was signed into law in 2008.

O'Hear (2007) provides this description of the functions of the Second Chance Act:

> Grant recipients . . . must develop a reentry strategic plan containing performance outcomes, one of which must be a *50 percent reduction in recidivism rates over five years* [emphasis added]. Other required performance measures include increased employment, education, and housing opportunities for offenders released back into the community. Grant recipients must collaborate with corrections, health, housing, welfare, education, substance abuse, victims services, employment services, and law enforcement agencies, and convene reentry task forces comprised of diverse agencies and community organizations. Priority must be given to applicants who provide prerelease reentry planning and continuity in the provision of services. (pp. 2–3)

The preceding represents an extremely tall order for any agency to undertake, let alone fulfill. The ultimate joker in the deck is the 50% reduction in recidivism over 5 years—a very unlikely accomplishment. The criminological literature has long shown that reductions in recidivism following participation in prison- or community-based programs are never large, if indeed they can be attributed to those programs. O'Hear (2007, p. 9) concluded that "although rehabilitative programs will never eliminate recidivism entirely, the achievement of demonstrably *high* reductions in recidivism may be necessary if the reentry movement is to grow and prosper over the long run." So, the Second Chance Act of 2007 is, on the face of it, a good idea that may prove to have limited success.

The second legislative proposal was the Second Chance Act for Ex-Offenders of 2007 (H.R. 623). Due to lack of support, this bill was never reported out of committee. It was reintroduced in 2009 as H.R. 1529, the Second Chance for Ex-Offenders Act of 2009. This is a potentially very important piece of legislation in that it "would permit expungement of records of certain nonviolent criminal offenses" (Second Chance Act, 2009, p. 1). H.R. 1529

> amends the federal criminal code to allow an individual to file a petition for expungement of a record of conviction for a nonviolent criminal offense if such individual has:
>
> (1) never been convicted of a violent offense and has never been convicted of a nonviolent offense other than the one for which expungement is sought;
> (2) fulfilled all requirements of the sentence of the court in which conviction was obtained;
> (3) remained free from dependency on or abuse of alcohol or controlled substance for a minimum of one year and has been rehabilitated, to the court's satisfaction, if so required by the terms of supervised release;
> (4) obtained a high school diploma or completed a high school equivalency program; and
> (5) completed at least one year of community service."

At this writing (December, 2009), this bill has not been signed into law.

If it becomes law the judiciary will not run many risks with the 2009 act. It applies only to first offenders with nonviolent offenses, who have completed all sentence terms, who do not abuse alcohol or drugs, who are high school graduates, and who have completed a year of community service. Those parameters represent what may be required to get this act on the books. If so, it is the thin edge of the wedge and its provisions may be amended over time. It is definitely a good start.

Travis (2005, p. 310) has offered recommendations for a national policy on prisoner reentry:

• Make efforts to reduce the high incidence of rearrest among prisoners immediately following their release. A safety plan should be developed that clearly specifies the goals of reentry and the procedures necessary to achieve those goals. Supervision services should be front-loaded. If the ex-prisoner requires assistance with housing, substance abuse treatment, physical health maintenance, or mental health treatment, arrangements should be made in advance to ensure that these services are available soon after release.

- Maintain a prisoner's strong family ties. Attention to these issues can begin while the individual is still confined, then be followed up by community agencies. There should be a strong focus on child welfare and reuniting families upon release.
- Create full-employment prisons where meaningful work is performed and skills learned can be translated to the real world of work. Skills learned should be those that will be of value to the community.
- Public health should be a major mission of corrections. Institutions should be able to detect and treat serious communicable diseases and create links for postrelease community health services. The major focus here would be on HIV/AIDS, sexually transmitted diseases, tuberculosis, and hepatitis C.
- No prisoner should be released to a homeless status. Public housing policies should be amended to allow prisoners in appropriate cases to return to their families. Community agencies should assist in resolving conflicts arising from the ex-prisoner's reunion with the family.
- Restore the right to vote and provide certificates of good conduct or rehabilitation. Create *reentry courts* (see below) to oversee the reentry process.
- Communities must become heavily involved in reintegration. Reliance will have to be placed upon families, faith-based organizations, and the business sector to play a constructive role in supporting reintegration. These entities cannot necessarily be expected to voluntarily undertake these tasks. Therefore it will be necessary to create a *justice intermediary* (see below) to broker these services.

Travis (2005) predates Robinson (2008) in summing up the value of these proposed remedies. "The rationale for these expenditures is not a rehabilitation rationale—these efforts may or may not reduce a prisoner's propensity to reoffend—but a risk reduction rationale" (p. 312).

Travis (2005, pp. 344–351) also recommended a jurisprudence, a system of law, governing the reentry–reintegration process. What follows represent only portions of what a new jurisprudence might look like, but they are clear recommendations for amending existing legislation and proposing new legislation.

- Create incentives for reentry preparation. An inmate could gain a reduction in sentence by showing (1) successful participation in prison activities related to postprison success (provided they existed), and (2) verifiable connections to family, work, housing, and other relevant community support systems.

- Devolve supervision to local jurisdictions. The guiding principle here is devolution—the surrender of the power of central government to local government. The level of government closest to community life is local, not state, government. The functions most closely related to successful reentry (child welfare, public housing, job training) are carried out by local government. All community supervision should be carried out by a *justice intermediary* (see below).
- Redefine the purposes of revocation of parole/probation. Back-end sentencing (revocation) should be used as a way to promote successful reintegration. Violations should be directly related to the risk posed by the parolee/probationer. "A new period of incarceration for violating a condition of supervision would be justified only if it was integral to the overall plan of increasing the individual's chances of prosocial behavior. . . . [T]he severity of the sanction is less important in securing compliance with social norms than the consistency and predictability of a system of incentives and modest sanctions administered in a respectful manner" (Travis, 2005, p. 348). Following revocation, sentences should be served in local jails, not state prisons.
- Limit collateral sanctions. Some of these cannot be done away with and should be directly related to the offense charged. The focus should be on reasonable restrictions that are directly related to the safety risk posed by the offender (e.g., a child molester may not work for a child care agency; a driver's license should be suspended for a DUI).
- Create *reentry courts* (see below). These courts essentially perform the functions currently performed by parole agents. The mission of the court would be to keep track of a prisoner's progress in meeting the reentry plan's goals. Early release might be granted to a person who has made significant progress. The court would be authorized to order short sentences of confinement to local jails.

Here we will consider in more detail some of the solutions proposed for overcoming barriers to reentry and reintegration. It is important to keep in mind that all information in this area is fragmentary. *The Report of the Re-Entry Council* (2005) worthily proposes highly specific solutions to the major barriers facing the reentry process. It does not necessarily offer suggestions for arriving at those solutions. As we have seen, to this point very little concrete progress (e.g., the Second Chance Act) has been made.

## The Reentry Court

Petersilia (2003) has offered a good description of this proposed entity.

> Reentry courts use judicial authority to apply graduated sanctions and positive reinforcement and to marshal community resources to support the prisoner's reintegration. . . . The goal of reentry courts is similar to drug courts, in that both attempt to coordinate services and establish a seamless system of offender accountability and support. . . . Judges use a case management approach to track and supervise offenders upon release. . . . [T]he judge becomes a reentry manager . . . identifies and coordinates local services that will help offenders reconnect with their families and community, including employment, counseling, education, health, mental health, and other essential services. (p. 204)
>
> Most important, reentry courts explicitly give recognition to the fact that the offender will come back to live in the community. (p. 205)

The preceding description shows very clearly that the existence of a reentry court in the community could conceivably occupy the central role in the reentry–reintegration process. All necessary elements could be gathered under a single umbrella.

According to Maruna and LeBel (2003), reentry courts as currently envisioned are based on drug treatment courts and other problem-solving courts. The core elements include assessment and reentry planning; regular status assessment meetings; coordination of multiple support services; accountability to the community; graduated and parsimonious sanctions for violation of release conditions; and rewards for success, such as, early release from parole and graduation ceremonies (p. 92). Although that sounds balanced, it is a combination of a control approach and a treatment approach. It is a pathologizing approach and assumes that the ex-offender remains a bundle of deficits. As an alternative, Maruna and LeBel argue for what they call a "strengths-based" approach, one that asks "not what a person's deficits are, but rather what positive contribution that person can make" (p. 97). Strengths-based themes, they say, have been a hallmark of progressive criminal justice reforms since the 19th century.

> In the reentry context, the strengths *narrative* begins with the assumption that ex-convicts are stigmatized persons, and implicitly that this stigma (and not some internal dangerousness or deficit) is at the core of what makes ex-convicts likely to reoffend. . . . [T]he strengths para-

> digm calls for opportunities for ex-convicts to make amends, demonstrate their value and potential, and make positive contributions to their communities. (p. 97)

And further:

> The focus . . . would be on monitoring, recording, and judging what the individual has done to redeem him or herself through victim reparation, community, volunteer work, mentoring, and parenting. . . . True to its name . . . the reentry court could become a "court of redemption," through which a stigmatized person has the opportunity to formally "make good." (p. 100)

## Reentry Partnerships

The intention of this model, working with the reentry court, is to systematically organize all community resources that are relevant to the reentry process. Petersilia (2003, p. 199) notes that the U.S. Department of Justice established the Reentry Partnership Initiative (RPI) in 2001. At that time eight states participated in the program. She cites Taxman and her colleagues (Taxman, Young, Byrne, Holsinger, & Anspach, 2002) for a description of the project:

> The underlying premise of the reentry partnerships is that each component of the criminal justice system—police, courts, institutional and community corrections—plays a role not only in immediate offender processing and control, but also in long-term offender change. . . . [C]riminal justice agencies cannot do this alone, and must engage family, community service providers, the faith community and other sources of formal and informal support in reintegrating offenders. . . . The challenge is twofold: (1) how do we prepare incarcerated and recently released inmates to be productive, contributing members of the community, and (2) how do we prepare communities to support, sustain, and when necessary sanction offenders returning under a wide range of release conditions. (p. 200)

## Justice Intermediary

Although it is a highly optimistic proposal, Travis (2005, pp. 300–301) has recommended a "justice reinvestment" strategy that could conceivably fund reentry courts and reentry partnerships. The basic idea would be to reduce the current level of imprisonment (i.e., reductions in admissions) and share the savings with communities. "Sharing" would include the establishment, for example, of halfway houses, the creation or expansion of drug and alcohol treatment programs, expansion of services to families, and the like. These services would not likely be created without oversight and for this Travis (2005) recommended the establishment of a justice intermediary, a broker of services who would work both with corrections establishments and community agencies:

> A justice intermediary would represent a test of the justice reinvestment model by achieving reductions in prison admissions, drawing upon the surveys in corrections budgets, melding public and private funding into a single budget for prisoner reintegration, and . . . seek to reduce the stigma associated with criminal justice involvement. . . . [T]he justice intermediary would serve as a justice development corporation, brokering needed services, making investments in properties needed to support the transition from prison, and building local institutional support for a new strategy for prisoner reentry. (p. 306)

The justice development corporation mentioned by Travis is one element of this proposed mosaic. This would be a community entity funded, as he proposed, by savings from reductions in admissions to prison. "This is a justice version of devolution—the transfer of responsibility for a critical function from the state to a community-based organization" (Travis, 2005, p. 58).

## Health Care Partnerships

We emphasized in the preceding chapter the extremely poor health status of many prisoners. The establishment of a health care partnership would be an important element of a reentry program. Following a survey of discharge planning for HIV-infected inmates in 1999–2001, the Centers for Disease Control formed a partnership with the Health Resources and Services Administration to implement a multisite demonstration project to evaluate transition to the community. There were three components to the project: (1) assess the inmate's need for continuing health care following release; (2) prior to release, identify a community-based medical or case management provider for each inmate; and (3) schedule the inmate for a specific appointment (not a referral) with a health care provider. As of 2005, the evaluation of this project was incomplete (Travis, 2005, pp. 209–210).

In a more broadly based program, said Travis (2005, pp. 212–213), prisons would (1) provide immunizations, screening, treatment, and prevention programs for communicable diseases; (2) provide comprehensive treatment programs for addiction and mental illness; and (3) implement universal health discharge planning. However, he concluded, "the prognosis for substantial new investments in prison health care is admittedly poor" (p. 213).

## Restoration of Civic Identity

We have mentioned many of the rules, regulations, and restrictions that contribute to and reinforce the social exclusion of ex-prisoners. We have also mentioned the stigma of former criminal involvement that offenders carry. Imprisonment tends to weaken social capital and thereby limits access to future social networks and full participation in the activities of the community. If the reentry and reintegration process is ever to be fully complete, means must be found to restore not only the reality but the personal sense of civic identity. Maruna (2001) has stated that ex-prisoners should be able to remove the stigma attached to their former inmate status and gain "permission to legally move on from the past. . . . Without this right, ex-offenders will always be ex-offenders, hence outsiders, or the Other" (p. 165).

Travis (2005) has noted that in 1956 the National Conference on Parole "recommended enactment of legislation authorizing sentencing judges to 'expunge' criminal convictions. The . . . order of expungement would be far-reaching: 'The individual shall be deemed not to have been convicted' of the crime" (p. 262). The drafters of the Model Penal Code followed up this recommendation 6 years later, stating that

> a sentencing court would be authorized to enter an order relieving "any disqualification or disability imposed by law because of the conviction" once he had completed his sentence. Furthermore, under a second provision, if the offender had exhibited a period of good behavior, the court could issue an order "vacating" the judgment of conviction. (p. 262)

We have seen that, nearly a half century later, a weak version of the expungement recommendation is expressed in the Second Chance for Ex-Offenders Act of 2009 which, at this writing, has not become law.

Although words such as "vacating" and "expungement" do not fall easily on the retributivist ear, these recommendations are not as far-fetched as they sound. In the United Kingdom the Rehabilitation of Offenders Act has been law since 1974.

> Under this law, an offender is deemed "rehabilitated" and his convictions "spent" if he is not convicted of a new felony within three years of his first conviction. This act also allows offenders covered by its provisions to say, if asked, that they have not been convicted of a crime and that they do not have a criminal record. (Travis, 2005, p. 263)

Maruna (2001) has referred to this practice as "rebiographing."

> Even when asked "Have you been convicted of a crime?" the law allows a desisting ex-offender to say "No." In this liberating model, an ex-offender is therefore legally enabled to rewrite his or her history to make it more in line with his or her present, reformed identity. After several years of good behavior, the State essentially says, "You don't appear to be the sort of person who has a criminal record, therefore you needn't have one." (p. 164)

Provisions that sweeping are not likely to play well in the United States. Some small steps have been made in the United States. New York parole boards may issue a Certificate of Good Conduct after a designated period of arrest-free conduct has been noted. The certificate restores the offender's right to vote and removes other civil disabilities. California may issue a Certificate of Rehabilitation after a period of arrest-free living. However, parolees must submit a petition, have a court hearing, and submit testimony and formal records. Because the procedure is so cumbersome, few parolees make application (Petersilia, 2003, p. 217).

## Recognition Ceremonies

Many authors have recommended a formal ceremony for recognition of desistance from crime. These are variously called "redemption rituals" (Maruna, 2001), "elevation ceremonies," "certification processes," or "delabeling processes." As well as formally recognizing desistance from crime, these ceremonies could formally mark the end of supervision, and hence involvement with the criminal justice system. McAlinden (2005) recommends the use of "reintegrative shaming" to affirm the ex-offender's membership in a law-abiding society. Travis (2005) believes that the ceremony could be a standard function of the reentry court.

Perhaps their greatest contribution could be to facilitate the recognition of a new civic identity for ex-offenders and thereby reduce the distance between Us and Them.

> Properly conceived, reentry courts could provide the "elevation ceremony" recognizing completion of the sentence. They could provide a forum for the narrative of redemption, the "re-biographing" that Maruna identified as the key ingredient in the desistance process. . . . Whether America becomes the land of the second chance depends on a public commitment and a legal framework to support and recognize the thousands of individual journeys of former prisoners and other ex-offenders searching for a better life. (Travis, 2005, pp. 273–275)

## Conclusions

In the preceding chapter we outlined the multitude of barriers to reintegration of ex-convicts to society. In the present one we have considered some of the ways that those barriers may be overcome. *The Report of the Re-Entry Policy Council* is a remarkable document in that it carefully outlines what *must* be done to accomplish reentry. What it does not do is tell us *how* these goals are to be achieved. Of the two Second Chance Acts, the 2007 version offers grant support for reentry demonstration projects but contains a reduction-of-recidivism requirement that is impossible to meet. The 2009 version simply does not go far enough. It is aimed at nonviolent first offenders, persons who are at low risk and might desist anyway. The reentry courts, which have been successfully used with drug offenders, is a very good idea in that its function is to manage all aspects of the reentry process and could be very comprehensive in coverage. The reentry court and its allied features such as a justice intermediary, reentry partnerships, health care partnerships, and procedures for restoration of civic identity probably represent the best avenues to pursue in overcoming the barriers to reintegration.

# V

# RECRUITMENT

## Chapter 11

# The Unknown Sex Offenders

*Bringing Them in from the Cold*

In this chapter and in the following chapters we switch the focus away from criminal offenders and concentrate on sex offenders exclusively. Our focus henceforth will be on how to encourage this resistant population to take advantage of and participate in treatment and other activities designed to assist them in improving the quality of their lives as they find their way out of involvement in the criminal justice system.

## The Candidate Population

The Bureau of Justice Statistics (BJS) (2009) reported that, in 2007, there were 826,097 sex offenders on parole and 4,293,163 on probation. In 1994 the BJS reported that 234,000 sex offenders were under the "care, custody or control of correctional agencies in the United States" (Bureau of Justice Statistics, 1996). Of these, 60% (140,400) were under conditional supervision in the community. At this writing, 15 years later, that figure must number several hundred thousand offenders. To this point we have gone to considerable length to illustrate the barriers to reentry faced by both criminal and sex offenders, as well as indicating that additional, quite severe conditions are frequently imposed upon the latter.

As we have shown in earlier chapters, continuation or initiation of treatment of mental illness in ex-prisoners is considered one of the major elements of the reentry and reintegration process. Rightly or wrongly, sexual deviation is considered to be a mental illness, and categories for official labeling of this status are available in the DSM-IV-TR (American Psychiatric Association, 2000) and the ICD-10 (World Health Organization, 2007). Labeling is only possible if the ex-prisoner was prosecuted for a sex offense. That individual might or might not be mandated to attend a treatment program, either in prison or the community. Many prisons offer treatment programs on a voluntary basis. A prisoner may decline to participate with no consequences. Many communities do not offer a sex offender treatment program and that condition of community supervision cannot be met. If, on the other hand, the prisoner was a sexual deviant prosecuted for a nonsexual criminal offense, knowledge of the sexual disorder might never be known and treatment would not be an issue. A large proportion of identified or unidentified sex offenders on parole or probation may not have attended a treatment program and may not seek one upon reentering the community. Thus we can assume that a fairly large number of ex-prisoners in the community have unmet treatment needs.

## Common Sources of Referral

These should come from three sources: parole, probation, and self-referral.

### *Parole*

Since the offender will have served one or more terms in jail or prison, records will be most complete from this source. While there is typically great duplication in these records, they will provide the most complete information on official records of criminal activity, background history, psychological test data, medical history, treatment records, and institutional behavior. Despite this, these records will have to be supplemented. Middle-age and older offenders are most likely to be found in this group. Depending upon the length of their incarceration(s), they are the most likely to be institutionalized and resistant to change.

### *Probation*

Most first-time offenders will come from this source. The amount of information available on probationers varies greatly. For some, all the practitioner will have is a referral sheet. For others, particularly those who have served multiple probation sentences, records will be more complete, containing police reports, victim statements, offender statements, and possibly psychological test data and, on occasion, treatment reports. These records will typically require considerable augmentation. The clientele in this group will be primarily composed of young to early middle-age adults with a small group of older offenders who were prosecuted for the first time for historical offenses. While there will be resisters among probationers, they constitute the group most likely to be amenable to a rehabilitation program.

### *Self-Referrals*

Sex offenders are typically not enthusiastic about referring themselves to a treatment program. Their appearance will likely be a result of what Sampson and Laub (1993) would call formal or informal social control. They may be referred by official sources in lieu of prosecution or they may be pressured by a spouse, other family members, friends, or employers. A very small number will recognize that they are in trouble and will refer themselves. In our judgment, this will be the smallest group of referrals. Their ages will range from early adulthood to old age.

## The Unknown

There is a much larger group of sex offenders who have not been prosecuted and who are not known to the authorities. Fortney, Levenson, Brannon, and Baker (2007) reported that only "thirty-six percent of victims who experienced rape/sexual assault . . . indicated that their victimization had been reported to the police" (p. 11). The reverse of that statement says that 64% of rapes/sexual assaults are never reported. The size of this population, of course, is unknown. If we assume, probably correctly, that it is fairly large and add to it the number of unidentified sex offenders exiting custody to community supervision, we can conclude that there is a candidate population of considerable size.

## Who Gets Treatment?

The reality is—a very small number of successfully prosecuted sex offenders. Previously we presented some statistical data from 2004. Those data showed that only 11% of prosecuted sex offenders were mandated to treatment, representing a mere 3% of all sex crimes reported in that year. If prisons offer treatment programs that can be declined without penalty, some prisoners will decline even though that may affect early release. Other prisoners will serve the complete sentence ("max out") and be released with no supervision conditions at all. If a probationer or parolee returns to a rural or semirural community where treatment is unavailable, or where the nearest treatment available is too far away to be realistically attended, no treatment will occur. We must conclude that there is a very large population of sex offenders who require services and are receiving none at all.

## In from the Cold?

We have argued to this point that there is a huge candidate population who could benefit from psychological intervention, however limited. Given what we know of this population, what is the likelihood that they can be encouraged to come in from the cold and accept those services? Sadly, it is unlikely that a large number would come forward. These are people who lead secret lives; who do not wish to talk about their behavior, their interests, or their motivation; and who do not wish to be identified and become part of someone's records, however confidential those records are supposed to be. Both of us have spoken to many sex offenders over the years who will say of their deviant sexual orientation, "If you take that away from me, what will I have left?" What they are saying in a remark such as that is that their sexually deviant behavior *is* their sexuality, their form of sexual relatedness. They will often admit that it may be wrong, in fact very wrong, but it is what they know how to do. They may or may not feel remorse or guilt about it. That they may not wish to talk about this in detail is hardly surprising.

Examined from a different perspective, this problem becomes more understandable. These offenders, because they are people like the rest of us, use sexual deviation in the pursuit of primary goods. These goods are defined as states of affairs, states of mind, personal characteristics, activities, or experiences sought for their own sake, and which are likely to increase psychological well-being. Looked at in this light, sexually deviant behavior, though distasteful in many ways, may conceivably be viewed as a means to enhance a sense of peace, of relatedness, of happiness. There is nothing mysterious about that. The task of the treatment model that we will propose in subsequent chapters is to assist offenders in securing many of the very same primary goods by legal and prosocial means. It is important to remember that many sex offenders, like most of us, lead quite conventional lives apart from their sexual deviance. Many are married, are raising children, have jobs, have friends, are financially responsible, and are well respected in their communities. The major task is to redirect their sexual behavior into conventional channels as well. The question is, How do we bring them in from the cold? In what follows we describe several means that could be used to accomplish that goal.

## The Public Health Approach

Reframing sexual deviance as a public health problem has two major goals. First, it is carried out as a very public enterprise that clearly specifies what needs to be done to target sexual abuse. Second, treating sexual deviance as a public health issue demystifies it. It says that sexual deviance is a behavior problem that can be easily understood but less easily managed. Most importantly, it says that sexual deviance is a health problem that is everybody's business, not just the business of the criminal justice or mental health professions.

Laws (2003, 2008) has provided a detailed description of the public health approach to sexual deviance. In this approach there are three levels of prevention.

### *Primary*

At this level the aim is to prevent deviant behavior from ever starting. The onus of prevention is placed upon potential perpetrators. Primary prevention would target adults about sexual abuse in general, about its magnitude, about who is at risk for abusing and being abused, and how to intervene and confront abusers. Among adults there are two target audiences. The first are persons who are aware of or suspect that abuse may be occurring in their midst. The second are persons who are at risk of committing sexual abuse. Persons who have no formal criminal history of sexual deviance are part of this second audience.

### *Secondary*

this level intervention is provided to persons who have begun engaging in deviant sexual behavior. The target population would be children, adolescents, and adults. Ideally we would seek early identification and intervention. Indications that persons might be likely to profit from this level of intervention would include unusual sexual interest or activity in children, nonnormative adolescent sexual behavior, or incest and/or opportunistic offending in adults. At this level the assumption is that while sexually deviant behavior is evident, it is not stable or chronic and may be amenable to treatment. Again, persons not known to the police as sexual deviants are actively offending and should be contacted and offered treatment.

### *Tertiary*

At this level we find the criminal justice and/or forensic mental health approach: to keep offending from reoccurring. Here we are dealing with chronic sex offenders with entrenched deviant sexual interests and a history of sexually criminal behavior. These are the persons most often seen in prisons, security hospitals, and under intensive supervision in the community. For this population intensive treatment would be recommended and would include cognitive-behavioral therapy, behavior therapy, and medication. The goal at this level is to stop the behavior and keep it stopped. Unfortunately, small though it may be, this is the population that is well known to criminal justice authorities and is most available to forensic mental health professionals. Valuable resources are expended on this group, the one least likely to profit from the intervention.

## *How to Accomplish This*

If we are to attempt to bring potential and actual sex offenders in from the cold and persuade them to accept services to address their problems, we need to find practical and workable ways to do this. There are two approaches available. The first is a macrolevel approach, a proposal for a nationwide effort to address sexual abuse. The second is a microlevel approach, an effort that precisely specifies the actions undertaken.

### *Macrolevel*

McMahon and Puett (1999) proposed what appears to be the ideal macrolevel approach. They recommended that the Centers for Disease Control (CDC) establish a panel to advise the CDC on a national response to sexual abuse. The issues to be considered would be the following.

#### RESEARCH, SURVEILLANCE, AND EVALUATION

They recommended establishing a standardized system for reporting to state agencies; identifying risk factors for sexual abuse; determining the parameters of "normal" sexual behavior at various life stages; and offering courses on sexual abuse by universities to widely publicize the problem in the academic world.

#### PUBLIC EDUCATION AND AWARENESS

Research findings should be made available to the public and policymakers; an agency should be created to deal only with sexual abuse; the media should be required to address sexual abuse frankly rather than sensationally; a consensus should be developed among experts; and education should be provided to the medical and mental health professions, the public, and the media.

### POLICY ISSUES

Elevate sexual abuse on a national public health agenda; encourage collaboration among agencies; seek foundation and federal funds to support research and evaluation; develop career incentives; and encourage political activism among survivors.

While not pie in the sky, it is clear that the preceding recommendations are extraordinarily complex and difficult to implement. There are significant barriers to the macrolevel approach.

- There is no common reporting system, hence, no surveillance system.
- There is no spokesperson in public health to champion this issue.
- Foundations do not typically support sexual abuse prevention.
- The media is interested only in the lurid and sensational, not the norm of everyday sexual abuse.
- The sociolegal attitude toward sex offenders prevents them from stepping forth to seek treatment.
- The general public attitude is that sexual abuse is something that is happening to someone else, on another street, in another town, certainly "not in my backyard."

In order to implement the macrolevel model, a national will, an effort resembling a crusade, is needed, and we do not seem to have that will. We will spend billions of dollars to prevent crimes we say that we care about (property, interpersonal, terrorism), but we do not seem to value preventing sexual abuse other than verbally. Preventing or diminishing sexual abuse is very costly in terms of focus, time, and money to set up a system, then to monitor, evaluate, and maintain it. It can be done and it should be done.

## *Microlevel*

There are two approaches at the microlevel that we wish to consider, one from the United States and the other from Germany. Both use similar approaches and both report some success in bringing sex offenders in from the cold.

### STOP IT NOW! (2000A, 2000B)

This is a community-based public health organization. It is not a treatment program but can make referrals for treatment. From Stop It Now's perspective, adults, not children or other victims, are responsible for perpetrating sexual violence and are responsible for stopping it. The overall purpose of the project is to increase both awareness and knowledge in sex offenders and the general public. They also teach families and friends how to confront abusers.

In 1995 Stop It Now! conducted a random telephone survey to determine what ordinary citizens knew about sexual abuse. They found basic knowledge lacking in several areas. They established focus groups in order to organize information to guide their eventual choice of interventions. They used "social marketing" to attract attention to their activities. This included radio and TV spots, articles in newspapers, advertising in city buses, and the opening of a website. They conducted workshops, conferences, and training for dealing with abusers. Finally, they established a toll-free telephone line for abusers to call in.

The Stop It Now! campaign contained these sequential components:

- Media and outreach campaign reaches abuser.
- Abuser calls helpline for information.
- Staff assigns a confidential ID number.
- Abuser agrees to evaluation for treatment.
- Abuser contacts lawyer.
- Abuser chooses to enter legal system with recommendations for treatment.

Stop It Now! conducted three follow-ups on social marketing in 1997, 1999, and 2000. They found that abusers *will* call for help. There was an increase in basic knowledge about sexual abuse expressed by adults. However, adults needed better skills to take direct action, to report their own abuse, and to learn to confront abusers. Some abusers turned themselves in, but the numbers were not large.

What does the Stop It Now! experience tell us? It seems to us that the model demonstrates that it is possible to get something, however minimal, done at the local level, and not at great expense. It tells us that we must not wait for governments to do something. They will acknowledge that there is a problem, then leave it to the police, the courts, and corrections to take action. It tells us that we need to adopt the social marketing model as a good way of getting the information to the people who need it.

## PREVENTION PROJECT *DUNKELFELD*

German forensic clinicians and researchers also acknowledge that official statistics do not tell the whole story. The official figures are referred to as the *Hellfeld* (light field), those offenders who are out in the open and known to the authorities. The balance, representing the cases not reported, are referred to as the *Dunkelfeld* (dark field), those offenders who are out in the cold and unknown to the authorities. The latter group, they say, form the largest number of offenders against children. Using the language of public health, they say that preventive efforts must focus upon primary prevention in the case of potential offenders, and secondary prevention in the case of self-referred offenders in the *Dunkelfeld*.

The Prevention Project *Dunkelfeld* (Beier et al., 2009) distinguished two types of child molesters:

- Persons who show no sexual preference disorder but who, for various reasons, sexually abuse children (e.g., sexually inexperienced adolescents; the developmentally disabled; persons with antisocial personality disorders).
- Those who do show a sexual preference disorder, either pedophilia or hebephilia.

The project clinicians noted that community-based programs with the proper diagnostic and treatment services for this clientele are scarce in Germany.

The project is ongoing at the Institute of Sexology and Sexual Medicine at the Charité in Berlin. The Charité-Universitätsmedizin Berlin is the medical school for both Humboldt University and the Free University of Berlin. The institute adopted a prevention approach using a media campaign to encourage self-identified (but unregistered) pedophiles and hebephiles to seek professional help through their program.

The project was initiated in 2005. An extensive media campaign communicated the following messages:

- Empathy for the particular situation of the participant.
- No discrimination based on sexual preference.
- Confidentiality and anonymity regarding all collected data.
- No requirement to express guilt or shame.

They adopted the slogan: "You are not guilty because of your desire, but you *are* responsible for your sexual behavior. There is help! Don't become an offender!" The social marketing campaign targeted print media, city billboards, and TV spots. A website was developed to provide easy access to information.

Persons responding to the media campaign contacted the research team by telephone. At the initial contact the staff attempted to express trust and empathy for the caller. A PIN was assigned to each caller who identified himself as a pedophile or hebephile, expressed interest in the project because of distress related to his sexual preference, and/or expressed an interest in consulting a clinical expert. Respondents appearing for an initial consultation were questioned about:

- Criminal and sexual history.
- Sexual fantasies and behaviors.
- Sociodemographic data (age, education, employment, family status, number of children).
- Former experience with health professionals.
- How they handled information about their sexual preference.

The response to the program offering was impressive. About 15–20 individuals per month contacted the Berlin office. By the end of 2008, there had been 800 contacts. Half of this group traveled to Berlin for assessment. The majority of the applicants were pedophiles and hebephiles. Almost half had already committed child molestation in the *Dunkelfeld*. At the end of 2008 half of the assessed group were invited to participate in a 1-year treatment program "to ensure impulse control."

> The treatment program integrates cognitive behavioral options, sexological tools (e.g., including adult sexual partner if applicable), and medicinal options: all participants are offered additional medication and are informed about effects and side-effects of medication like SSRI and anti-androgens. (Beier et al., 2009, p. 854)

Treatment is offered in individual and group settings. No data on program efficacy was provided.

Even in the absence of hard data, the apparent success of Berlin Prevention Project *Dunkelfeld* is indeed impressive. First, it shows that the public health approaches of primary and secondary prevention and social marketing all work if properly applied. Second, it is extremely impressive that, in a period of 3 years, the project was able to contact 400 child molesters who were hitherto unknown to the criminal justice system. Beier et al. (2009) offered the following commentary on the project:

> This study has demonstrated that potential perpetrators of CSA [child sexual abuse] may be reached for primary prevention via a media campaign. The success of the media campaign is believed to be founded on the combination of scientific respectability, the general media alertness regarding child abuse, and professional public relations. Furthermore, the favorable legislation in Germany regarding mandatory reporting of CSA offences must be considered crucial for its success: According to German law it would be a breach of confidentiality to report either a committed or a planned CSA offence. The relevance of the first results of the Berlin Prevention Project *Dunkenfeld* (PPD) to current policy is that a significant number of pedophilic or hebephilic individuals who are not under supervision of the legal system are motivated and willing to participate in a treatment program aiming to prevent child sexual abuse if they can trust . . . the pledge of confidentiality by experts specialized in assessment and therapy of their disorder. (p. 863)

The obvious conclusion is that it *is* possible to bring them in from the cold.

## Conclusions

According to data presented by the BJS, there is potentially a huge candidate population of sex offenders under community supervision. A large number of these individuals could profit from treatment but only a very small number actually enter, let alone complete, these programs. There is a much larger group who are unknown to the authorities. The chapter describes two public health approaches to this population. One, a macrolevel approach, would require a huge governmental investment and commitment to attack sexual abuse. This is unlikely to happen. The other, a microlevel approach, has shown promise. In the United States, Stop It Now! has shown that a program of social marketing can attract public support and bring a few offenders into treatment. In Germany, the Berlin Prevention Project *Dunkelfeld* has shown considerable success in attracting potential and active offenders into a psychiatrically based assessment and treatment program.

## Chapter 12

# Blending Theory and Practice

## *A Criminological Perspective*

In this book we are proposing to accomplish a difficult but not impossible task. Our goal is to present a workable scheme, a combination of ongoing assessment, ongoing supervision, treatment, and realistic follow-up, to foster desistance from crime in sex offenders. In an earlier chapter we indicated that, at present, there is no systematic plan in forensic psychology for encouraging desistance in this population. Our task is made more difficult because our aim is to incorporate information from one discipline, criminology, into another discipline, forensic psychology, in order to remedy this deficiency.

In some respects the two disciplines resemble each other in their assessment of problems in criminal behavior. However, each approaches those problems in different ways, using different methods, different terminology, and with different goals in mind. The transition from one to the other will show this relatedness but the transition will not be seamless.

In terms of criminological information and guidance, we prefer the age-graded theory of informal social control advanced by Sampson and Laub (1993; Laub & Sampson, 2003) and the narrative theory of desistance advanced by Maruna (2001). The Sampson and Laub theory suits our purposes because it is a longitudinal examination of career criminality across the life course. We have shown that there are other theories and empirical investigations that are somewhat similar but none that extend over a period of 60 years and none that provide the wealth of detail available in the age-graded theory. We indicated in earlier chapters our conviction that desistance from sexual crime proceeds in the same manner for sex offenders as it has been shown to do with criminal offenders. That being so, much of what Sampson and Laub accomplished will suit our purposes in obtaining information on the past lives of sex offenders, their present circumstances, and what might be expected to occur in their future lives. It is in the present and the future lives that our interest resides, to monitor and encourage the "continuity and change" that Laub and Sampson (2003) describe.

It is also in the present and future lives that Maruna's (2001) work comes into play. If we are to encourage and assist desistance processes in sex offenders, it seems to us that it is crucial that they begin to develop and refine a new narrative identity for themselves. In this respect the autobiographical accounts that Maruna describes, used in conjunction with the life course history taking developed by Sampson and Laub, provide useful information for supervision and treatment interventions. Many investigators disparage efforts such as this as too loose, too subjective. However, narrative research methods have been shown to be useful for empirical examination of cognitive processes (see, e.g., Ward, Louden, Hudson, & Marshall, 1995).

It is our expectation, as Maruna (2001) observed, that life scripts will emerge from this effort. However, rather than seeing two dramatically different types of scripts as he saw in the Liverpool Desistance Study, what we are likely to observe is a script that unfolds in conjunction with, and complements, the development of a new narrative identity. Any professional who has worked intensively with sex offenders for a long period of time will instantly recognize that what we are proposing will not be easy to accomplish.

Again, the life-course-persistent offenders are not our target population. Our interest is in the vast majority of sex offenders who are not necessarily going to become persisters. We are under no illusions about either the nature of this clientele or their potential dangerousness. These are not poor little lambs who have lost their way. Rather, they might be more reasonably seen as fallible, faulted human beings who have never found their way.

## A Picture of the Offender's Life Course

We would now like to present information on materials and procedures that may be used in supplementing a Good Lives rehabilitation program. Following the lead of Sampson and Laub, we will construct a picture of each offender's life course, from childhood (about age 10) to his or her current age. This will be accomplished through a variety of means: official records, existing histories and reports, self-report inventories and questionnaires, and interview self-report. These will be explained in more detail below. Here we should state a major caveat. Sampson and Laub (1993) have correctly observed that, no matter how inventive or resourceful the contemporary clinician/researcher may be, it is no longer possible to obtain the wealth of data such as the Gluecks did, and certainly not by the intrusive means that they used.

We believe that the following elements taken from the desistance literature may be usefully added to the assessment and treatment interventions described in the following chapters.

### *Primary Assessment*

The first major task will be to establish a basic timeframe that illustrates the fundamental features of an offender's life course.

#### *Timeframe 1*

A good model for this purpose would be Laub and Sampson's (2003) *Life History Calendar* (see Figure 6.2 in Chapter 6). This method of charting allows the user to plot the frequency of major life events (vertical axis) across the years from age 10 to, perhaps, age 70 (horizontal axis). The vertical axis includes items such as marriages, children, family, housemates, employment, residences, arrests, and convictions. This is a frequency count and will serve as an *aide-memoire* for further exploration by various means. The advantage of this method is that it provides at a glance the occurrence of major events in the offender's life course. Possibly a major use will be to determine the points at which turning points and desistance may be detected. The *Life History Calendar* can be only partially completed by use of official records. It must be supplemented by offender self-report and, if possible, cross-checked from other sources. Several of these sources may be independently validated.

##### OFFICIAL CRIME DATA

It is likely that state rap sheets in the United States may not have complete information on arrests and convictions. Laub and Sampson (2003) remarked that FBI rap sheets were more complete. Probation and parole officers are able to access these sources. Persistence across the life course should be immediately evident, as will intermittency of offending, as well as apparent desistance. These issues can be explored more completely in interview.

*Rap Sheet Problems.* Rap sheets are more often than not extremely vague on the specification of the offense. The citation might be only the number of the statute violated and/or the name of the offense. Disposition is often missing. These gaps might be closed in interview or via consultation of police and victim statements.

#### TIME UNEMPLOYED

States maintain rolls of unemployment benefits paid. These are particularly important in this case as the number of benefit periods will provide an indication of job stability over time. Here we are looking at frequent job changes, type of work, and length of unemployment periods.

#### TIME ON WELFARE

Some individuals will be maintained on welfare benefits for varying periods of time. This provides another measure of job stability as well as economic dependency.

#### INSTITUTIONALIZATION

Rap sheets will not contain information on periods of confinement in mental hospitals or periods spent in alcohol and/or drug rehabilitation centers. Official records accompanying a referral may or may not contain this information. Offenders might admit to time spent in a rehab center but be more unwilling to volunteer information on mental hospitalization. How many of these confinements were there? Is it possible to obtain a diagnosis? Does this individual have a co-occurring mental disorder that contributes to criminal behavior?

### *Timeframe 2*

A second approach to a description of the life course would be the *Life Story Interview* (McAdams, 1995). A modified version of this instrument was used by Maruna (2001) to examine the identity narratives of criminal offenders. Unlike the more formal *Life History Calendar,* this instrument asks the individual to "play the role of storyteller about your own life—to construct for us the story of your own past, present, and what you see as your own future" (Maruna, 2001, p. 1). This will prove a daunting task for nonexpressive and somewhat inarticulate offenders. Therefore, recording of their responses and preparation of a transcript is recommended. The major advantage of an instrument such as this is in periodic readministrations. In these repeats subtle changes in the story can be detected (re-storying) and, most importantly, changes that represent identity reconstruction should be evident. Thus it is possible to observe the desistance process unfolding.

The *Life Story Interview* was obviously not developed for use with criminal offenders. The manuscript that we have contains a long set of guidelines apparently intended to be used by the interviewer. It is intended to "arrive at some fundamental principles of life-storytelling as well as ways of categorizing and making sense of life stories constructed by healthy adults living at this time in history and in this place. . . . We are not trying to figure out what is wrong with you. Nor are we trying to help you figure out what is wrong with you" (McAdams, 1995, p. 1). This sort of language is not appropriate for use with offenders who will neither understand the statement very well nor believe its supposedly harmless intent. All similar statements in the interview must be modified to avoid offending sex offender interviewees or making them suspicious. We suggest use of eight of the nine sections of the interview. Following are some samples from each section. The quotations shown are from the interview format (McAdams, 1995), modified by us as appropriate.

### LIFE CHAPTERS

"We would like to begin by thinking about your life *as a story*. . . . Think about your life story as having at least a few different chapters. . . . I would like you to describe for me each of the main chapters of your life story. . . . [D]escribe *briefly* the . . . contents of each chapter. As a storyteller here, think of yourself as giving a plot summary for each chapter" (p. 1). The purpose of this section is to establish the story's outline. Here the structural context of family life will emerge as well as initial information on the social processes of school (was the individual attached?) and peer relationships (was the individual delinquent?).

### CRITICAL EVENTS

"We would like you to concentrate on a few key events that may stand out in bold print in the story. A key event should be a specific happening, a critical incident, a significant episode in your past set in a particular time and place. It is helpful to think of such an event as . . . a specific moment in your life story which stands out for some reason. . . . I'm going to ask you about 8 specific life events. For each event, describe in detail what happened, where you were, who was involved, what you did, and what you were thinking and feeling. . . . Also, try to [say] what impact this event has had in your life story and *what this event says about who you are or were as a person.* . . . [B]e specific" (p. 2). These events will provide a picture of the myths that the interviewee has created about himself as well as whether his behavior agrees with these myths and stories.

*High Point.* "[This] . . . would stand out in your memory as one of the best, highest, most wonderful *scenes* or moments in your life story. Please describe in some detail a [high point], or something like it, that you have experienced some time in your past" (p. 2). Here we should see some evidence of major turning points (see below).

*Low Point.* "Thinking back over your life, try to remember a specific experience in which you felt extremely negative emotions, such as despair, disillusionment, terror, guilt, etc. You should consider this experience [as] one of the low points in your life story. Even though this memory is unpleasant . . . be as honest and detailed as you can be" (p. 2). Here we may see evidence of junctures that led to persistence in crime rather than turning away from it.

*Turning Point.* "It is often possible to identify certain key turning points—[events in] which a person [experiences important] change. . . . I am especially interested in a turning point *in your understanding of yourself.* . . . If you feel that your life story contains no turning points, then describe a particular [event] in your life that comes closer than any other to [being] a turning point" (p. 2). Here the interviewer should be alert to positive statements about marriage or conjugal relationships, children, job quality and stability, and choice of prosocial relationships or situations. Negative influences may emerge as well.

*Earliest Memory.* "Think back now to your childhood, as far back as you can go. The memory [doesn't have to be important] in your life today. . . . [W]hat makes it (important) is that it is the first or one of the first memories you have, one of the first scenes in your life story. These should be detailed enough to qualify as an event" (p. 3).

*Important Childhood Scene.* "Now describe another memory from [later] childhood that stands out in you mind as especially important. . . . It may be a positive or negative memory" (p. 3). Here look for early evidence of antisocial conduct.

*Important Adolescent Scene.* "Describe an event from your teen-aged years that stands out as being especially important" (p. 3). Look here for evidence of early criminal behavior.

*Important Adult Scene.* "Describe an event from your adult years [age 21 and beyond] that stands out as being especially important" (p. 3). Is there now evidence of a developed criminal lifestyle?

*One Other Important Scene.* "Describe one more event, from any point in your life, that stands out in your memory as especially important" (p. 3).

### LIFE CHALLENGE

"Looking back over the various chapters and scenes in your life story . . . describe the single greatest challenge that you have faced in your life. How have you faced, handled, or dealt with this?. . . . How has this had an impact on your life story" (p. 3). Here we may observe the person's ability to self-regulate (a critical feature of our treatment), his tolerance of frustration, and general self-management skills.

### INFLUENCES ON THE LIFE STORY

Our concern here is with two influences:

*Positive.* "Looking back over your life story, please identify the single person, group of persons, or organization/institution that has or have had the greatest positive influence on your story. Please describe this person, group, or organization and the way [these] have had a positive impact on your story" (p. 3). Again, interviewers should be alert to turning point information.

*Negative.* "(P)lease identify the single person, group of persons, or organization/institution that has or have had the greatest negative influence on your story. . . . [How] have they had a negative impact on your story?" (p. 3). Look here for turning points that contributed to persistence.

### ALTERNATIVE FUTURES

"I would like you to imagine two different futures for your life story" (p. 4).

*Positive.* "Please describe what you would like to happen in the future for your life story, including what goals and dreams you might accomplish or realize in the future. Please try to be realistic" (p. 4). Look here for information on "knifing off" the past.

*Negative.* "Please describe a highly undesirable future for yourself, one that you [think] could happen to you but you hope does not happen. Again, try to be pretty realistic" (p. 4). Failure to knife off may emerge here.

### PERSONAL IDEOLOGY

These are questions about fundamental beliefs and values. These may or may not be useful with criminal offenders.

- "Please describe in a nutshell your religious beliefs or the ways [that] you approach life in a spiritual sense" (p. 5).
- "Please describe how your religious or spiritual life, values, or beliefs have changed over time" (p. 5).
- "Do you have a particular political point of view? Are there particular issues or causes about which you feel strongly?" (p. 5).
- "What is the most important value in human living?" (p. 5).
- "What else can you tell me that would help me understand . . . your philosophy of life?" (p. 5).

### LIFE THEME

"Looking back over your entire life story with chapters and scenes, [going back] into the past as well as the imagined future, [do you see] a central theme, message, or idea that runs throughout the story? What is [that] major theme?" (p. 5). Again, does the person's behavior agree with the story he constructed about himself? Look especially for continuity of nondeviant behavior.

### OTHER

"What else [do I need to] know to understand your life story?" (p. 5).

We have included considerable detail on the *Life Story Interview* for good reason. This document, it seems to us, is an ideal vehicle for use with sex offenders. It has been our consistent experience over the years that sex offenders like to tell you their story. They have, in many cases, told it often, and often to disbelieving audiences. Our experience has been that, if the interviewer is open to what they have to say, is gently prompting but not confrontational, they will, more often than not, provide considerable information. Denial will often be present but may erode in subsequent retellings.

We stated above our expectation that a script will eventually emerge from this procedure. As Sampson and Laub and Maruna remind us, desistance is a dynamic process that is always in motion. Readministration of the later phases of the *Life Story Interview*, particularly *Life Challenges, Influences on the Life Story*, and *Alternative Futures*, should provide windows on this process.

### *Self-Regulation Worksheet*

This is an instrument developed for use in conjunction with *The Self-Regulation Model of the Offense and Relapse Process: Volume 3* (SR-3; Yates, Kingston, & Ward, 2009). This manual is a guide to assessment and treatment planning using the integrated Good Lives/Self-Regulation Model for treatment of sex offenders. The worksheet package is intended as a plan for the development of a Good Lives intervention. We include mention of it here because its structure nicely supplements and expands the categories of the *Life Story Interview*. For example, the SR-3 worksheets cover the following 10 domains of primary goods: Life, Knowledge, Play and Work, Human Agency, Inner Peace, Relatedness, Community, Spirituality, Happiness, and Creativity. This information will be treated at greater length in the Good Lives treatment section below.

## ***Secondary Assessment***

This section can be expanded to accommodate the specific needs of any treatment program. We believe that, at minimum, two secondary areas need to be covered: sexual interest and self-control. Practitioners may wish to add measurements in other areas such as intelligence and personality.

### *Sexual Interest*

It is all but mandatory to include a measure of sexual interest or preference in a sex offender treatment program. Most agencies and clinics will be unable to afford the expensive instrumentation and time-consuming procedures of penile plethysmography or polygraphy. Typically a self-report measure, an admittedly fakeable device, is substituted. If this is the choice, we would recommend the *Clarke Sexual History Questionnaire—Revised* (SHQ-R). The original SHQ (Paitich, Langevin, Freeman, Mann, & Handy, 1977) was a 225-item questionnaire that measured the frequency, desire for, and disgust with a wide range of sexual behaviors, including deviant behavior. Twenty-four scales were derived from factor analysis of the items. The SHQ was reported to be relatively free of bias from age, education, intelligence, social desirability, and defensiveness. A more recent version is the *Clarke Sex History Questionnaire for Males—Revised* (SHQ-R; Langevin & Paitich, 2002). It is similar to the original, contains 23 scales, a demographics section, and 508 questions in a multiple-choice format. It may be computer-administered. The authors state that the SHQ-R is intended to help evaluate the offender's risk to others and his potential for rehabilitation by determining his specific sexual experiences. While it is conceivably possible to fake such an instrument, it is very difficult to do so consistently with such a large item pool. A faked profile would immediately be at variance with known history.

### *Self-Control*

In our review of criminological theories in Chapter 4 we mentioned the centrality of the construct of self-control in Gottfredson and Hirschi's (1990) *General Theory of Crime.* We also reported that subsequent empirical research, particularly Pratt and Cullen's (2000) meta-analysis, validated many of Gottfredson and Hirschi's contentions. We think it wise to include a measure of self-control in our treatment program for two reasons. First, sex offenders are an emotionally volatile population and many offenders provide evidence of very poor self-control. Second, one of the keystones of the Good Lives Model (GLM) of treatment is assessment of self-regulation (e.g., Ward et al., 2004).

A number of studies testing aspects of Gottfredson and Hirschi's (1990) general theory (e.g., Arneklev et al., 2006) have used the measure developed by Grasmick et al. (1993) and we suggest its use here. The Grasmick et al. (1993) measure is a 24-item self-report scale containing four items each in the six domains said to be characteristic of low self-control: impulsivity, preference for simple tasks, risk-seeking behavior, preference for physical rather than mental activities, self-centeredness, and poor anger control. The items are endorsed on a 4-point Likert scale. Grasmick et al. (1993), Armstrong (2005), and Arneklev et al. (2006) have all found the low self control scale useful in explaining criminal behavior. We acknowledge that the low self-control scale was developed to test a theory of general criminal behavior, not specifically deviant sexual behavior. We include it here solely because it shows promise for evaluating the assertions that we will make regarding self-regulation.

## Conclusions

This chapter suggested that two major features of our favored criminological theories be incorporated into the assessment model that we will propose below. These are the *Life History Calendar* (Laub & Sampson, 2003) and the *Life Story Interview* (McAdams, 1995; Maruna, 2001). Both of these instruments are useful in obtaining a picture of an offender's life course, embracing both the past and the present. Careful use of the instruments could provide a window on the desistance process and help to identify turning points in the individual's life. Such instruments are easily integrated into the GLM. We have also suggested supplementing them with two additional measures, a detailed self-report on sexual behavior and an assessment of self-control.

We have now reached the end point of our evaluation of the relationship of criminological theory and research on desistance and the potential contribution of forensic psychology to that effort. This chapter has considered how elements of criminological theory could be accommodated in a forensic psychological program to foster desistance from sexual crime. The chapter has focused upon only the initial assessment preceding treatment. Related approaches will be described below in the Good Lives treatment section.

# VI

# DESISTANCE-FOCUSED INTERVENTION

**Chapter 13**

# The Good Lives Model of Offender Rehabilitation

## *Basic Assumptions, Etiological Commitments, and Practice Implications*

The Good Lives Model (GLM) is a strength-oriented rehabilitation theory or framework that aims to equip offenders with the internal and external resources to successfully desist from further offending. It assumes that all individuals have similar aspirations and needs and that one of the primary responsibilities of parents, teachers, and the broader community is to help each of us acquire the tools required to make our own way in the world. Sometimes this process goes horribly awry. It then falls to the community and state to repair the damage by way of providing educational, vocational, and psychological capital to deprived individuals. In the case of offenders, the responsibility of the state and community to supply such resources is accompanied by the implementation of criminal sanctions.

The GLM is a rehabilitation theory and as such is a hybrid or mixed theory containing ethical (i.e., principles and rules that stipulate how people should act toward others), metaphysical (i.e., concerning the nature of human beings and their world), epistemological (i.e., concerning what counts as knowledge and science), methodological (i.e., how to obtain the relevant ethical and scientific knowledge), etiological (i.e., what causes crimes), and practice assumptions that are intended to guide policymakers and program developers when they decide how best to intervene with offenders (Ward & Maruna, 2007). The GLM is a strength-based rehabilitation theory because it is responsive to offenders' particular interests, abilities, and aspirations. It also directs practitioners to explicitly construct intervention plans that help offenders to acquire the capabilities to achieve the things that are personally meaningful to them.

The core idea at the heart of the GLM is that correctional reintegration and rehabilitation efforts should be based on the concept of *practical reasoning*. Practical reasoning involves judgments concerning the worthiness of an individual's goals and the best way to effectively achieve them through coordinated action. The concept of practical reasoning is distinguished from theoretical reasoning by the fact that it is concerned to guide *action* rather than specify norms for forming and evaluating beliefs. Audi (2006) has captured the difference between the two types of reasoning well in his statement that "practical reasons might be said to be reasons *for acting*; theoretical reasons might be described as *reasons for believing*" (p. 1). Correctional programs involve both types of reasoning but in our view the emphasis ought to ultimately be on practical reasoning because of its close connection with individuals' goals and subsequent actions. After all, the aim of intervening with offenders is to encourage them to act differently—any changes in their cognitive and emotional processes are only useful insofar as they result in socially acceptable outcomes (Ward & Nee, 2009).

To foreshadow our later detailed description of the GLM we would first like to summarize the basic ideas comprising this new rehabilitation theory. The best research evidence and theories point to a conceptualization of human beings as *practical decision makers* who have the following characteristics: they are physically embodied organisms who formulate plans and intentionally modify themselves and their environments in order to increase their chances of achieving their goals. The environment confronting human beings typically includes social, cultural, biological, and physical materials that provide the resources necessary to implement their plans successfully. Thus, from the viewpoint of the GLM, the overall purpose of correctional rehabilitation ought to be to help offenders acquire the core competencies constituting valued activities such as being intimate, managing stress, and so on, and to be able to effectively coordinate their goals and adjust them depending on the prevailing contingencies of the world. In other words, rehabilitation initiatives ought to be agency-centered while accepting the reality that effective and adaptive actions depend on the accessibility of opportunities and social supports. In Chapter 14 we examine the relationship between the GLM and desistance ideas in greater detail.

The GLM is agency-centered (i.e., concerned with individuals' ability to select goals, formulate plans, and to act freely in the implementation of these plans) because it is founded on the ethical concepts of human dignity and human rights. Human dignity is ultimately grounded in the capacity of human beings to act in pursuit of their own freely chosen goals in ways that reflect their status as human agents (see Chapter 16). Furthermore, in order to be able to successfully function as agents human beings require certain freedom and well-being goods, such as freedom of movement, freedom of conscience, problem-solving abilities, adequate physical and mental health, and sufficient knowledge of themselves and the outside world. Human rights function as protective capsules that ensure the resources required for people to make their own decisions are available and that they are not unjustifiably restricted from living lives they freely choose. While we appreciate the fact that offenders face legitimate restrictions on their freedom of movement and some of their other rights, their access to the majority of the core freedom and well-being goods should be guaranteed by virtue of the fact that they are human beings and as such are protected by human rights norms.

Once it is accepted that it is ethically obligatory to acknowledge the agency status of offenders, and that engaging them as fellow members of the moral community is the right way to relate to them, it follows that intervention programs ought to be mindful of this requirement. Furthermore, the scientific evidence from cognitive science, evolutionary research, motivation, social psychology, and clinical psychology also indicates the remarkable abilities of human beings to actively control aspects of themselves and their environments in goal-enhancing ways (Clark, 2008; Gibbs, 2006; Johnson, 2007; Robbins & Aydede, 2009). In a rather elegant manner, the ethical obligation to acknowledge the agency of offenders and the scientific evidence underlining this feature of human brings converge in the GLM's stress on promoting offenders' goals alongside reducing their ability to harm other people. Furthermore, there is also a surprising resonance between the GLM and the agency and social factor strands of desistance theory and research that we discuss in Chapter 14.

In the rest of this chapter we outline the fundamental assumptions of the GLM concerning the most appropriate way to effectively rehabilitate or reintegrate offenders. Our intention is to provide a reasonably detailed summary of the GLM as well as to reformulate it slightly in accordance with a stronger agency orientation. In the most recent description of the GLM, offender agency was seen as only one of a number of primary goods comprising human well-being (Ward & Maruna, 2007). As with all the goods hypothesized to comprise well-being, Ward and Maruna (2007) argued that while human beings need to have a minimal degree of agency or autonomy in their lives, individuals could legitimately vary in the degree to which they endorsed it as an overarching value. That is, some people might want lives characterized by high levels of independence while others may have a more collective orientation to their personal and social lives. We no longer think things are quite so simple and argue that the capacity for agency is a cornerstone of human functioning and resultant sense of meaning. To this end, we make a distinction between agency in the sense of self-determination of goals and an ability to act in ways that change the world in accordance with such goals, and autonomy simply as an absence of external coercion. In our view, because of their physical embodiment and significant degree of dependency on other people, human beings are vulnerable agents, but agents they are. Therefore, therapists and correctional workers ought to exhibit a profound respect for the self-determination capacities of all people, including offenders, and should always seek to build capabilities and provide resources that restore, augment, or create such capabilities in their practice. Basically, our job is to help offenders become more reflective, caring, and responsible citizens through the provision of social and psychological resources.

## The GLM of Offender Rehabilitation

Rehabilitation theories are composed of *three* levels of ideas: (1) a set of general assumptions concerning the ethical values guiding rehabilitation, the nature of human beings, conception of risk, and the aims and purpose of rehabilitation practice; (2) a set of general etiological (causal) assumptions that account for the onset and maintenance of offending; and (3) the practice implications of both of the above. In our view, it is helpful to think of the three levels as ordered in terms of their degree of abstractness, with the general aims and values providing a conceptual foundation for the subsequent levels (etiology and practice). Thus any specific therapy goals will depend in part on what are considered to be the general causes of offending, and the kinds of causes sought depends in part on what the aim of rehabilitation is. If the aim is simply to protect the public, then factors relevant to offender well-being will not be identified and therefore are unlikely to be evident in intervention programs. On the other hand, if the entitlements of both offenders and members of the public to primary goods are accepted, then researchers and clinicians will be concerned to discover how and why well-being and freedom factors are related to offending and effective intervention. In this kind of scenario it is to be expected that practice will have a dual focus on risk reduction and offender agency and well-being interests. Each level of the GLM is discussed in greater detail below.

### *General Comments*

The GLM was formulated as an alternative approach to correctional interventions that has the conceptual resources to integrate aspects not well addressed by the Risk–Need–Responsivity Model (RNR; Andrews & Bonta, 2007) perspective, such as the formation of a therapeutic alliance, agency concerns, and motivating individuals to commit themselves to therapy and ongoing desistance from offending (Ward & Gannon, 2006; Ward, Mann, & Gannon, 2007; Ward & Maruna, 2007; Ward & Stewart, 2003). The GLM has been most extensively applied to rehabilitation work with sex offenders, and therefore the assessment process and interventions consistent with the GLM have been developed in the most detail with this particular population (McGrath, Cumming, & Burchard, 2009). It important to note, however, that the GLM is a general rehabilitation theory that is applicable to a wide range of problems, including other types of criminal behavior, and is not restricted to use with sex offenders. It has recently been applied to individuals convicted of violent, non-sex-related crimes (Langlands, Ward,& Gilchrist, 2009; Whitehead, Ward, & Collie, 2007), young offenders (Robertson, 2008), offenders with a personality disorder (Brookes, 2008), substance-dependent offenders (Blud, 2007), indigenous offenders (Spivakovsky, 2007–2008), and individuals with medical disabilities (Siegert, Ward, Levack, & McPherson, 2007).

The GLM is an example of a positive or strengths-based approach to rehabilitation, although it was developed independently of the positive psychology movement. Positive psychology is a relatively recent scientific approach to the study of human behavior that focuses on examining the nature of human well-being and happiness, and identifying the factors that promote these states (Seligman, 2002; Seligman & Peterson, 2003). The origins of positive psychology can be traced back to an ancient Greek view that human beings are naturally inclined to seek happiness through the perfection of their specific qualities. It was thought that people could only reach a state of personal fulfillment if their potentialities were realized and integrated within a good life plan. A primary aim of positive psychology is to enhance human well-being, in part by highlighting individual strengths rather than singling out, and possibly aggravating, psychosocial deficits (Aspinwall & Staudinger, 2003). Positive psychology is a strength-oriented approach in that a major goal is to furnish people with the psychological and social resources to effectively meet their needs and develop plans for living centered on their aspirations and interests. An expectation is that once equipped with these kinds of psychological and social capital (i.e., capabilities, skills, competencies, supports, and opportunities) it is more probable that people will lead deeply satisfying lives. Related to this constructive view of human nature is the claim that unhappiness and psychopathology are more likely to occur when such conditions are missing. In an allied sense, risk factors for any type of human harm can be conceptualized as partly having their origins in a lack of the necessary internal and external conditions to achieve important needs and goals.

There is an important distinction in the philosophical and psychological literature between happiness as a specific *hedonic* state of pleasure and an *overall* judgment of well-being, a view that one's life is going well and that all the various components or ingredients of a good life are cohesively related. According to this distinction, a person could be happy in the sense that he or she experiences pleasant states but still feels deeply unfulfilled. In this kind of situation, a person could be pursuing experiences and engaging in activities that momentarily make him or her feel good but ultimately be denying important aspects of his or her character and needs. Thus, in essence such individuals are not striving to realize their full potential as human beings. The emphasis on overall happiness logically implies a connection between personal meaning and the way investment in practical identities guides individuals' actions in the world. Arguably, all of us endorse a range of particular identities connected to social roles, personal characteristics, and our professions. According to Korsgaard (1996), conceptions of practical identity provide "a description under which you value yourself and find your life worth living and your actions to be worth undertaking" (p. 101). Thus individuals' sense of identity emerges from their basic value commitments, the goods they pursue in search of better lives. Interestingly, Korsgaard argues that when there are conflicts between different practical identities people have to work hard to establish some degree of unity in their lives and she suggests that a way of assisting this process is by focusing on our common humanity and our (shared) inherent dignity. Later in this chapter we talk about the importance of offenders constructing plans for living that unify their various values—arising from the way they pursue the various primary goods—and that help them to derive a coherent sense of self.

In summary, the objective of positive approaches to problematic behavior is to increase individuals' abilities to live meaningful, constructive, and ultimately fulfilling lives so that they can stop offending. One of the key assumptions of positive psychological theories is that people are naturally inclined to desire, and subsequently seek, certain outcomes (i.e., primary goods) and that they experience happiness if these goods are obtained. Antisocial or problematic actions are hypothesized to occur when individuals lack the internal and external resources to achieve their goals in socially acceptable and personally meaningful ways. Sometimes people are simply unaware of alternative means to obtain valued outcomes and sometimes they are not able to take advantage of opportunities to do so, or indeed there may be no such opportunities. In other words, crime and psychological problems are hypothesized to be related to difficulties meeting needs, or rather securing access to primary goods that satisfy those needs (Ward & Stewart, 2003). From the viewpoint of positive psychology, in order for individuals to resume, or begin, a life free from crime they first need to develop the inclination and ability to reflect critically on the things that really matter to them. The process of critical reflection involves an evaluation of the ends or goals sought, the fundamental values underlying these goals, and the means selected to achieve them. The next step is to acquire the capabilities to effectively implement an attractive and ethically acceptable plan for living that is realistic and has some chance of success. In essence, programs for offenders ought to offer them a chance to be better people with fulfilling lives. It is clear that the ethical and capacity-building components of correctional interventions converge in better lives plans, which in turn, rest upon individuals' capacity for agency.

## *Principles, Aims, and Values of the GLM*

### *Embodiment, Plasticity, and Cognitive Extension*

The first major set of theoretical assumptions of the GLM revolves around recent research and theory in cognitive science relating to the nature of human agency or self-governance. More specifically, this research suggests that (1) human agents' physical embodiment has a profound impact on their cognitive functioning and interface with the world; (2) human agents are characterized by plasticity of cognitive functioning; and (3) human agents have cognitive systems that incorporate both internal and external components (Ward, 2010). The above claims converge on a picture of organisms who are (naturally) designed to act in pursuit of biological, psychological, and social goals (Clark, 2008). We briefly discuss each of these assumptions in turn.

The claim that human beings are embodied is based on a unified conception of the mind and body and a rejection of dualism. That is, mental properties are thought to be causally dependent upon the body and their form determined in part by the experience of physical embodiment (Johnson, 2007; Ward & Nee, 2009). The dependence of mental properties on the fact of physical embodiment means that cognitive categories are frequently derived from sensory and motor experience. For example, the conception of "crooked thinking" arguably has its origins in materials that are deformed in some way, while the idea of balancing distinct viewpoints reflects the process of measuring different objects (Johnson, 2007). Furthermore, the body also plays an important part in altering the environment in ways that facilitate problem clarification and effective action. It is the interface between inner and outer resources that makes it possible for individuals to bring about goal-directed changes in the environment, and ultimately within themselves.

The dependence of goal-directed action and psychological functioning upon the body creates a source of vulnerability for human agents and underlines the need to ensure threats to physical integrity are efficiently managed. The provision of adequate food and water, safe and hygienic environments, freedom from physical danger, and accommodation are necessary ingredients of a good life. Typically, this means individuals need educational and vocational skills to be able to work in order to pay for these essential materials. The fact of being physically vulnerable agents points to our ultimate interdependence and reliance on each other for access to vital goods or at least to the means of providing them for ourselves. Offenders as embodied human agents also require (and have rights to—see Chapter 16) the materials needed to protect their physical integrity and subsequent ability to act in pursuit of their goals.

The second assumption concerning the nature of human beings and their capacity for agency trades on the view that they are cognitively versatile animals who are able to quickly adapt to novel situations and acquire new cognitive repertoires and tools with relative ease (Clark, 2008). This cognitive plasticity is related to the fact that human beings evolved in moderately changeable environments and therefore, evolutionarily speaking, could not rely on built-in solutions to adaptive problems (Sterelny, 2003). Instead, individuals' brains are scaffolded from the moment of birth by a suite of learning opportunities and deliberately engineered environments that allow each person to construct a self as well as the skills and competencies to pursue his or her vision of a good life. Human beings' sense of self is derived from the ability to effectively change the world and themselves in accordance with their personal commitments. According to research on the use of technology to enhance motor and sensory competency, modifying the extent of agency also changes individuals' sense of who they are (Clark, 2008; Korsgaard, 2009). Korsgaard (2009) argues that this is because actions reveal what people consider worthwhile seeking and what personal identities they are drawing from when deciding what to do and how to do it. Learning new ways to secure important outcomes can alter the nature of the self as well as the environment acted upon. The cognitive plasticity and interdependence of human beings indicates their social nature and the fact that in order to achieve the things that matter to them, people need to cooperate. In essence, humans are co-constructed through the delicate interplay between biological, psychological, social, and environmental variables (Tomasello, 1999). The work of self-construction is never finally completed because of its reliance on our actions. In brief, we are always seeking to realize valued outcomes and their achievement or nonachievement reflects what we are and who we are becoming. The constant, almost restless nature of human beings' agency quests also underscores the crucial role of social and cultural resources, such as technology, for successful goal completion. From a rehabilitation standpoint, the "soft" nature of human agency reminds correctional practitioners that enhancing offenders' abilities to achieve better life plans is likely to alter their sense of themselves in ways that are socially beneficial as well as personally fulfilling (Ward, 2010).

The third agency-related assumption builds on the fact of human beings' cognitive plasticity and claims that external cognitive resources such as language, computers, other minds, and social and cultural institutions under some circumstances can be viewed as part of peoples' (extended) minds. In a previous paper Ward has argued that human beings possess *hybrid* cognitive systems that extend into the physical and social world (Ward, 2010). In other words, we are not cognitively limited by the biological boundaries of skin and skull and are able to intentionally incorporate internal and external elements when engaged in cognitive tasks. Cognitive systems incorporating internal and external resources may be relatively enduring or constructed simply to solve a unique and temporary problem. The test for whether a component is part of a cognitive system is whether or not it is functionally integrated with a person's beliefs, attitudes, values, and cognitive operations. We do not have the space to fully explain this complex and novel idea but point out that it is logically connected to the previous two assumptions (see Ward, 2010). It is because human beings are physically embodied that they are able to use tools of various kinds to change themselves and their world. Furthermore, it is their cognitive plasticity and soft agency that enables people to actively incorporate internal and external cognitive resources when engaged in problem-solving activities. The implications of this assumption for offender rehabilitation is that it makes sense to focus our efforts on what matters to people and to realize that external social and cognitive resources may well be actively recruited in offenders' problem-solving routines and strategies. If offenders are quarantined in environments that only contain others like them and few prosocial models, the chances are that their beliefs, values, and actions will continue to be antisocial in nature.

*Primary Human Goods*

The above set of three presuppositions of the GLM centered on human embodiment and agency are the most fundamental ones. The following assumptions are really derived from them. The biological nature of human beings, and the dependence of psychological properties on physical processes and structures, means that in order for individuals to function adaptively their basic needs have to be met (Deci & Ryan, 2000). Furthermore, the biological and psychological evidence suggests that all people, including offenders, are naturally inclined to seek certain goals, or what we have called *primary human goods* (e.g., relatedness, creativity, physical health, and mastery; see Ward & Maruna, 2007; Ward & Stewart, 2003). Primary goods have their origins in human nature and have evolved through natural selection to help people establish strong social networks and to survive and reproduce. Arnhart (1998, p. 29) labels these goods "natural desires" because "they are so deeply rooted in human nature that they will manifest themselves in some manner across history in every human society." Primary human goods are linked to certain ways of living that, if secured, involve the realization of potentialities that are distinctively human. These goods all contribute to a happy or fulfilling life but are intrinsically valuable in themselves.

In essence, *primary* goods are states of affairs, states of mind, personal characteristics, activities, or experiences that are sought for their own sake and are likely to increase psychological well-being if achieved (Kekes, 1989; Ward & Stewart, 2003). That is, they have intrinsic value and represent the fundamental purposes and ultimate ends of human behavior. In addition to these primary goods, *instrumental* or secondary goods provide particular ways (i.e., means) of achieving primary goods, for example, certain types of work or relationships. For instance, it is possible to secure the primary good of relatedness by the way of romantic, parental, or personal relationships. The notion of instrumental goods or means is particularly important when it comes to applying the GLM to offending behavior as it is assumed that a primary reason individuals commit offenses is that they are seeking primary goods in socially and often personally destructive ways. That is, the means chosen to achieve offenders' goals are problematic but not necessarily the goals themselves.

The psychological, social, biological, and anthropological research evidence provides support for the existence of at least 10 groups of primary human goods (see Aspinwall & Staudinger, 2003; Cummins, 1996; Deci & Ryan, 2000; Emmons, 1999; Linley & Joseph, 2004; Murphy, 2001; Nussbaum, 2000), including the following.

### LIFE

The primary good of life incorporates physical needs and factors that are important for healthy living and physical functioning, such as food, water, a physically healthy body, and so on. Examples of instrumental (secondary) goods to attain this primary good include engaging in physical exercise, being diet-conscious, and managing specific health problems, such as high blood pressure.

### KNOWLEDGE

This primary good is based on the notion that human beings are inherently curious and possess the desire to understand aspects of themselves, their natural environments, and other people. The good of knowledge satisfies this need and includes acquiring wisdom or information such as facts, theories, or ideas, and striving to answer questions pertaining to the meaning of information or events or the way objects function. Examples of instrumental (secondary) goods to attain this primary good include asking questions; attending school; participating in training, vocational, or self-study activities; or belonging to a discussion group.

### EXCELLENCE IN PLAY AND WORK

This primary good refers to the desire to engage in leisure or fun activities for their own sake and to strive for mastery at work-related and leisure or recreational activities. The notion underlying this primary good is that human beings seek to enjoy and to be good at a range of work-related and leisure activities and tasks. As such, the underlying idea of this good involves both engaging in activities for the purpose of enjoyment and the desire to achieve mastery in the areas of work and play. Examples of instrumental (secondary) goods to attain this good include participating in competitive sports; undergoing apprenticeships, training, or mentoring programs; and hobbies.

### AUTONOMY

The primary good of autonomy refers to the desire to formulate one's own goals and to seek ways to realize these through actions and activities of one's choice without facing undue interference from others (moderated by cultural and social norms). Examples of instrumental (secondary) goods to attain this primary good include seeking employment that allows for autonomy, achieving financial independence, asserting oneself and one's needs, and attempting to dominate, control, or manipulate others.

### INNER PEACE

The primary good of inner peace refers to emotional self-regulation and the ability to achieve a state of dynamic emotional equilibrium and competence. Emotional competence is basically the application of self-regulation processes to the emotional domain and consists of a number of skills such as awareness of one's emotional state, the capacity to identify other's emotions, the ability to use the emotional vocabulary of one's culture, the capacity to respond empathically to others, the capacity to manage aversive emotions through a range of adaptive strategies, and the capacity for emotional self-efficacy. Examples of instrumental (secondary) goods to attain this primary good include engaging in activities to achieve a balanced lifestyle, building positive relationships with others, learning emotional control and other self-regulation skills, physical exercise, sexual activity, and substance use.

### RELATEDNESS

The good of relatedness refers to the natural desire of human beings to establish warm, affectionate bonds with other people. It is noted that these relationships range from intimate, romantic relationships to close family relationships to platonic relationships and friendships. Activities such as disclosure, support, sexual activity, physical contact, spending time together, sharing interests, and so on, constitute the goods of relatedness. Examples of instrumental (secondary) goods to attain this primary good include establishing and maintaining intimate or romantic relationships, establishing and maintaining friendships with others, spending time with family, having and parenting children, and participating in community groups.

### COMMUNITY

The primary good of community refers to the desire human beings have to belong to social groups and to feel connected to groups that reflect their interests, concerns, and values. It is the sense of being part of a wider social and/or cultural network, of contributing to a larger social unit, and of being able to rely on this larger group to meet one's own needs. Examples of instrumental (secondary) goods to attain this primary good include belonging to a social service organization or special interest group (e.g., a political party), engaging in volunteer work, or being part of a neighborhood group.

### SPIRITUALITY

The primary good of spirituality refers to the desire to discover and attain a sense of meaning and purpose in life. The definition provided here is not restricted to participation in organized religious activities, but reflects seeking religious truths and involvement, a spiritual connection with a transcendent being or reality, or simply the experience of being part of a larger whole. In short, this good refers to a variety of activities in which participation provides a broad sense of purpose and direction in an individual's life. Examples of instrumental (secondary) goods to attain this primary good include belonging to a church or spiritual group, practicing one's religious or spiritual beliefs, or living one's life according to particular values, such as nonviolence.

### HAPPINESS

The primary good of happiness refers to a hedonic (pleasure) state or the overall experience of being content and satisfied with one's life, and includes the subgood of sexual pleasure. Examples of instrumental (secondary) goods to attain this primary good include establishing particular relationships that result in happiness and pleasure, or engaging in activities such as sex, eating, or playing sports in which the goal is at least partly associated with attaining feelings of contentment or pleasure.

### CREATIVITY

The primary good of creativity refers to the desire for novelty and innovation in one's life, the experience of doing things differently, or engaging in a specific activity that result in an artistic output or other novel or creative product. Examples of instrumental (secondary) goods to attain this primary good include work, parenting, gardening, painting, playing a musical instrument, and so forth.

Although this list is extensive it is not meant to be exhaustive, and we are not wedded to the list of primary goods outlined above. However, we argue that the available research indicates that the goods listed are likely to appear in some form on any list generated (Aspinwall & Staudinger, 2003; Cummings, 1996; Emmons, 1999, 2003; Nussbaum, 2000; Ward & Stewart, 2003). It is also possible to subdivide the primary goods noted above into subgroups. For example, the good of relatedness could be further divided into goods such as the provision and experience of mutual support, sexual activity, personal disclosure, physical comfort, and emotional reassurance.

An especially significant characteristic of the GLM is that the goods are plural rather than singular, and therefore a fulfilling life will most probably require access to all the primary goods even though individuals can legitimately vary in the way they value or rank them. This means that there are multiple sources of motivation and that each has their origin in the evolved nature of human beings. It is also important to emphasize that the goods referred to in the GLM are *prudential* (i.e., related to personal interests) rather than moral goods. That is, they are experiences and activities that are likely to result in enhanced levels of well-being rather than morally good actions. There is no assumption in the GLM that individuals are inherently or naturally good in an ethical sense. Rather, the presumption is that, because of their nature, human beings are more likely to function well if they have access to the various types of goods outlined above.

### *Values and Practical Identities*

A major assumption of the GLM is that rehabilitation is a value-laden process and involves a variety of different types of values including prudential values (What is in the best interests of individual clients?), ethical values (What is in the best interests of the community when individuals' interests conflict?), and epistemic or knowledge-related values (What are our best practice models and methods?). The construction of a more adaptive narrative identity involves orienting individuals to the range of primary goods, helping them understand how the problematic pursuit of these legitimate goals led them to illegal behaviors, and providing them with the psychological and social resources to secure better lives in ways that are personally satisfying and socially acceptable. Prudential goods provide the fundamental goals toward which individuals strive. Epistemic goods are utilized to devise methods of achieving them that are reliable and responsive to the environments in which they are embedded. Thus, values and facts are inextricably linked.

The plural nature of the goods sought is likely to result in their differential weightings or endorsement by individuals. While all the primary goods may need to be present to some degree (i.e., meet a threshold requirement) if persons are to achieve good lives, there could be significant differences in the experiences, objects, and activities they consider most important. The existence of a number of practical identities also means that each of us will draw from a variety of distinct value sources when faced with decisions about how best to act (Korsgaard,

2009). For example, a person may value being a father, psychologist, scientist, citizen, and member of a political party and each of these practical identities will exert some normative (i.e., what is considered worthwhile to pursue) pressure on his actions and life. Unfortunately, it is frequently the case that the aims and subsequent actions arising from the value commitments of each of these practical identities conflict. The relevance of variation in value endorsements is that if offenders' sense of themselves and what really matters depends upon the things they most value, then correctional practitioners ought to identify what primary goods are most heavily endorsed by the offenders in question, and in particular how they are expressed in their lives (Archer, 2000; Emmons, 2003; Clark, 2007).

According to the GLM, natural desires motivate individuals to act in ways that they think will satisfy them. Through a process of socialization and construction of practical identities people acquire norms (i.e., rules of how to act to achieve a valued goal) and their associated practices (i.e., sequences of coordinated actions that are based on these norms) that shape how desires are expressed. Because of the fact that human beings are thinking animals, there is a reflective gap between the experience of a desire to act in pursuit of a natural good or incentive, and actually doing so (Korsgaard, 2009). This reflective gap allows individuals space to critically evaluate desires and to decide whether or not they are worthy of fulfillment—whether they are really of value. Arguably, problematic actions such as sexual offending partly arise because individuals make faulty judgments, which reveal a lack of forethought or knowledge concerning the relevant facts and the real value of the proposed actions. Examples of faulty value judgments are when sex offenders believe that children benefit from sex with adults or that women enjoy sex under any circumstances.

Thus, the process of rehabilitation requires not just the targeting of isolated risk "factors," but also the holistic reconstruction of the "self." The GLM emphasizes the overarching construct of personal identity and its relationship to individuals' understanding of what constitutes a good life. According to theory and research on identity development and personal strivings, individuals' self-conceptions directly arise from their basic value commitments and the way in which they are expressed in their daily activities (Deci & Ryan, 2000; Emmons, 1999). In other words, people acquire a sense of who they are and what really matters from what they do. What this means for correctional practitioners is that it is not enough to simply equip individuals with skills to control or reduce their risk factors. It is essential that they are also given the opportunity to acquire a more adaptive personal identity, one that gives them a sense of meaning and fulfillment.

### *Goods and Risks*

According to the GLM, correctional interventions should aim to (1) promote offenders' aspirations and plans for better lives as well as (2) manage/reduce risk their risk to the community. This assumption has both normative and pragmatic strands to it. Normatively, the assertion that interventions should promote well-being alongside the reduction of risk reflects the ethical foundation of the GLM in human rights theory and practices (see Chapter 16). Pragmatically, it is assumed that because criminogenic needs and human needs are causally related (see below), the promotion of adaptive approach goals (i.e., goals that reflect desires for certain outcomes to occur rather than to be avoided—the latter is an avoidance goal) should also reduce dynamic risk factors. Thus a major aim of correctional reintegration work is to help individuals to construct life plans that have the basic primary goods, and ways of effectively securing them, built into them and does not involve inflicting harm on others. According to the GLM, risk factors represent omissions or distortions in the internal and external conditions required to implement a good lives plan in a specific set of environments. Installing the internal conditions (i.e., skills, values, beliefs) and the external conditions (i.e., resources, social supports, opportunities) is likely to reduce or eliminate each individual's set of criminogenic needs. From an agency standpoint, in order to be able to engage in effective action, offenders (like all human beings) require a range of competencies and external resources. Some of the required competencies and resources will involve knowing how to achieve certain outcomes, and in addition, being presented with a meaningful opportunity to do so, while others are reliant upon a grasp of what is ethically and prudentially worthy of pursuit. Criminogenic needs are dynamic risk factors that can be conceptualized as difficulties in these prerequisites of effective action (e.g., impulsivity is a problem adequately reflecting and acting on the basis of a coherent set of goals—see below).

### *Ecological Selves*

As discussed above, according to the GLM, people are multifaceted beings comprised of a variety of interconnected biological, social, cultural, and psychological systems, and are interdependent to a significant degree. What this entails is that complex animals such as human beings can only flourish within a community that provides emotional support, material resources, education, and even the means of survival. The complexity of human functioning means that an adequate explanation of something as important as crime will require multiple levels of analysis and theoretical perspectives. In particular, the interdependency of human behavior points to the necessity of adopting an ecological framework. This is because of peoples' reliance on other life forms and cultural resources as essential tools. According to Steiner (2002, p. 2), "Ecology is, by definition, the reciprocal relationship among all organisms and their biological and physical environments. People are organisms." In our view, thinking of the cultural, social, and personal circumstances as ecological components helps to keep in mind the fact that human beings are animals who purposively interact with their environment and develop in a dynamic and interactive manner. Therefore, offending emerges from a network of relationships between individuals and their local environments, and is not simply the consequence of individual psychopathology or psychological deficits.

The fact that human beings are interdependent, and that therefore a satisfactory understanding of behavior will always involve an appreciation of the contexts in which they exist, has important implications for therapists when designing reintegration programs. Thus, according to the GLM, any assessment and intervention should take into account the match between the *characteristics* of the individual and the likely *environment* where he or she will be living. In other words, when seeking to promote adaptive functioning it is necessary to grasp the specific contexts in which individuals live and the unique challenges they face. The idea of context-free intervention, then, is clearly a mistake. This assumption nicely coheres with desistance theory and research and paints a picture of rehabilitation that contrasts with traditional risk reduction approaches (see Chapters 4, 5, and 6). Rather than viewing the offender as essentially a self-contained deviancy machine (or bearer of risk—see below), and therefore treatment as intended to restore, repair, or, more frequently, to manage the offender's faulty system, the aim is to locate him or her within a social network. Intervention consistent with the GLM is viewed as furnishing individuals with some of the agency scaffolding and resources required to establish important social bonds and to engage meaningfully with the world. Once this is successful, it is assumed that the natural contingencies associated with social and personal life will take over and promote desistance from further crimes. We will develop the relationship between the GLM, sex offender therapy and desistance in detail in Chapters 14 and 15.

## The Nature of Risk

Because people are both embedded within, and examples of, complex systems, risk is viewed as multifaceted rather than purely individualistic in nature (Denny, 2005). In our view, risk is best viewed in contextual terms rather than conceptualized purely as constituted by individual deviancy. Thus it is to be expected that an adequate risk management plan would need to take into account individuals' particular lifestyles and environments. Even dynamic risk factors that can be viewed as located "inside" individuals (e.g., impulsivity, aggressiveness) are only meaningful in their specific, cultural, and situational contexts. This is because such traits are always expressed in response to particular environmental cues such as interpersonal threats or powerful, appetitive stimuli (e.g., food or sexual characteristics). As such, etiological theories need to be explicitly ecological and multisystemic when seeking to formulate explanations of offending and its consequences, and the cultural dimensions of risk need to be considered when planning therapeutic interventions (see Lynch, 2006).

The trouble with psychometric approaches to risk assessment and management is that they have a tendency to identify risk primarily in terms of individuals' deviancy and to view offenders as essentially bearers of risk (Ward & Maruna, 2007; Ward & Stewart, 2003). By "bearers of risk" we mean that in some sense risk is seen as inhering within individual offenders and, to a lesser extent, their environments. A difficulty with such a static conceptualization is that it fails to appreciate how risk can be created by correctional interventions and policies that effectively isolate offenders, such as community notification or geographical restrictions (Vess, 2009). It is easier to motivate offenders by taking their personal aspirations and concerns seriously and designing intervention programs that reduce risk while building strengths. For example, increasing a sex offender's intimacy skills and opportunities to engage in relationships with adults is likely to lessen the chances he will experience emotional loneliness and start to fantasize about having sex with children (Marshall et al., 2006).

### *The Nature of Intervention*

Finally, according to the GLM, an intervention plan should be *explicitly* constructed in the form of a good lives conceptualization or plan. In other words, it should take into account individuals' strengths, primary goods, and relevant environments, and specify exactly what competencies and resources are required to achieve these goods. An important aspect of this process is respecting the individual's capacity to make certain decisions him- or herself, and in this sense, accepting his or her status as an autonomous individual. This is in direct contrast to previously recommended practice in the treatment of offending behaviors, where therapists were cautioned not to allow offenders to participate in decision making (e.g., Salter, 1988). Using the GLM, we believe that each individual's preference for certain primary goods should be noted and translated into his or her daily routine (e.g., the kind of works, education, and further training, and types of relationships identified and selected to achieve primary goods). This assumption is both normative and pragmatic. Normatively, we argue that individuals should not be forced to undergo changes in their character or core sense of self against their wishes. Pragmatically, we doubt whether such a thing is really possible, as a normal response to perceived coercion is defiance ("reactance" in social psychological terms) and possibly an attempt to reassert a sense of agency using whatever ways are at hand (Aronson, Wilson, & Akert, 2009). In other words, self-change necessarily involves the motivation to change and requires that the client is invested in the process (see Maruna, LeBel, Mitchell, & Naples, 2004). Even if there is no moral obligation for correctional practitioners to respect client autonomy and choice (and we argue that there is), rehabilitative success still likely requires it.

This final assumption has substantial implications for the nature and character of rehabilitative interventions. The GLM should be understood in the tradition of "rights-based" rehabilitation (Ward & Birgden, 2007). That is, whereas some rehabilitation interventions are normatively justified on the grounds that the needs of the community outweigh the rights and liberties of the individual offender, others have justified rehabilitation itself as being the "right" of the prisoner or probationer (Lewis, 2005; Ward & Birgden, 2007). That is, although no one should be obligated to undergo rehabilitation, the *state* is itself obligated to provide such help to those who want to change their lives. The GLM falls squarely in this tradition. Individuals take part in the GLM—as they might take part in education or other forms of self-improvement—because they think that such activities might either improve the quality of their lives (intrinsic goal) or at least look good for judges, parole boards, and family members (extrinsic goal).

## Etiological Assumptions of the GLM

As stated earlier, the etiological component of a rehabilitation theory flows logically from its basic assumptions, is general in nature, and functions to give correctional workers a cognitive map or general overview of the broad causes of antisocial behavior. The etiological framework outlined here integrates aspects of various preexisting theories of criminality in a way that is user-friendly for practitioners and (crucially) clients in a therapeutic situation. After all, etiological explanations need to be empirically valid, but also practically useful. They need to "make sense" to rehabilitation participants and lead naturally to practical intervention strategies. Like all behaviors, criminal behavior is a product of complex interactions between *biological* factors (influenced by genetic inheritance and brain development), *ecological* niche factors (i.e., social, cultural, and personal circumstances), and *psychological* factors. The role of an etiological theory is to organize these complex factors into a parsimonious and elegant "story" that is readily understandable by others.

According to the GLM, goals are usefully construed as primary human goods translated into more concrete forms, and as such are typically the objects of intentions and actions. Goals are the ultimate and intermediate ends of any actions and collectively give shape to people's lives insofar as they create a structure of daily activities that represent what is of fundamental importance to them. Goals ultimately express the values individuals hold and are buttressed by beliefs about the social world and the person him- or herself. Problems in the scope of these goals, and the planning necessary to achieve them, can involve social, biological, and psychological impediments. For example, a parent values the role of caregiver and the various constituent activities of such a role including bathing, clothing, teaching, feeding, loving, disciplining, and protecting his or her child. The various parenting practices outlined above collectively give an individual parent a sense of identity because they are oriented around the personally endorsed values of care and protection. A lack of knowledge or skills can make it extremely hard for a person to successfully achieve the goals of good parenting.

In terms of practical identities, goals are typically thematically linked to concrete identities and the various roles and tasks they imply. For example, as a psychologist a person has responsibility for the assessment and treatment of psychological disorders. Each of these domains of professional practice is linked to actions, guided by particular goals, such as conducting an interview competently, interpreting psychological tests, or assisting an individual to overcome his or her fears of intimacy. Alternatively, the practical identity of being someone's romantic partner generates a variety of tasks such as providing emotional support, spending time together, and maintaining a household. In other words, goals are typically clustered together under specific descriptions; these descriptions are ultimately anchored in practical identities (Emmons, 1999; Korsgaard, 2009).

Criminal behavior can be partly understood as the product of distortions in an individual's value/belief system. Yet, the origins of these distorted self-narratives are always in the person's cultural and social environment. Self-identity is not constructed in a social vacuum (see Presser, 2004). Each of us draws on available cultural narratives in constructing our own worldviews. Thus, changing behaviors necessarily requires paying attention to both psychosocial functioning and ecological/cultural influences simultaneously.

According to the GLM there may be a number of distinct problems within the various domains of human functioning that can result in offending behavior: emotional regulation difficulties, social difficulties, offense-supportive beliefs, empathy problems, and problem-solving deficits. Yet, such individuals' underlying personal motivations/goals are rarely inherently bad. Instead, as stated above, it is the means used to achieve these goods that are deviant. The value of this understanding is that it helps to focus clinical attention on primary goods, the ultimate underlying motivating factors, and away from an exclusive focus on the psychosocial difficulties with which individual clients are struggling. That is, there are likely to be distortions in the internal and external conditions required to achieve the primary goods in socially acceptable and personally satisfying ways. Yet, the GLM-guided analysis goes beyond deficit-based etiological theories (i.e., theories that focus on what individuals lack) by encouraging clinicians to think clearly about just what it is that the person is *seeking* when committing the offense. This information has direct treatment implications and can provide a powerful way of motivating individuals to engage in therapy; the aim is to help them to secure human goods that are important to them, but to do so in ways that are socially acceptable and also more personally satisfying. The latter point is especially important, as most of the causal factors implicated in crimes involve self-defeating attempts to seek personally valued goals and consequences. The GLM can explain why this is so and provide clinicians with a clear understanding of where the problems reside in an individual's life plan.

From the perspective of the GLM, there are two routes to the onset of offending, each reflecting individuals' agency, a direct and an indirect route (Ward & Gannon, 2006; Ward & Maruna, 2007). The *direct* pathway is implicated when offending is a primary focus of the (typically implicit) cluster of goals and strategies associated with an individual's life plan. This means the individual intentionally seeks certain types of goods directly through criminal activity. For example, an individual may lack the relevant competencies and understanding to obtain the good of intimacy with an adult, and furthermore may live in an environment where there are few realistic opportunities for establishing such relationships. Thus, the actions constituting offending can be regarded as means of striving for fundamental goods. It must be stressed that the person concerned may be unaware of the primary good that is being sought, and could simply be concerned with engaging in criminal behavior. In other words, sometimes the goals that actually motivate human actions (e.g., efforts to establish a sense of autonomy or power) are invisible to the individual in question. This lack of awareness is often due to the absence of personal reflectiveness evident in many offenders and what you often find instead is a more concrete manifestation of the good. For example, rather than citing a quest for relatedness or intimacy as a desired goal, an offender might state that he or she is looking for a "good partner." Typically such formulations are either simply alternative descriptions of the primary good or else particular, concrete examples of the good in question.

The *indirect* route to offending occurs when the pursuit of a good or set of goods creates a ripple effect in the person's personal circumstances and these unanticipated effects increase the pressure to offend. For example, conflict between the goods of relatedness and autonomy might cause the breakup of a valued relationship and subsequent feelings of loneliness and distress. The use of alcohol to alleviate the resultant emotional turmoil could lead to loss of control in specific circumstances, and this might increase the risk of offending. In this type of situation there is a chain of events initiated by the goods conflict that ultimately results in offending. These indirect or ripple effects are particularly evident when two practical identities a person is invested in conflict and cause him or her uncertainly about how best to act. An example of this conflict of identities is when an offender values both his role as a worker and as a husband. The two identities can on occasions clash and in some circumstances the pressure to work longer hours in order to get a job done might interfere with his responsibilities as a partner. Lack of self-reflectiveness can cause a state of dissonance and erratic or contradictory actions, and in some situations, ultimately result in antisocial actions such as a sexual offense.

From the standpoint of the GLM, criminogenic needs are conceptualized as *internal* or *external obstacles* that frustrate and block the acquisition of primary human goods. What this means is that the individual concerned lacks the ability to obtain important outcomes (i.e., goods) in his or her life, and in addition, is frequently unable to think about his or her life in a reflective manner. As stated earlier, it is possible to construe criminogenic needs as deficiencies in agency and the conditions that support agency rather than purely as dysfunctional mechanisms. We suggest that there are four major types of difficulties often evident in individuals' life plans. These types of problems are overlapping but conceptually distinct. It is also important to note that the real problem resides in the secondary goods rather than in the primary ones. In other words, it is the activities or strategies used to obtain certain primary goods that create problems, not the primary goods themselves (i.e., primary goods are sought by all humans).

First, an individual who has problems with the *means* he uses to secure goods may be using inappropriate strategies to achieve the necessary primary goods needed for a good life. He may act in ways that violate important social and ethical norms, and as a consequence of this fact, experience disapproval, disappointment, and frequently frustration at the outcome. Second, an individual's life plan might also suffer from a lack of *scope* with a number of important goods left out of his or her plan for living. For example, the good of work-related competence might be missing, leaving the person concerned with chronic feelings of inadequacy and frustration. From an agency perspective, he might be insufficiently informed about the conditions required to support a set of aspirations or be under the influence of a single practical identity (e.g., his identity as a worker might trump all others).

Third, some people may also have *conflict* (and a lack of coherence) among the goods being sought and their associated practical identities and therefore experience acute psychological stress and unhappiness (Emmons, 1999). An example of conflict in a life plan is where an attempt to pursue the goal of autonomy through controlling or dominating a partner makes it less likely goods related to intimacy will be achieved. Fourth, a final problem is when a person lacks the *capabilities* (e.g., knowledge, skills) to form or effectively implement a life plan in the environment in which he or she lives, or to adjust his or her goals to changing circumstances (e.g., impulsive decision making). For example, a submissive individual may lack the skills to assert himself sufficiently to get his basic needs met from others. This lack of capability may lead to increased subjective emotional experiences of frustration and humiliation, which may be relieved or comforted through aggressive release. The problem of capability deficits has both internal and external dimensions. The internal dimension refers to factors such as skill deficits while the external dimension points to a lack of environmental opportunities, resources, and supports.

In summary, the etiological commitments of the GLM are *general* in form and stem from a view of human beings as creatures capable of reflective agency, usually acting under the conceptual constraints of a range of practical identities. That is, human beings are goal-seeking, culturally embedded animals who utilize a range of strategies to secure important goods from their environments when occupying personally valued social or cultural roles (e.g., partners, workers, citizens, playmates, artists, helpers). When the internal or external conditions necessary to achieve valued outcomes associated with practical identities are incomplete or absent, individuals tend to become frustrated and may engage in antisocial behavior. The etiological commitments serve to orient correctional workers and require supplementation from specific theories to supply more fine-grained explanations of antisocial behavior and particular types of offenses.

## Implications of the GLM for Practice

From an agency perspective, a major aim of intervention is to (initially) scaffold individuals' agency attempts to achieve valued outcomes that are ethical, legal, and personally meaningful (to the offender). What this means in practice is that therapists ought to try to identify what practical identities and associated goods and strategies have been associated with individuals' offending, and what aspirations they have for the future. This analysis is both backward (examining the offense and associated history and circumstances) and forward looking (what does the person want in the future?). The expectation is that practitioners relate to offenders as fellow agents and engage them in a dialogue about what kind of things are important to them and how such values are related to their criminal actions.

From the viewpoint of the GLM, there ought to be a direct relationship between goods promotion and risk management in rehabilitation work. In brief, a focus on the promotion of specific goods or goals is likely to automatically eliminate or modify commonly targeted dynamic risk factors (i.e., criminogenic needs). That is, assisting individuals to achieve goods via nonoffending methods may function to eliminate or reduce the need for offending. There are three strands to our argument.

First, the pursuit of primary human goods is implicated in the etiology of offending. By virtue of possessing the same needs and nature as other people, offenders actively search for primary human goods in their environments (e.g., relationships, mastery experiences, a sense of belonging, a sense of purpose, and autonomy). The active search for primary goods is usually carried out under the guidance and constraints of a person's practical identities, and, as such, there will be patterns or themes evident in his sexual offending actions. In some circumstances (e.g., through a lack of internal skills and external conditions), this can lead to antisocial behavior. Second, we argue that therapeutic actions that promote approach goals will also help to secure avoidance goals. This occurs because of the etiological role that goods play in offending, and also because equipping individuals with the internal and external conditions necessary to effectively implement a good life plan (i.e., a plan that contains all the primary goods and ways of achieving them that match the individual's abilities, preferences, and environment) will also modify their criminogenic needs. Third, it is easier to motivate individuals to change their offense-related characteristics by focusing on the perceived benefits (primary goods) they accrue from their offending and by exploring more appropriate means (secondary goods) to achieve what is of value to them. By proceeding in this manner, individuals do not need to abandon those things that are important to them—only to learn to acquire them differently. Identifying the practical identities that are associated with their sexually abusive actions should help offenders to grasp the meaning of their actions, and to look beyond the harm done to their underlying values (e.g., need for intimacy motivating a sexual offense against a child).

A critical therapeutic task involves managing the balance between the approach goal of promoting personal goods and the avoidance goal of reducing risk. Erring on the side of either goal can result in disastrous social and personal consequences for the therapist and client. Simply seeking to the increase the well-being of a prisoner, parolee, or probationer without regard for his or her level of risk may result in a happy but dangerous individual. Alternatively, attempting to manage an individual's risk without concern for goods promotion or well-being could lead to punitive practices and a defiant or disengaged client (see Maruna et al., 2004; Sherman, 1993).

A related consideration concerns the attitude of the therapist to the client and the importance from the perspective of the GLM of adapting a constructive, humanistic relationship (see Chui & Nellis, 2003). The fact that the offender is viewed as someone attempting to live a meaningful worthwhile life in the best way he can in the specific circumstances confronting him reminds correctional workers that their clients are not moral strangers. That is, like us, individuals who commit offenses act from a common set of goals stemming from their underlying human nature. They warrant our respect for their capacity to change and the fact that their offending is directly or indirectly associated with the pursuit of the ingredients of a good life. The fact that they have committed harmful actions does not suggest that they are intrinsically bad or destructive individuals. It is only the rarest of individuals whose motives are purely psychopathic and sadistic. Even the most destructive actions (e.g., the military slaughter of innocent civilians) are often motivated by ultimately noble goals, albeit through misguided and distorted means. The focus on achieving primary goods speaks directly to clients' self-interest and incentives for engaging in treatment. Individuals may be persuaded to change their behavior for primarily self-regarding reasons rather than any charitable feelings for the "good of society." This is especially true, considering that in many cases, individuals feel that "society" has been anything but charitable to them. From a therapeutic perspective, it is the fact that such individuals are motivated to change and *engage* in the treatment process that is critical. Thus, even if some rare individual was intrinsically "evil" (e.g., psychopathically sadistic and unconcerned with others), it does not mean that he cannot be treated according to the GLM. By focusing on the promotion of client self-interests (in personally satisfying but also socially acceptable ways), the GLM could conceivably work with those with no empathy at all (if such individuals exist).

The GLM recommends that there should be some degree of tailoring of therapy to match individual clients' particular life plans and their associated risk factors (i.e., problems with the internal and external conditions). In other words, the individual's particular strengths, interests, values (weightings of goods), social and personal circumstances, and home environments should be taken into account when constructing a rehabilitation plan. Although GLM interventions may still be implemented in a systematic and structured way (like current standard RNR programs), therapeutic tasks within standard program modules should be shaped to suit the person in question based on his own life plan. For example, while an individual might receive a standardized social skills module, individualized self-directed tasks might be geared to his particular needs and issues.

Another area where attention needs to be paid is to the language of treatment. Modern intervention texts repeatedly use language such as "deficit," "deviance," "distortion," and "risk" (e.g., see Salter, 1988). All such words are associated with negative evaluations or expectancies. The GLM is a positive model, based on the assumption that people are more likely to embrace positive change and personal development, and so the kinds of language associated with GLM interventions should be future-oriented, optimistic, and approach-goal focused.

Applying the GLM to offender treatment requires the delineation of several considerations that could underlie the construction of a treatment program. These are:

1. Prisoners and probationers are whole individuals and more than the sum of their criminal records. They have expertise and a variety of strengths that can benefit society. Interventions should promote and facilitate these contributions whenever possible.

2. At the same time, many prisoners and probationers are likely to have experienced adversarial developmental experiences, and have lacked the opportunities and support necessary to achieve a coherent life plan.

3. Consequently, such individuals lack many of the essential skills and capabilities necessary to achieve a fulfilling life.

4. Criminal actions frequently represent attempts to achieve desired goods but where the skills or capabilities necessary to achieve them are not possessed (direct route). Alternatively, offending can arise from an attempt to relieve the sense of incompetence, conflict, or dissatisfaction that arises from not achieving valued human goods (indirect route).

5. The absence of certain human goods seems to be more strongly associated with offending: self-efficacy/sense of agency, inner peace, personal dignity/social esteem, generative roles and relationships, and social relatedness.

6. The risk of offending may be reduced by assisting individuals to develop the skills and capabilities necessary to achieve the full range of human goods.

7. Intervention is therefore seen as an activity that should *add to* an individual's repertoire of personal functioning, rather than an activity that simply *removes* a problem or is devoted to *managing* problems, as if a lifetime of grossly restricting one's activity is the only way to avoid offending (Mann, Webster, Schofield, & Marshall, 2004).

In other words, a more "holistic" treatment perspective is taken, based on the core idea that the best way to reduce risk is by helping individuals live more personally fulfilling, successful, and productive lives. In addition, therapy is tailored to each client's good lives plan while still being administered in a systematic and structured way. For normative and practical reasons, individual clients need only undertake those treatment activities that provide the ingredients of their own particular plan. At stake here is both the development of a therapeutic alliance and the fit between therapy and clients' specific issues, abilities, preferences, and contexts. In the GLM, risk factors are regarded as internal and external obstacles that make it difficult for an individual to implement a good lives plan in a socially acceptable and personally fulfilling manner. Thus, a major focus is on the establishment of skills and competencies needed to achieve a better kind of life, alongside the management of risk. This *twin focus* incorporates the strengths of the relapse prevention and capabilities approaches to treatment. It is also much easier to motivate individuals if they are reassured that the goods they are aiming for are acceptable; the problem resides in the way they are sought. Of course, sometimes individuals mistake the means (secondary goods) for the end (primary goods), and it may be necessary to spend quite a bit of time exploring the goods that underlie their offending behavior and the specific problems in their life plan. In the GLM approach, the goal is always to create new skills and capacities within the *context* of individuals' life plans and to encourage fulfillment through the achievement of human goods.

## GLM Misconceptions

There are four common misconceptions associated with the GLM: (1) that the GLM has no research support, (2) that adopting the GLM means having to drop the empirically tested RNR model, (3) that the GLM ignores risk reduction and management, and (4) that the GLM places the offenders' interests above those of the community.

First, the GLM *has* in fact received empirical support internationally, and there are a number of programs in the United Kingdom, the United States, Canada, and Australasia that have developed treatment programs that are consistent with the GLM rehabilitation theory (Eldridge & Findlater, 2009; McGrath et al., 2009). Second, dropping the RNR in favor of the GLM would be a grave and costly mistake. The RNR has shown itself to hold some worthy and empirically supported principles. Instead, the GLM should be used *in conjunction* with the RNR in an attempt to further improve current rehabilitative practice. More accurately, we suggest that the principles of risk, need, and responsivity are embedded within the GLM core assumptions but that it provides a broader and more constructive rehabilitation framework (Ward & Maruna, 2007). Third, on a related point, to perceive the GLM as ignoring or downplaying the issue of risk is mistaken, since the GLM is intended to act as a further grounding mechanism for the RNR approach. Fourth, the GLM does not place the needs of the offenders above those of the community. Grounding an already empirically supported approach (the RNR) within a more restorative approach is one of the surest and safest ways of ensuring that we reduce further offending to the community. Thus, it is high time that such misconceptions were laid to rest since they discourage creativity and the potential exploration of a new wave of rehabilitative theory that may be even more effective than the RNR approach alone.

## Conclusions

In this chapter we have outlined the basic assumptions, etiological commitments, and practice implications of the GLM. Our concern is to stress the focus of the GLM on the possibility of better lives for offenders and therefore underline the importance of agency considerations rather than simply reduction of risk factors. In our view, the GLM provides a supple and broad rehabilitation framework that looks to the world both outside the correctional contexts and to the future as well as the past. It has the theoretical resources to provide practitioners with a conceptual map to guide all aspects of their clinical work with sex offenders and also help steer the professional activities of other correctional workers and community volunteers as well. In the next chapter we will map the GLM onto desistance theory in order to demonstrate how it is able to incorporate this important body of ideas and research and thus provide a rehabilitation vantage point that transcends simply therapeutic concerns.

*Chapter 14*

# The Good Lives Model and Desistance Theory and Research

## *Points of Convergence*

In this chapter we aim to map desistance theory and research findings onto the GLM theory of offender rehabilitation. We have chosen the GLM because it is an example of a systematic theory of rehabilitation and reintegration that is strength-based, risk-oriented, and yet reaches beyond the parameters of the psychological. More specifically, we argue that the GLM has the conceptual resources to incorporate desistance ideas by virtue of its stress on agency, interdependency, and development. In other words, there is a natural resonance between desistance theory and the GLM because of their overlapping theoretical ideas and broad way of conceptualizing the relationship between human beings and their social world. In fact, the GLM has some desistance concepts built into it, but they are underdeveloped. Clearly there are distinct theories of desistance each with varying emphasis on the types of factors thought to be causally related to cessation from further offending. But, as demonstrated in the earlier chapters, there is relative agreement in the field that any account of desistance needs to address developmental, social, and agency variables and an overlapping consensus that the truth of why individuals permanently refrain from further offending lies in the interaction between social encounters and opportunities

---

Portions of this chapter appeared in Ward and Maruna (2007). Reprinted by permission of Taylor & Francis Group.

and psychological capacities (e.g., skills, reflectiveness, agency). It is not enough to be presented with social capital, such as a job or a promise of an intimate relationship. Unless an individual evaluates such opportunities as worthy of his or her investment, they are likely to wither and leave behind disappointment and frustration.

First, we analyze the differences between desistance theory and research and rehabilitation theories. Second, we investigate the reasons why attempts to apply desistance theory to practice so far have not been entirely successful. Third, we outline how it is possible to expand on the basic assumptions, etiological commitments, and treatment implications of the GLM to include desistance-oriented practice. The primary aim of this chapter is to provide the theoretical framework for the following chapter, where we describe in some detail a desistance-influenced application of the GLM to the assessment and treatment of sex offenders.

## Desistance Theories and Rehabilitation Theories

Desistance theories and rehabilitation theories address different but overlapping phenomena, from unique conceptual perspectives involving distinct social actors. The phenomena in question relate to offending and its associated problems, such as impulsivity, substance abuse, cognitive distortions, social alienation, unemployment, and dysfunctional relationships. Rehabilitation practitioners try to help offenders make significant behavioral changes by utilizing a range of therapeutic technologies and practices. Ideally, such intervention initiatives ought to be accepting of offenders' agency status and thus acknowledge their ability and right to make key decisions for themselves. From a desistance perspective, the changes underpinning crime cessation frequently occur outside the direct orbit of influence of practitioners but still involve intentionality on behalf of actors within the offenders' wider social and personal worlds—employers, girlfriends, family, friends, and so on. By "intentionality" we mean actions that are consciously directed toward the achievement of a goal. Thus, what is considered natural change in desistance terms really only means change that is outside the direct sphere of action of correctional agents. This makes sense, as crime arguably represents actions directed at achieving valued outcomes such as the acquisition of material goods or power, or at least the least bad outcomes, and thus necessarily involves intentionality rather than being the consequences of random effects and movements. What is "natural" in this sense means what happens independently of professional activity (Raynor & Robinson, 2009). However, the fact that natural desistance occurs independently of the actions of correctional personnel is of crucial importance and offers practitioners an untapped arena to capitalize on in their attempts to encourage offense-free lives. If offenders relinquish antisocial goals and inclinations because they have found satisfying jobs or become romantically involved with people they care about, then it follows that any social initiatives that make these events more possible are to be encouraged.

We explicitly analyze the relevance of natural desistance and offender rehabilitation later in this chapter. For now, the vital take-home message is that there is more occurring within the universe of offender change than what happens in a treatment center or group. Just what this "more" amounts to has been discussed earlier in the book and will also become apparent later in this chapter. In brief, important events such as being offered a job or starting a new relationship can initiate a cascade of changes in offenders' lives and move them further away from a life of crime to one of social acceptability and integration. The possible mechanisms mediating the transformation from a criminal to a law-abiding lifestyle are numerous and include the establishing of greater social bonds, stronger agency, turning points, or a change in self-narrative (Gottfredson & Hirschi, 1990; Maruna, 2001; Moffitt, 1993; Sampson & Laub; 1993; also see Chapters 2, 3, 4, 5, and 6).

The distinct, but overlapping, nature of the crime-related phenomena in question revolves around the way they are conceptualized within the two perspectives. Practitioners in traditional sexual offending programs typically aim to equip sex offenders with an array of cognitive and behavioral strategies for reducing their dynamic risk factors or criminogenic needs. The problems in question usually include such things as deviant sexual interests and arousal; social skill and intimacy deficits; distorted beliefs, attitudes, and thinking processes; emotional incompetence; sexual dysfunction; vocational difficulties; self-regulation deficits; and lifestyle imbalance (to use the "traditional" deficit-based language; see Ward, Polaschek, & Beech, 2006). From a desistance viewpoint, factors such as age, marriage, work and job stability, military service, juvenile detention, prison, education, cognitive transformation/self-constitution, the Pygmalion effect, knifing off, spirituality, fear of serious assault or death, and sickness and incapacitation are investigated and their relationship to cessation from reduced offending documented (Farrall, 2002; Maruna, 2001; Maruna & Farrall, 2004; Laub & Sampson, 2003; McNeill, 2006; Petersilia, 2003; Sampson & Laub, 1993; Travis, 2005; Weaver & McNeill, in press). A number of the two sets of research and intervention targets overlap such that an argument can be made that they are simply representations of the same phenomena approached from different standpoints (see below). That is, despite appearances, some of the phenomena targeted by rehabilitation researchers and some targeted by desistance researchers are actually identical in kind. The reason for the different language and formulation of the phenomena is that correctional practitioners concentrate on deficiencies whereas desistence researchers pay more attention to the presence of protective factors, essentially a deficit versus strength emphasis. For example, a lack of intimacy deficit may be causally related to a sexual offense whereas a sound marriage could protect an offender from committing further sexual crimes. Thus, we suspect that one of the major reasons for the varying representations of what are arguably similar factors resides in the professional disciplines of sex offender therapists (social workers, psychologists) and desistance researchers (criminologists). Therapists seek to identify and reduce an offender's risk of reoffending whereas desistance researchers set out to explain why some individuals decide to turn their lives around and stop offending.

The point is that both therapeutic and desistance perspectives converge on similar factors, but have different interests and agendas. Because of the overlap it is possible to use the findings from desistance research to more directly inform offender rehabilitation and treatment. The question is, What is the most effective way to achieve this goal? It is not a straightforward task and the relationship between what has been termed "natural desistance" and therapist-assisted change is complex. Despite this complexity, we will argue that a strength-based rehabilitation approach (i.e., the GLM) provides a better fit with desistance theories than alternative, more traditional, approaches to rehabilitation and that programs dominated by risk management concerns effectively seal themselves off from capitalizing on these exciting ideas for facilitating crime reduction.

## Desistance and Practice

Desistance theorists and researchers have written eloquently about the need both to take advantage of natural desistance processes and to direct rehabilitation efforts to the factors associated with desistance (e.g., McNeill, 2006; McNeill et al., 2005; Porporino, 2008). A notable feature of rehabilitation-focused strands of such work has been a recommendation to tailor assessment and intervention activities to the personal circumstances and needs of individual offenders rather than adopt a one-size-fits-all approach. We briefly consider two applications of desistance research to offender rehabilitation: a criminological and a psychological account.

Criminological desistance researchers typically stress the necessity of ensuring that offenders have social capital (relationships, opportunities, etc.) as well as human or psychological capital (skills, capabilities) if they are to have a realistic chance of successfully adopting an offense-free life (McNeill, 2004). What this amounts to in practice is extending the focal point of rehabilitation to agents, relationships, and institutions outside of the program setting, for example, to family relationships, work opportunities, mental health care, and so on (Travis, 2005). McNeill et al. (2005) explicitly draw from the work of researchers such as Maruna (2001) and convincingly argue that a desistance-oriented treatment approach should be founded on essential practice skills including skills required to build strong treatment alliances, to target strengths as well as risk, and to deliver empirically supported programs. Frequently such theorists are critical of the narrow focus of traditional correctional programs on individual risk factors and a corresponding tenuous grasp of relevant ethical issues and problems. Failure to grant sex offenders the basic entitlements of citizenship and the conditions required to live fulfilling lives is ethically unjustified as well as practically self-defeating (see Chapter 16). As stated above, a notable feature of criminological desistance suggestions for practice is their recommendation that damaged family and community relationships ought to be an explicit focus of practice attention (McNeill, 2009). The reason for this is that there is little point helping offenders acquire psychological capital if they lack opportunities to apply these skills.

While criminologists with a strong applied background such as McNeill (2006, 2009) make some excellent suggestions for importing desistance ideas into practice with offenders, ultimately their recommendations remain overly general and are not sufficiently detailed to guide the construction and implementation of intervention programs for groups such as sex offenders. We suggest one possible reason for this problem is a lack of an adequate psychological conception of agency and the conditions that make the exercise of agency possible, such as nutrition, accommodation, education, physical safety, cognitive skills, emotional competency, and social scaffolding (see Chapters 14 and 16). It is not that such factors are ignored—far from it; it is just that the theoretical resources that such theorists draw from do not include a rich view of human nature informed by biology and psychological theory and research. Rather, the stress tends to be on the social and cultural underpinnings of crime, which are important but are not the only causal influences relevant for understanding human action and identity. From the naturalistic perspective endorsed by the GLM, individuals have innate inclinations to desire and seek certain outcomes (see Chapter 13). The claim is that individuals' level of well-being is crucially reliant upon their basic human needs being met and this requires the availability of a complex suite of psychological, social, and environmental resources. However, it is not enough simply to meet basic needs because not every possible means of satisfying them is necessarily personally fulfilling or socially or ethically acceptable. Part of adaptive functioning is to learn to critically evaluate desires emerging from needs and at times to reject them as unworthy of pursuit and attempt to transform or disregard them. This may mean finding other ways of achieving the good in question, or, more accurately, the activities and outcomes that secure the good (e.g., seeking intimacy with an adult rather than with a child). That is, a critical task is to understand what it is the person wants and needs, and if accepted by the offender, assisting in the construction of the social and psychological resources required to make this possible. Thus, from the viewpoint of the GLM offender, rehabilitation is simultaneously a capacity-building and a normative (i.e., value-laden) business. The process of establishing offender competencies involves using the arsenal of therapeutic techniques available to psychologists and practitioners and does not simply rely on what resources an agent happens to possess. From a psychological perspective, skill deficits are often linked to impoverished learning environments or traumas of some kind. The metaphor of a scaffold is helpful because it enables us to distinguish between two related but distinct dimensions of support for people with skill deficits: (1) the intensity of support and (2) the duration of support. The *intensity* of support refers to the strength and extensiveness of a scaffold—just how far does it extend around a person's life and what domains of living does it cover? The *duration* of support offered by a scaffold refers to the length of time that support will be needed in order to shore up a person's agency efforts. Because human beings are embodied agents who possess considerable cognitive plasticity, they are able to utilize internal and external resources to achieve their goals. People vary in terms of the resources and support they require from others to assist them in the pursuit of their goals, although because of their inherent vulnerability and interdependence all human beings require some degree of scaffolding.

In summary, criminological desistance theories are strong on the role of social and cultural factors in accounting for crime cessation but are weaker when it comes to explaining why people (and offenders) are motivated to desire and seek certain outcomes, and what such "natural" motivation implies for both intervention and desistance initiatives.

A recent psychological application of desistance theory to offender rehabilitation was made by Porporino (2008). In his examination of correctional programs Porporino is critical of what he labels "blind empiricism" and the treatment of offenders in a narrow, mechanical way that overlooks the importance of the construction of a new prosocial identity. He is also critical of the assumption that evidence-based programs are actually responsible for reduction in offending rates. Porporino (2008) points out that

> a central feature of the risk/needs paradigm is that it perpetuates the notion of "fixable" dynamic risk factors, and programs become the *means to that end.* But we are really not sure about how to fix these "factors" (Bourgon, Hanson, & Bonta, 2008), and besides, there is at best only theoretical supposition that the same factors that might be implicated in why offending starts are also those that might underpin desistance if we reverse them. (p. 11)

He argues that we ought to develop programs that encourage offenders to reflect on their lives in new ways and to adopt goals that are personally motivating and congruent with desistance processes. Explicitly integrating ideas from the GLM, Porporino states that offending continues because individuals seek to meet their needs through inappropriate means, have life plans that contain conflicting elements and restricted scope, or lack the internal and external resources to live fulfilling and prosocial lives. He draws from positive psychology to support his argument for a more constructive strength-based approach to offender rehabilitation. Porporino states that, as people like us, offenders "strive towards possible future selves" that are socially and personally valued, competent, meaningful, coherent, unique, and cared for by others (p. 21). Thus, he asserts that providing offenders with the resources and motivation to constructively achieve their goals is also likely to reduce their desire to commit further crimes.

Poporino's paper is full of exciting ideas and demonstrates a fusion of desistance research with psychological interventions and theory. From our perspective he does a very good job of sketching out a new direction for correctional practice that incorporates positive psychological concepts and desistance findings. Ultimately, though, Porporino's paper is intended more as a clearinghouse for a range of empirically founded rehabilitation principles, strength-based rehabilitation conceptions, and desistance theory. It is not a systematic theory of rehabilitation and was never intended to be so. The GLM framework fleshed out below is such a theory and is entirely consistent with the spirit and many of the ideas evident in Porporino's erudite reflections on correctional programs.

Another good recent attempt to integrate the psychological and social aspects of desistance is evident in a paper by Serin and Lloyd (2009). In general terms, this work is supportive of the GLM and the need to include both internal and situational factors in any explanation of the desistance process. In our view, however, Serin and Lloyd do not develop the notion of agency sufficiently or fully explore the implications of practical reasoning for offender rehabilitation. One of the challenges for psychological approaches to desistance is to look beyond the preoccupation with risk factors and skill deficits to the concrete details of individual lives and the persons who live them. Desistance theory provides a wonderful source of ideas and research to therapists, which promises to enrich their vision of the rehabilitation process (see Chapters 4 and 6) . What is currently lacking in the literature, however, is an explicit and integrated attempt to create a bridge between the predominantly psychological field of correctional rehabilitation and the broader criminological field of desistance. The aim is to create such a bridge in this and the next chapter.

A final point to consider is the relationship between the "natural" desistance process and desistance that is indirectly or directly triggered by the intentional actions of correctional staff. As stated above, natural desistance occurs within the social ecology of offenders and does not seem to be particularly influenced by the actions of correctional professionals. Taking such findings into account, it may be tempting to disregard the efforts of therapists and program providers, and to locate the real source of desistance in such events as obtaining a job, starting a new relationship, or finding somewhere safe to live. Rehabilitation could be viewed as simply an additional extra, something that may be useful for nudging offenders into taking up external opportunities and not a powerful source of change in its own right. We think this view is a mistake and runs the risk of misrepresenting what treatment actually is and how it could work.

There are reasonable grounds for concluding that rehabilitation programs for offenders are effective in reducing recidivism rates (see Chapter 9). What is not so evident, however, is how they actually generate change. A virtue of the GLM's focus on practical reasoning and its assumption that crime can be understood as involving inappropriate ways of seeking primary goods is that programs can be viewed as focused and powerful ways of strengthening or instilling the core conditions of agency. The claim is that all people are naturally inclined to need and seek certain primary goods using a range of strategies that are socially and culturally acquired. Sometimes, however, the use of ineffective or counterproductive cognitive and behavioral strategies arising from impoverished or flawed good lives plans can result in personally frustrating and/or socially unacceptable actions. By participating in well-structured programs such individuals are more likely to be able to engineer, or take advantage of, "natural" desistance opportunities and processes in the future. Traditional, RNR-type treatment programs may promote offender capabilities, albeit in a generic sense, and it is likely that many of the skills learned are then transferred into the offender's world, outside the narrow confines of the treatment room. Some individuals might require more scaffolding than others in acquiring the capacities necessary to construct and put into action a plan for living that is adaptive and meaningful. Sometimes a greater need for professional input is a legacy of offenders living in particularly impoverished social environments with minimal social capital and sometimes it is because they possess few psychological resources of their own. In either of these situations rehabilitation programs can be helpful, with the former setting out to instill psychological skills and the latter concentrating on creating social opportunities and supports.

What we are suggesting is that the differences between natural and professionally assisted desistance may reside in the psychological and social resources available to specific individuals rather than representing qualitatively distinct routes to crime cessation. All human beings require help from other people to acquire and utilize the psychological capabilities and social resources necessary to realize their aspirations whether this involves completing job training, participating in social activities, or remaining crime-free. Exactly what kind of help is needed or is likely to be most useful will be a function of their personal characteristics and situation.

If what we have proposed makes sense, then it follows that a model such as the GLM is ideally placed to integrate desistance ideas while still advocating for the utility of treatment programs for some offenders. What rehabilitation options are offered to offenders should depend on their specific needs and capacities (i.e., psychological capital) in conjunction with their social and physical circumstances (i.e., social capital). It may be that following a period of intensive (community) social support and vocational skills training a person with a criminal history will be able to satisfactorily cope with the day-to-day demands of living an offense-free life. Alternatively, a person needing more ongoing specialist interventions because of major social and self-regulation skills deficits may require participation in a variety of intervention programs to help him to translate his personal goals and interests into tangible benefits. From a rehabilitation viewpoint, the key point is that the level and duration of support needed by individuals ought to be based around their capacity to act in service of their goals in ways that are ethically permissible and meaningful.

## The GLM and Desistance: An Integrated Framework

Desistance research and theory and offender rehabilitation initiatives direct their attention to many of the same phenomena but with different aims in mind. Traditionally, treatment programs derived from the RNR theory of offender rehabilitation formulate goals in deficit terms and thus concentrate resources on the reduction and management of risk. The fact that such programs are deficit-oriented means that there is often a failure to recognize any common ground that exists between themselves and desistance-inspired interventions. Strength-based treatment programs tend not to suffer from this problem because of their stated aim of capitalizing on offenders' abilities and interests, and consequently seeking to build capabilities to enable them to effectively pursue their personal goals. The treatment purpose of positive programming is to *achieve* certain outcomes such as intimacy within a relationship rather than to *avoid* reoffending.

The GLM is a rehabilitation theory *not* a treatment program, but it does have significant practical implications for the assessment and treatment of sex offenders. Its purpose is to provide a theoretical framework or map for practitioners working with offenders and to outline broad strategies that can inform the construction and implementation of *specific* assessment and intervention activities. In other words, the function of a rehabilitation theory is to help practitioners to decide what to target, how to go about working with offenders, and how to justify intervening in their lives in ways that are personally challenging and constraining. In order to achieve these practical and ethical aims a rehabilitation theory needs to contain a number of assumptions and conceptual levels covering its goals, etiological commitments, and practice implications.

The GLM is a coherent, systematic rehabilitation theory that addresses the full range of tasks confronting practitioners and provides a theoretical and ethical justification for these tasks (Ward & Maruna, 2007). In our view, because of this breadth the GLM is easily able to accommodate desistance concepts and therefore extend its applicability from purely practice concerns to the further reaches of reentry and reintegration. And, as argued above, desistance theory is essentially concerned with describing and explaining the processes of reentry and reintegration and the factors that promote them and sustain crime cessation. Important factors associated with successful reentry and reintegration include maintaining links with family, dealing with accommodation matters, ensuring offenders have adequate physical and mental health care, supplying employment assistance, and providing education or training opportunities (O'Hear, 2007; Petersilia, 2003; Robinson, 2008; Travis, 2005). While supporters of rehabilitation and desistance frameworks both hope to reduce reoffending, their analytic foci are different. In brief, the GLM is *a rehabilitation* theory because it is designed to guide practitioners in the assessment and delivery of therapy to offenders in community and prison correctional settings. It can also deal with *reentry* matters because its major analytical construct is that of good or better lives and as such it is directed toward offenders' lives outside of correctional contexts and into the future (O'Hear, 2007; Re-Entry Policy Council, 2005; Robinson, 2008). Furthermore, the GLM is capable of handling the issue of *reintegration* because of its stress on building better lives for offenders, which acknowledges their interdependency with others and the value of being socially embedded within intimate relationships and communities. According to the GLM, individuals' practical identities are in part derived from social and cultural resources and therefore they necessarily point to peoples' social dependencies (O'Hear, 2007; Ward & Marshall, 2007; Ward & Stewart, 2003).

It is true that the desistance-relevant aspects of the GLM have not been sufficiently elaborated, and also that it is at heart a rehabilitation theory. However, we believe it has the conceptual flexibility to incorporate desistance ideas, and in this enriched form is ideally placed to give researchers and practitioners a comprehensive practice map. Moreover, it is a map that goes beyond guidance on therapeutic issues and program content to suggesting ways of creating social and psychological capital that supports desistance from offending. We will now discuss the different levels of the GLM and their assumptions, pointing out explicit links to desistance research and theory. In particular, we hope to demonstrate how the ideas of Laub and Sampson (2003) and Maruna (2001) cohere with the GLM's core concepts of agency and social and physical interdependency.

## Principles, Aims, and Values

### Embodiment, Plasticity, and Cognitive Extension

In the following discussion of desistance concepts and the GLM we repeat some of the ideas outlined in Chapter 13 in an abbreviated form to ensure that the reader is able to grasp their theoretical overlap and possible convergence.

According to the GLM, human beings are physically embodied and use their bodies to change themselves and the world in accordance with their goals. In turn, individuals' goals are derived from their practical identities, which are constructed through a process of socialization and personal experience. Some aspects of individuals' practical identities are derived from physical characteristics such as gender or physical prowess, while others are based on religion, class, profession, or other social roles (Nussbaum, 2000, 2006). However, the GLM stipulates that because human beings are evolved animals they come into the world with a range of natural desires that motivate them to seek certain outcomes—natural preferences, if you like. Due to a combination of cognitive and behavioral flexibility people learn to use a variety of internal and external tools to further their agency efforts and to increasingly shape and engineer their social and physical environments (Sterelny, 2003). In essence, we are self-constituting beings that both create their environments and are shaped by them in turn. Because of the dynamic, constant nature of this process of self-constitution through actions that seek to secure valued outcomes, people are dependent on the goodwill and support of others.

It is possible to identify three strands in desistance theory, those that stress the importance of maturation, agency, and social relationships (McNeill et al., 2005; Maruna, 2001). Theorists have sometimes contrasted objective desistance factors (e.g., a job or marriage) (Glueck & Glueck, 1968; Giordano et al., 2004; Laub & Sampson, 2003) with a subjective sense of meaning, arguing for the primacy of one over the other (Bottoms et al., 2004; Weaver & McNeill, in press). More recent theoretical work has emphasized the interaction between all three sets of desistance factors and the fact that it is in the interfaces between these variables that desistance exerts its effect (McNeill et al., 2005; McNeill, 2009; Porporino, 2008). According to the GLM, offenders' core values enable them to capitalize on, or create, objective events that reflect their practical identity. There is no separation: people constitute themselves through actions which necessarily involve opportunities and objective events. Because of its stress on the importance of the past in fashioning practical identities and the associated socialization and acculturation processes, the GLM also has a strong developmental focus without adopting a fatalistic tone. There is arguably a red thread that runs through offenders' lives from the past to the future, linking core values, life plans, identity, and ultimately meaning. Furthermore, the GLM's stress on agency and the importance of reflectiveness is entirely consistent with desistance theorists' emphasis on "turning points" (Sampson & Laub, 1993; Laub & Sampson, 2003) or critical events that create a sense of crisis in offenders and ultimately prompt them to reevaluate their lives and reconstruct their identities. Identity reconstruction (Maruna, 2001) works through the location of the primary goods (see below) that are most important to offenders and an analysis of alternative ways to seek them. Practical identities are constituted by practices and ways of acting in the world and inevitably involve norms that regulate specific actions, dress, habits, and so on. What we are saying is that the process of constructing new narrative identities, or redemptive scripts (Maruna, 2001), can be unpacked in terms consistent with the GLM's basic assumptions about agency and identity. The flexibility of human beings, and their natural press to seek certain outcomes and to view their lives as meaningful and unified, is likely to contribute to self-reflection following crises or turning points. It goes without saying that adequate self-control is a consequence of possessing the capabilities needed to be a reflective and effective agent, and correspondingly a lack of self-control will be reflected in problematic ways of seeking primary goods (Gottfredson & Hirschi, 1990).

### *Primary Human Goods*

The GLM assumes the existence of a rich psychological architecture derived from a combination of natural selection and human beings' capacity for self-constitution through the modification of internal and external systems (see Chapter 13). According to the GLM, people are naturally inclined to seek a range of primary goods that have intrinsic value to them through the construction of secondary goods, which are basically the concrete ways of pursuing the more abstract primary goods. For example, a person might seek the goods of intimacy through having sex with a child or by way of establishing a relationship with an age-appropriate adult. Primary goods are experiences, activities, or outcomes that are sought for their own sake but they can be realized in a number of ways. In a real sense the devil is in the detail and it is through social learning that individuals construct practical identities and formulate specific ways of achieving primary goods. Practical identities are comprised of beliefs, norms, and practices that organize individuals' actions under a coherent description, for example, being a parent, lover, psychologist, or gang member. At the level of the abstract primary good, there is a degree of universality apparent in people's motives and their associated actions. However, at the level of everyday actions, there is frequently a bewildering variety of ways of seeking and realizing these abstract values.

As stated above, desistance theorists do not typically provide fine-grained analyses of the psychological variables associated with desistance and instead concentrate their efforts on explicating the social and cultural dimensions of cessation from offending (for an exception, see Porporino, 2008). A consequence of this analytic preference is that it is unclear exactly why offenders would be motivated to develop redemptive scripts or new practical identities. Or if they are, what the basis of this motivation might be. The GLM can add value to reintegration, reentry, and rehabilitation frameworks by virtue of its naturalistic assumptions, which are buttressed by scientific theory and research. However, both the GLM and desistance theorists agree on the importance of social learning for identity construction and the importance of social capital in helping offenders to turn their lives around. Secondary or instrumental goods represent particular ways of living in the world and arguably each identity is clustered around different primary goods: parenthood around the primary goods of relatedness and community; professional roles around mastery; romantic relationships around relatedness and pleasure; and so on. In fact, we argue that all of the desistance factors can be conceptually mapped onto both primary goods and criminogenic needs.

We do not have the space to demonstrate this mapping in detail but will engage in a preliminary analysis for the following desistance factors: work, impulsivity (i.e., lack of self-control), marriage, education, cognitive transformation, and fear of injury or sickness (Laub & Sampson, 2003; McNeill et al., 2005; Maruna, 2001; Porporino, 2008; Travis, 2005). One thing to note is that the desistance factors represent practices rather than abstract values, and therefore it is probable there will be connections to a plurality of goods. For ease of discussion, we will just highlight the primary goods most clearly relevant to the desistance factor under discussion. The desistance factor of *work* is related to the good of excellence at work or mastery (Uggen, 2000) and the related criminogenic need is unemployment (Andrews & Bonta, 2007). Lack of *self-control* has been consistently found to be associated with reoffending and can make it extremely difficult for offenders to participate in prosocial relationships and to achieve vocational goals (Gottfredson & Hirschi, 1990). Poor self-control is plausibly connected to the primary goods of inner peace and autonomy and can be conceptualized from a criminogenic viewpoint as impulsivity or poor self-regulation (Hanson & Morton-Bourgon, 2005). *Marriage* is arguably linked to the primary good of relatedness (Giordano et al., 2004; Laub & Sampson, 2003) and the associated criminogenic needs are intimacy deficits or antisocial peers. The factor of *education* is usefully approached through the primary good of knowledge (O'Hear, 2007) and the relevant criminogenic need could be offense-supportive beliefs and attitudes (Gannon & Polaschek, 2006). The next desistance factor on our list is *cognitive transformation* (Giordano et al., 2004; Maruna, 2001), whose closest primary goods would be autonomy and spirituality in its broadest sense of personal meaning. Autonomy is relevant because it involves the capacity to be self-directed and to reflect on one's life while spirituality entails the conviction that one's life is a meaningful one. A matching criminogenic need would be impulsivity or problems in controlling and organizing ones actions (Andrews & Bonta, 2007). Finally, *fear of injury or sickness* would be linked to the primary goods of health (physical integrity and intact functioning) and inner peace (Travis, 2005). The relevant criminogenic need is not obvious but could be offense-related beliefs or inappropriate anger depending on the circumstances (Craig, Brown, & Beech, 2008). From the viewpoint of the GLM, emotions function to alert individuals to beneficial or harmful situations, and are conduits of value experiences. Critical appraisal of their secondary goods can lead individuals to reject practical identities and lifestyles linked to offending. In these situations you would expect offenders to experience more negative emotions and fewer positive emotions when confronted with crime-related cues and situations. In other words, identity change is intimately linked to changes in emotional experience, and this in turn is arguably a consequence of adopting a redemptive or prosocial practical identity (Giordano et al., 2007).

What the above analysis reveals is that the domains of life identified by desistance research as relevant for understanding cessation from offending can be viewed through a values/primary goods lens, and for many of these factors also unpacked in terms of a corresponding criminogenic need. In our view this makes perfect sense because desistance from offending is arguably generated by establishing adaptive ways of meeting needs and a subsequent identity and lifestyle that is socially acceptable. Both desistance theories and the GLM challenge the RNR's primary focus on criminogenic needs or offense-related factors. This is partly because of their emphasis on promoting social integration by way of offenders' agency concerns and aspirations. The assumption is that ultimately desistance from offending is best achieved by facilitating the construction and implementation of better life plans that are centered on offenders' practical identities and their associated goals and actions. It is assumed that helping offenders acquire social, psychological, and cultural resources to meaningfully participate in the life of the community (or communities) will result in reduced reoffending rates. The finding that most offenders, including sex offenders, stop offending without specialist psychological help confirms the desistance claim that natural processes and events are critical elements in persuading people to give up criminal lives (see Chapters 4 and 8). It goes without saying that obtaining offenders' consent and agreement on the best way to achieve their cherished goals and identities is ethically obligatory and practically prudent.

### *Values and Practical Identities*

We have already referred to values and practical identities above and so will make our comments here brief. Two additional, particularly important issues concern the plural nature of the primary goods and their relationship to practical identities, and the importance of reflectiveness in "making good" (Maruna, 2001).

We argued in Chapter 13 that human beings pursue a plurality of goods, and that for their lives to go well, all primary goods need to be present to some degree. We also proposed that the necessary conditions for agency require access to these goods and therefore all people have entitlements to a number of the primary goods to some (threshold) degree. Furthermore, it was suggested that practical identities develop around specific goods and that in many respects each primary good relates to a domain of human functioning and is associated with classes of practical identities. Different weightings of the goods by individuals will be reflected in distinct identities and sources of meaning. For example, the primary good of relatedness will be evident in practical identities such as friends, partners, parents, while the good of excellence is likely to be associated with identities pertaining to employment, for example, psychologist, train driver, or teacher. The relevance of these points for desistance is relatively straightforward. Attraction to specific primary goods and their manifestation in ways of living that are threatened by continued offending may create turning points for people (Giordano et al., 2002; Weaver & McNeill, in press). For example, females in their 20s who are involved in intimate relationships may see crime as a threat to a valued identity such as being a mother or partner. For another example, the opportunity to pursue a valued job could lead a young man to reconsider the wisdom of continuing to rob banks and decide to reform his ways. Conflict between the norms associated with particular identities and offending might create a crisis point and prompt serious reflection on the things that really matter to an offender. Access to social and psychological capital (McNeill, 2009; Ripple, Alexander, & Polemis, 1964), in conjunction with the desire to stop offending, could result in ongoing desistance from offending. It would be expected from a GLM viewpoint that the kind of goods and their associated identities should vary depending on the developmental stage, gender, and cultural identity of the individuals concerned. Thus the GLM and its assumptions about identity coheres well with desistance research and theory that indicates there are a variety of pathways in and out of offending, arguably associated with individuals' personal concerns and goals (Giordano et al., 2002; McNeill et al., 2005; see Chapters 4, 5, and 6).

The second issue we would like to enlarge on is the importance of reflectiveness and cognitive transformation for desistance from offending. While there has been some disagreement between desistance theorists concerning the causal role of identity transformation in the transition from offending, most agree that it is evident in some individuals at least (Laub & Sampson, 2003; Maruna, 2001). Certainly secondary desistance (Maruna & Farrall, 2004), which involves sustained lifestyle change and ongoing cessation from crime, seems likely to be partly a consequence of offenders adopting redemptive scripts and actively rethinking their values and life options (Maruna, 2001; Ward & Marshall, 2007). The GLM has strong roots in individuals' agency capabilities and their subsequent decisions about what values they endorse and how they should live. Additionally, the GLM can account for the *lack* of scrutiny of lifestyles and values evident in many offenders (and nonoffenders) by way of the concept of practical identities. Many of us passively adopt our values and their related practices, and it is only at times of crisis or after events that have particular salience to us that we think more systematically and deeply about what to do and who to be. Being imprisoned and participating in treatment programs could trigger this reflective process, as can the influence of friends or simply the accumulated pressures of an antisocial lifestyle. Whatever the reasons for deciding to desist from an offending lifestyle, the GLM is able to account for, and cohere with, desistance theorists' insistence on the critical role of agency and its subsequent effects on those individuals who decide to make good and transform themselves and their lives. A nice feature of the GLM is because it works with a self-constituting conception of agency and identity, it can account for the effects of external factors that prompt change such as a marriage or a crisis of meaning only evident to an offender (Ward et al., 2007).

### Goods and Risks

According to the GLM, practitioners ought to seek to promote offenders well-being alongside the targeting of risk factors. What this means in practice is that a good lives plan with the core goods and their associated identities should be formulated, and the internal and external conditions required to successfully implement it noted. The aim is to make sure that the capacity-building process also reduces risk; certainly, for most criminogenic needs, this is the case (see Ward & Maruna, 2007). For example, strengthening an individual's capacity to function as a self-determining agent should also reduce his level of impulsivity.

Desistance theorists and researchers set out to identify the determinates of crime cessation and are primarily involved in descriptive and explanatory tasks rather than the normative one of providing guidance for intervention. However, some theorists have explicitly addressed the implications of desistance research for offender rehabilitation and recommended that desistance factors and processes should be deliberately cultivated to facilitate offenders' social integration and agency strengthening (McNeill, 2009). A problem has been a lack of a theoretical framework or theory to focus and justify such intervention-directed efforts.

Typically, a list of desistance factors is detected and sometimes causal processes postulated that explain why such factors are likely to promote crime reduction and their absence to be associated with offending (Laub & Sampson, 2003; Maruna, 2001; Travis, 2005). The GLM can provide a theoretically grounded and systematic theory to explain why promoting strengths such as work or a sound marriage is desirable and should increase an offender's chances of remaining offense-free (Warr, 1998). It also has the resources to explicitly guide and coordinate specific intervention efforts across a wide range of correctional professionals.

### *Ecological Selves and the Nature of Risk*

A common criticism of RNR-type correctional programs by desistance researchers and theorists is that they are rigid and based on a one-size-fits-all treatment philosophy (Farrall, 2002; McNeill et al., 2005; Porporino, 2008; Raynor & Robinson, 2006). It is alleged that there is a lack of attention to the contextual nature of human action or an appreciation of the multifaceted nature of crime. Furthermore, given the contextual and dynamic nature of crime, it also follows (it is argued) that risk too should be conceptualized in this manner rather than characterized as inhering essentially within individual offenders. We agree with these criticisms. In our view, the overly mechanical and bureaucratic approach of the RNR to offender treatment and risk is based on an implicit individualism. A consequence of this reliance is sometimes a tendency to overpathologize individual offenders and neglect the important role of external and systemic influences in the creation of crime-facilitative circumstances. In other words, from a desistance perspective it is imperative to take offenders' unique set of circumstances into account when seeking to understand factors that reduce crime and enhance prosocial functioning.

The GLM, by virtue of its core assumptions, understands human beings as interdependent, multifaceted, and possessing "soft selves" that are self-creating in important respects. What this view amounts to when it comes to risk and the nature of the self is an awareness that correctional interventions at the primary, secondary, and tertiary levels need to take account of individual offenders' personal associations and circumstances. In other words, it is necessary to grasp what practical identities and their associated values are of relevance for individual offenders and discern how such identities are socially and culturally scaffolded by external factors such as friends, employment, or local organizations (Korsgaard, 2009; Weaver & McNeill, in press; see Chapters 11 and 12). Therefore, the GLM can function as a practice conduit for desistance ideas and is able to accommodate both situational and personal factors in correctional interventions.

### The Nature of Intervention

Desistance theorists and researchers have recently begun to explicitly think about the intervention implications of their findings (e.g., McNeill, 2006; Porporino, 2008). Their stress on the importance of social (opportunities, supports) (Laub & Sampson, 1993; McNeill, 2006) and psychological capital (skills, capabilities) (McNeill, 2006; Porporino, 2008) means that there is some degree of impatience with traditional RNR interventions that are primarily aimed at protecting the community rather than respecting the inherent dignity and moral status of offenders. As discussed in Chapter 16, human rights confer both entitlements and obligations and so acknowledging the rights of offenders to certain freedom and well-being goods does not mean overlooking their duty to the community to respect the interests of others. Thus interventions based on desistance research would focus on providing offenders with the internal and external resources to secure a number of personal goods including meaningful work, social supports and opportunities, caring relationships, physical health, a safe environment, freedom of choice (suitably modulated), and so on (McNeill, 2009). At the fulcrum of any interventions would be *recognition respect* for the agency of the offenders and refusal to use coercive measures to advance the interests of members of the community (Darwell, 2006).

The GLM is ethically underpinned by human rights theory and a subsequent commitment to respect the right of moral agents to be self-determining as long as they do not unjustifiably violate the rights of others in the process of doing so (see Chapter 16). Intervention plans based on the GLM involve the construction of good lives plans that are centered around favored identities and their core values, for example, mastery or caring. The aim is to assist offenders in the acquisition of psychological, social, and material resources to advance their aspirations while also reducing their risk for further violence. Thus it is evident that the GLM and desistance-oriented programs are both strength-focused and systemic in nature.

## Etiological Assumptions

The focus of desistance theories is on the identification of variables that are associated with crime cessation and an explanation why they work in this way. Thus they are not intended to be etiological theories in the ordinary sense of the term. However, it is possible to tease out etiological implications from desistance theories such as those of Laub and Sampson (2003) and Sampson and Laub (1993). In essence, desistance theories concentrate their explanatory efforts on three sets of factors: maturation, social relationships, and cognitive transformation. As discussed earlier, Sampson and Laub (1993) and Laub and Sampson (2003) explain offending by failure in the mechanisms of formal and informal social control. They argue that inconsistent, abusive, or negligent parenting can result in children who lack the capacity to establish close social bonds and who are disinclined to take the interests and well being of other people into account when pursing their own goals. Furthermore, such antisocial proclivities may result in close association at school with delinquent peers and subsequent academic failure and persistent norm violation in both school and community settings. The logical implication for intervention of this view for the etiology of crime is to assist offenders to become more socially invested and to develop stronger social motivations and capabilities. Cognitive transformation desistance theorists such as Maruna (2001), Giordano et al. (2002), and Marranci (2007) agree that such developmental variables play an important role in creating criminal vulnerabilities but add that a crucial part of the reintegration puzzle resides in a change in narrative identity. For Maruna, it is the transformation of self, the generation of a new self-identity, that is the key to offenders adopting prosocial lifestyles and making good. In his study, individuals who developed redemptive identity scripts were more committed to a life without crime than those who had condemnation scripts. In other words, the ability of offenders to reflect on their lives and to commit themselves to new practical identities, alternative ways to achieve their values, was crucial to eventual success.

The GLM takes into account the goal-seeking nature of human beings and the dependence of identity on action and its embedded values and associated goals. Who people are, what they stand for, and what matters to them becomes apparent through their actions and the effects of such actions on the environment and themselves. For example, a rapist who demeans his victims may be revealing aspects of his identity as an aggrieved male who believes he has the right to control women's sexuality and will. The rapist's actions express humiliation-related goals and their supervening values (e.g., agency, entitlement) while their effects change aspects of his relationship to the victim and the community. As stated in Chapter 13, there are four major types of difficulties evident in individuals' life plans: problems of scope, means, conflict, and capacity. These flaws constitute the forms of criminogenic needs and can manifest internally or externally. According to the GLM, there are two primary, goal-related pathways to sexual offending, a direct and an indirect route

(Ward et al., 2006). In the direct route an offender is hypothesized to be intentionally seeking a specific type of good, for example, intimacy or mastery, through sexually abusive actions. In the indirect route, a combination of events, frequently triggered by lifestyle imbalance, results in a sexual offense. An example of an indirect route is when a person overworks, drinks to deal with the accompanying stress, argues with his partner, drinks more, loses his job and relationship, and down the line rapes a woman. In both offense pathways goals are involved but in quite different ways. (The evidence for these pathways and the associated flaws in offenders' good lives plans is presented in Ward et al., 2004, 2006.) The goals adopted by offenders can be traced back to their practical identities (e.g., partner, male, worker), which can be viewed as an integrated combination of instrumental and primary goods (see Chapter 13). The implicit or explicit good lives plans endorsed by offenders are usually grounded in primary goods and their corresponding identities and specific actions. Offenders, like all human beings, are characterized by cognitive and behavioral plasticity and are capable of intentionally structuring their environments and themselves to help them to achieve their desired outcomes. Thus at the heart of the GLM is a conception of offenders as agents capable of endorsing ultimate ends and constructing and implementing plans for achieving them.

What are the points of convergence between desistance theories and the etiological commitments of the GLM? In our view, there are five major areas of agreement (Farrall, 2002; Giordano et al., 2002; Glueck & Glueck, 1968; Maruna, 2001; Maruna & Farrall, 2004; Maruna et al., 2005; Laub & Sampson, 2003; McNeill, 2006; Petersilia, 2003; Sampson & Laub, 1993; Travis, 2005; Weaver & McNeill, in press). First, offending and desistance are viewed as partly a result of offenders' exercise of choice and therefore agency. Second, if a decision to desist from further offending is to be successfully translated into sustained actions, offenders require the internal and external resources to formulate and implement their plans for living. It is the connection between goals and actions, and the necessary resources needed to achieve them, that brings desistance theory and the GLM into alignment. As argued earlier, the only real difference between "natural" desistance processes and therapy-assisted desistance resides in the type, and possibly the degree, of scaffolding required. Ethically justified, personally effective, and meaningful actions depend on a variety of psychological, social, and material goods. Third, such plans for living (good lives plans) reveal aspects of offenders' identities, the core values they are committed to, and their corresponding lifestyles. It is what individuals *do* in the commission of their offenses and whether or not their actions are supported or constrained by their environments that sustain or weaken deviant identities. Fourth, a crucial level of analysis when attempting to understand the reasons for a persons' sexual offending and whether it is likely to continue is that of *meaning*. That is, it is important to clarify what identity descriptions best capture their values and their relationships to the subsequent actions that aim at realizing these values in their lives. Fifth, people commit crimes in specific contexts and give up offending, in part, because they are provided with opportunities to do so. This assumption is directly derived from a conception of ecological selves and the necessary reliance of people on each other for need satisfaction.

## Implications for Practice

The common ground evident between desistance theories and the GLM in the practice arena arises from their core and etiological assumptions outlined above. In a nutshell, both are future-oriented, individualistically rather than group-focused, contextual, strength-based, and holistic perspectives that set out to help offenders resume or begin meaningful and socially productive lives (see Chapters 4, 6, and 13). Furthermore, there is a shared commitment to offenders' inherent dignity and an awareness that this entails ensuring that any interventions are respectful of their agency and responsive to the interests of the whole community.

We will now briefly discuss each of these shared assumptions. There is an acknowledgment by the GLM and desistance theory that people are products of their past as well as being open to the future. In order to understand the reasons individuals commit offenses and how these reasons cohere with practical identities and values, practitioners ought to be mindful of their developmental history (Glueck & Glueck, 1950, 1968; Sampson & Laub, 1993). There is a particularly strong emphasis in desistance research and theory on the impact of family and early relationships on offenders' subsequent social and psychological functioning (see Chapter 4). However, because both perspectives accept the (partial) self-constituting nature of human agents, they also recognize that change is possible and ultimately rooted in the capacity for self-determination alongside the provision of social and psychological capital. In other words, the GLM and desistance theories are both backward and forward looking. Forward-looking theories that are constructive in nature can reasonably be expected to engender hope and optimism for change in offenders, and as such, the GLM suitably enriched by desistance concepts is able to facilitate the change process (Burnett, 2002).

There is agreement between the GLM and desistance theories that intervention programs ought to be tailored to take account of the specific talents, aspirations, and circumstances of individual offenders and their lives (Farrall, 2002; Ward & Maruna, 2007; Weaver & McNeill, in press). There is little point in adopting a one-size-fits-all approach, in part because it ignores the kinds of beings we are and also because such a broad approach is unlikely to be that effective in promoting desistance. Attention to the social and personal circumstances of offenders' lives also means intervening where necessary to repair damaged relationships with family, peers, or the wider community. This point is nicely stated by McNeill (2009) who asserts that "it follows that supporting desistance requires probation services . . . to repair the bonding social capital represented in family ties" (p. 35). McNeill suggests that repairing damaged social relationships and creating positive connections with the community can "create channels for the generative activities that seem to be important to those desisting from crime" (p. 35). An additional aspect of working with offenders in their social ecologies is to actively counter punitive attitudes toward offenders and rehabilitation efforts (see recommendations by Travis, 2005, Ch. 11).

Another point of agreement between the GLM and desistance theories is that care should be taken when attempting to persuade individuals to give up crime to look to build strengths rather than simply eradicate, control, or manage risk. The research literature on motivation is clear that the best way to get people engaged in the process of behavior change is to focus on approach goals that are personally meaningful (e.g., Amodeo, Kurtz, & Cutter, 1992; Emmons, 1999; Gorman, Gregory, Hayles, & Parton, 2006; McMurran, 2002). Simply demanding that offenders participate in challenging treatment or change programs so that they are less harmful is not an attractive option (Mann et al., 2004; McMurran & Ward, 2004; Ward & Gannon, 2006). What is also required is that there is a possibility of a more fulfilling life and the perception that practitioners care about them and are personally invested in assisting them with their journey (McNeill et al., 2005). From a desistance viewpoint, attempts to motivate individuals to give up their offending lives should take advantage of turning points, hooks for change, or current dissonance arising from the consequences of offending (Giordano et al., 2002; Vaughan, 2007).

The GLM and desistance theories share a view that an effective rehabilitation strategy ought to be holistic in its orientation and attend to individuals' array of social, material, and psychological needs as well as their range of life circumstances. What this means in practice is that therapists ought to pay greater attention to the individual, environmental, and social contexts of offenders' lives and their criminal actions (Farrall, 2002). Both theoretical perspectives criticize traditional RNR programs for focusing too narrowly on factors directly linked to offending and neglecting offenders' values, goals, and hopes for their lives. A first point concerns the difficulty of motivating people by negative goals such as crime cessation (McMurran & Ward, 2004). A second issue is that if intervention works by reconnecting or connecting people with valued social and personal networks, then long-term desistance requires casting a wider net than is typically done (Farrall, 2002). Helping offenders reevaluate their values and goals and to construct practical identities that are truly redemptive in nature necessitates creating dialogues based on mutual respect and openness. Such dialogues are unlikely to be concentrated on discussions of criminogenic needs or reoffending patterns. Rather, we suspect the topics raised will be those of work, children, wives, husbands, sports teams, hobbies, religion, and so on (see, e.g., the *Life History Interview* in Chapter 12). If risk is to be a focus, it should be configured in ways that link up with the topic of growth, not of containment and restriction. The holistic orientation of both desistance theories and the GLM has this kind of emphasis.

Finally, according to both desistance theory and the GLM, creating a sound therapeutic alliance with correctional clients is a pivotal component of effective intervention and should not be viewed as of lesser importance than the application of therapy strategies and techniques (McMurran, 2002; McNeill, 2006). This is as much an ethical as a technical task and may entail working politically to ensure offenders' basic human rights are protected and, ultimately, that their citizen privileges are not unreasonably restricted or even lost (Birgden, 2008; Lippke, 2002; Uggen, Manza, & Behrens, 2004; Vess, 2009; Ward & Birgden, 2007) Too often, rehabilitation research ignores the role of therapist interaction effects in impacting client self-concept (Ward & Maruna, 2007). Working collaboratively with clients in developing treatment goals results in a stronger therapeutic alliance; therapist features such as displays of empathy and warmth, and encouragement and rewards for progress, facilitate the change process (Leibrich, 1994; Marshall et al., 2003; Ward & Stewart, 2003).

The GLM and desistance ideas can help negotiate the tension inevitably present in correctional contexts between moral condemnation and a desire to assist offenders achieve more fulfilling lives. Both theoretical perspectives are able to help because of their recognition that offenders have value as human agents, and also by making their offending intelligible in the light of the pursuit of human goods (see Chapters 13 and 16). The respect that prisoners and probationers are owed as human beings, in conjunction with the understanding that the establishment of a therapeutic relationship requires trust and openness, means that therapists need to create a constructive and positive environment. Thus, recognition of offenders' moral equality and their status as fellow human beings with the same needs and aspirations as the rest of us makes it easier to establish strong therapeutic alliances. Furthermore, restorative justice practices and communicative theories of punishment may also be helpful in pointing out ways that offenders can repair their relationship to the community, and hence pave the way to eventual reentry and reacceptance (Birgden, 2008; Duff, 2001; Johnstone, 2002; Raynor & Robinson, 2009; Travis, 2005).

## Conclusions

In this chapter we have explored similarities between desistance theories and the GLM, and concluded that they share a number of core assumptions concerning the aims, causes, and nature of rehabilitation, reentry, and reintegration. In our view, the GLM is able to incorporate desistance ideas and therefore is ideally placed to provide a systematic framework for guiding practitioners in working with offenders. In fact, we suggest that by virtue of its core assumptions and their implications for etiology and practice, the GLM actually contains some nascent desistance concepts. More specifically, we propose that the Good Lives–Desistance Model (GLM-D) can help therapists to build the psychological and social capital needed by offenders to live better lives and as such to redeem themselves in both the community's and their own eyes.

The GLM makes a significant difference to the way practice is carried out with offenders and is *not simply a positive gloss on traditional sex-offending treatment approaches and programs* (Ward & Maruna, 2007). Strengthening the desistance elements of the GLM adds a further dimension to therapeutic work and moves practice significantly beyond the straightforward cognitive-behavioral skill acquisition nature of contemporary programs for sex offenders (Whitehead et al., 2007). In essence, a GLM-D program seeks to tailor an intervention plan around an offender's core values and associated practical identities. The good lives plan unfolds from this value center and incorporates all of the various goods required to function as a reflective and effective agent within specific environments. Where possible, local communities and resources are recruited and the objective is to assist in the building of a better life rather than simply trying to contain risk. For example, an individual's treatment plan could be based on his desires to learn a trade (e.g., become a mechanic) and establish a romantic relationship. The skills required to become a mechanic, such as mechanical knowledge of engines, effective work habits, at least a reasonable degree of social and communication skills, and affective and self-control competencies, may reduce risk while consolidating the offender within a social network.

All of these factors are established desistance variables (see Chapter 5). Access to workmates and hobbies that cohere with his interests might further open up opportunities to meet potential partners who are law-abiding and supportive. The result of such a plan will hopefully be a life that is fulfilling, meaningful, ethically acceptable, and socially productive (Burnett, 2002; Maruna et al., 2004; Warr, 1998; Whitehead et al., 2007).

We consider assessment and therapy according to the GLM-D in some detail in the next chapter. We finish this chapter with an overview of an intervention structure based on the GLM-D. There are five phases to a GLM-D rehabilitation framework. We now briefly describe each of these phases before examining them in detail in the next chapter.

The *first phase* when intervening with offenders from the standpoint of the GLM-D involves the detection of the social, psychological, and material phenomena implicated in individuals' sexual offending. This requires a careful analysis of offenders' level of risk, their living circumstances, physical and social problems, and psychological capabilities around the time of their offending and stretching into their past as well. Offenders are likely to have multiple problems such as poverty, substance abuse, lack of accommodation, high levels of impulsiveness and aggressive behavior, and so on (see *Life History Calendar,* Chapter 12; Laub & Sampson, 2003; McNeill et al., 2005).

In the *second phase* of the GLM-D, the function of offending (i.e., what the individual expected to achieve via his offending) is established through the identification of primary goods that are directly or indirectly linked to the sexually abusive actions. In addition, the identification of the *overarching good* or value around which the other goods are oriented should also be ascertained. This step requires that practitioners identify the practical identities endorsed by offenders and clarify how they are causally related to their sexually abusive actions. It is anticipated that the core goods (e.g., mastery or caring) will be translated into more concrete values and tasks that directly connect with the offenders' general life circumstances and their offense-related actions.

In the *third phase* of the GLM-D rehabilitation process, the selection of the practical identities and their overarching good(s) or value(s) is undertaken and made a focus of a plan. As discussed earlier, frequently practical identities are aligned with the primary goods and in a sense simply flesh out the abstractness of the good in question. In effect, practical identities and their goals, strategies, and practices provide the detail needed to effectively work with an offender. For example, an individual might nominate knowledge and relatedness as the two most important goods and decide that going to university and establishing a relationship with a woman are means to these ends.

In the *fourth phase*, a greater level of detail is added to the above developing plan and the selection of secondary goods or values that specify how the primary goods will be translated into ways of living and functioning undertaken. In this step, identification of the contexts or environments in which the person is likely to be living while in the community during or following treatment is conducted. For example, the practical identity of being a university student (and partner in a relationship) is now examined with respect to a possible environment and the educational, social, psychological, and material resources required to make this possible are noted. The GLM-D is a regulatory and pragmatic model, so it is imperative that the probable environments a person will be living in are identified and their potential to provide the required resources to realize the good lives plan ascertained.

In the *fifth phase*, the practitioner constructs a detailed intervention plan for the offender based on the above considerations and information. The plan will be holistic, specify the internal and external conditions required to successfully implement it, revolving around offenders' core values and their associated practical identities, and the various tasks for correctional practitioners will be carefully detailed. Dynamic risk factors or criminogenic needs are indirectly targeted when cognitive-behavioral techniques and social interventions are utilized in the acquisition of offender competencies. Thus, taking into account the kind of life that would be fulfilling and meaningful to the individual (i.e., primary goods, secondary goods, and their relationship to ways of living and possible environments), the evaluator notes the capabilities or competencies he requires in order to have a reasonable chance of applying the plan. Practical steps are then taken to organize the various actors involved and to put the good lives plan into action. The offender is consulted in all the various phases and in a robust sense he drives the content of the plan if not its form. Furthermore, the practitioner seeks to balance the ethical entitlements of the offender with those of victims and members of the community. Some offenders may require intensive therapeutic input while others may have enough psychological and social capital to be able to take advantage of "natural" desistance factors such as employment opportunities, supportive community groups, or a welcoming and caring family (see Chapters 9 and 10 on these issues). More often than not, a combination of interventions may be what is needed.

In the next chapter we outline how the assessment of therapeutic work with sex offenders could proceed if the GLM-D framework were adopted. To reiterate, the GLM is essentially a rehabilitation theory and therefore intended to assist practitioners in the design, construction, and delivery of intervention programs for a variety of offenders. What we have attempted to achieve in this chapter is expand on those elements that resonate with desistance ideas and practice suggestions. In our view, the incorporation (or elaboration) of desistance concepts gives the GLM greater breadth and moves it away from a secondary treatment orientation. Thus it is not enough for a sex offender program to enhance an offender's empathy skills or equip him with the ability to cope with stress or emotional loneliness. Beyond these essential tasks practitioners should be looking to create social supports and opportunities, and to help create ways of living that follow from a personally significant, and ethically acceptable, (redemptive) practical identity (Maruna, 2001). Practitioners need to work with criminological, biological, psychological, therapeutic, and political resources to aid in the desistance process. Inevitably this will entail working collaboratively with a wide range of professionals and members of the community. It may also involve them in ethical and political debate alongside the application of technologies of behavioral change.

## Chapter 15

# The Good Lives–Desistance Model

## *Assessment and Treatment*

Our aim in this chapter is to give an overview of the various general intervention strategies involved in assessing and treating sex offenders from a GLM-D standpoint. This is not a therapy manual and therefore we will not be outlining in great detail how to assess and work with sex offenders. Rather, the level of discussion will be more strategic in nature and is intended to provide therapists with the knowledge to be able to recruit existing cognitive and behavioral treatment techniques in the service of desistance-oriented intervention, based on offenders' particular Good Lives Plans (GLP). After describing the assessment and treatment issues and strategies we will present three small case studies that should give practitioners a concrete idea of how GLM-D treatment could work. However, before diving into a discussion of intervention ideas, we would like to make a few general observations founded on the preceding chapters. The purpose of doing this is to summarize the core ideas derived from criminological desistance theory and the GLM-D in the book so far.

A first point is that we assume the validity of distinguishing between two distinct, overlapping normative frameworks evident in the criminal justice system that are often conflated (Ward & Langlands, 2009): a response to crime (punishment) and rehabilitation initiatives that follow this response. Each of the two normative frameworks revolves around a core set of values, ethical (relating to the coordination of competing interests) in the former, and prudential (relating to self-interests and well-being) in the latter. The aim of a just response to crime is to arrive at a solution that balances the harm inflicted on offenders in response to the damage they have done with their interests and those of the rest of the community. Theories of punishment are designed to provide a justification of the structure of penalties arrived at that is reasonable and not arbitrary (see Chapter 16). The aim of rehabilitation is to assist offenders to reenter society, and ultimately to become productive and accepted citizens rather than be regarded as predators by members of the general community. In part, a critical piece of the rehabilitation puzzle is to enable offenders to live fulfilling and happy lives. Although punishment and rehabilitation are underpinned by contrasting sets of values (ethical vs. prudential), each is also subject to the influence of both types of values. When administering punishment it is important to take offenders' welfare into account and when working therapeutically it is imperative to ensure that any intervention plans are ethically acceptable. Although the two frameworks are overlapping in that there are elements in some forms of punishment (e.g., restorative justice) and rehabilitation (e.g., cognitive restructuring) that have some components of the other, generally speaking they remain distinct criminal justice perspectives with their own cluster of practices (Ward & Salmon, 2009). This is an important issue because if punishment and rehabilitation practices are conflated, then it is easy to focus on risk management concerns at the expense of offenders' well-being and search for meaning and fulfillment. It is easy to do this because risk management within the criminal justice arena is about public protection and typically involves imposing considerable burdens upon offenders, burdens that can plausibly be construed as aspects of punishment (Glaser, 2003). From a desistance perspective, rehabilitation is as much about promoting social reintegration and a sense of meaning as it is about risk containment. Therefore, it makes sense to distinguish between the two frameworks and it is also more consistent with the ethical approach rooted in equal dignity assumed in this book.

A second, somewhat related, point we would like to stress is that a primary concern of the GLM-D is on agency and the conditions that make it possible, that is, the provision of well-being and freedom goods. Practically speaking, it is difficult, if not impossible, for any person to be able to live the life he or she would like if these basic goods are missing or insufficiently provided. The necessary dependence of agency on the availability of freedom and well-being goods opens up questions concerning individuals' rights to these goods and what obligations the state and the members of the community have to each other to ensure that each person has access to them. In our view, rights to these goods are grounded in an ethical perspective emphasizing the inherent dignity and interdependence of all human beings, including offenders. All human beings have intrinsic value and therefore offenders' core interests are as important as those of others and vice versa (see Chapter 16). As embodied beings we all need well-being and freedom goods to possess the necessary conditions to exercise agency. This conclusion has significant implications for the type of intervention plans offered to individuals within the correctional system and how such plans are actually put into practice. The GLM-D and desistance approaches to rehabilitation accept this ethical requirement and therefore are better placed to promote constructive, more positive intervention options for offenders than RNR-type programs.

A third point that has emerged from the preceding chapters is the significant emphasis of both the GLM-D and desistance viewpoints on practical reasoning and its associated agency implications. All human beings are viewed as agents who act in pursuit of valued goals in ways they believe are likely to achieve them. Because dignity is premised on offenders' abilities to function as agents and the availability of the conditions (e.g., adequate food, security, education, options, resources) that make this possible, assessment and intervention needs to (1) be constrained by this requirement; and (2) be built around the provision of psychological and social capital needed to assist offenders to live lives they choose and that are ethically acceptable. What this amounts to in practical terms is that everything therapists do when intervening with sex offenders should reflect a concern to enhance their ability to achieve lives they want while ensuring that inevitable restrictions are ethically justified and proportional to the assessed level of threat or risk. In reality there are significant constraints on what is socially and physically possible for sex offenders within therapy and postrelease programs. Practitioners are not miracle makers but they are obligated to work toward the best possible outcomes for the men they treat founded on an appreciation of their inherent dignity and entitlements to the core conditions of agency this dignity entails. And if in the judgment of practitioners sex offenders are treated unfairly (e.g., an unjustified denial of rights), they ought to address these justice issues in appropriate ways. Once it is accepted that human rights and the concept of inherent dignity that grounds them applies to sex offenders, it is not possible ethically to work in narrow risk reduction ways or to tacitly accept that community protection is the only significant value that ought to guide practitioners in their work. Such ethical blindness is likely to result in poor practice and at the very least culpable negligence, and at the worst demeaning or harmful actions.

A fourth general implication for intervention relates to the detection of practical identities and the various primary goods that reside at the heart of such identities. According to the GLM-D, there are the following relationships between practical identities and subsequent sexually abusive and nonoffending actions. First, practical identities are shaped by social, cultural, and personal experiences that confront individuals during the course of their lives. Second, practical identities are constructed or "wrapped" around particular primary goods, for example, the good of knowledge arguably resides at the center of the practical identity of a researcher, or, in a more deviant case, a gang member who plans crimes (Whitehead et al., 2007). Third, practical identities are constituted by secondary goods and their associated practices, which are linked by a specific theme (reflecting the primary good). Thus, a researcher belongs to a specific discipline and has various tasks and assigned roles such as carefully designing and carrying out studies, analyzing the results, communicating the results to colleagues, and so on. An offending-related example might be a practical identity as an "enforcer" of gang norms and directives. Typically individuals will have a number of practical identities but one is likely to be more significant because it reflects the primary good that is most heavily endorsed or weighted by the person. If the identity and thus access to such a good is removed, there will probably be experiences of alienation, loss of meaning, and weakening of psychological and social integrity. Fourth, practical identities and their associated tasks and strategies for securing primary goods are translated into concrete actions in particular contexts. For example a researcher may feed data into a statistical package or a gang member might threaten an errant member with violence if he does not comply with gang rules. There is a need for individuals to *strive* to create unified lives because of inevitable conflicts between their various practical identities (Korsgaard, 2009). The possibility of constructing a unified self requires reflectiveness and agency capacities, all hopefully directed toward the primary values a person weights most highly and the ways they are sought. A lack of unity may result in fragmentation of identity, which in turn could lead to a loss of dignity and problematic actions such as substance abuse or sexual offenses. From the GLM-D standpoint, an important goal of offender interventions is to exploit or create turning points that arise from practical identity conflicts or frustrations.

Because the GLM-D is founded on the above assumptions it aims to *instill or repair* offenders' agency conditions by way of basic therapeutic interventions. When these conditions are already present it seeks to create the conditions for the *exercise* of agency by way of making available or taking advantage of opportunities that are linked to the adaptive expression of practical identities (secondary goods and practices). For example, a gang member whose primary identity is that of an offense planner could be provided with, and may choose to take up, an opportunity to study at a local educational institution.

Finally, correctional practitioners seek to determine what practical identities and their associated good are endorsed by the offender, what GLP captures these concerns most comprehensively, and how best to take advantage of natural desistance processes. Responding to the above questions also means that practitioners have to ascertain what psychological and social capital is required for a particular offender and what actors are needed to enable the GLP to be effectively implemented. A key assumption is of the interdependence of human beings and the fact that actions take place within a social context and involve combinations of internal and external resources.

Three general possibilities exist with respect to GLM-D-oriented practice:

1. Desistance factors such as a job, relationship, education, and so on may be available to an offender already. Possibly some degree of brokering by correctional practitioners with family and community agencies might be necessary, but there is no requirement for specialized sex offender therapy.
2. Some intervention may be needed to enable the offender to take advantage of desistance opportunities but this is more along the lines of repair or "recalibrating" (i.e., learning how to apply intact skills in different contexts or with some minor changes).
3. Intensive intervention work is required to instill the internal and external conditions required for an offender to be able to formulate and execute his GLP within a specific context. Typically in such cases, offenders lack important psychological capabilities and/or social supports and opportunities. In effect, therapy *artificially* assists normal socialization and engagement processes that members of the other two groups are able to enlist without much help.

For all three possibilities, the aim is to assist offenders to exercise agency and take opportunities in the social world to turn their lives around. The difference is that for the first group of offenders the experience of being in prison and the various consequences this entails function as turning points and causes them to critically reflect upon their values and actions (and identities) and consider the possibility of committing themselves to crime-free lives. The availability of friends, employment opportunities, and so on allows such offenders to transition into more generative lives. However, offenders belonging to the second and third groups need greater input from practitioners in the creation of psychological and/or social capital. Such therapeutic initiatives might involve family work, creating job placements, or providing educational opportunities as well as cognitive-behavioral skill training. At the heart of all three types of reentry and reintegration work is a view of practical reasoning based on the pursuit of valued outcomes in ways that reflect practical identities and social opportunities. Thus, the possession and exercise of agency capabilities that allow a person to decide how he or she wants to live is viewed by GLM-D as a necessary condition in seeking redemption and in adopting an offense-free life.

In the following description of GLM-D interventions with sex offenders we will be careful to distinguish among the three groups and their respective needs. Furthermore, our intention is to utilize assessment and intervention ideas derived from criminologically inclined desistance research presented in Chapter 13.

## Assessment

The purpose of GLM-D-guided assessment of sex offenders is to formulate a set of suggestions for intervention that take the form of a GLP. A GLP is essentially an offender's plan or conception for living that takes into account what he values and hopes to attain, his associated practical identities, and what will hopefully assist in enhancing his levels of well-being and sense of meaning. The GLP (or in therapeutic terms, a case formulation) also takes into account static and dynamic risk, criminogenic needs, self-regulation pathway, responsivity concerns, and other pertinent individual factors in order to construct a treatment plan that is individualized to the particular needs, preferences, lifestyles, and personal identities of offenders. This is pretty much state-of-the-art, accepted best practice in the field and we certainly acknowledge the importance of subjecting offenders to a thorough assessment process (Beech, Craig, & Browne, 2009; Craig et al., 2008; Marshall, Marshall, Serran, & Fernandez, 2006; Ward et al., 2006, 2007; Yates, 2007; Yates & Ward, 2008). We intentionally do not refer to the GLP as a *treatment plan* because some individuals will not participate in therapy programs, and additionally, even those who do will also receive desistance-oriented interventions that could not be considered to involve treatment in any meaningful sense of that term (e.g., attending a job training course, joining a sports club). The aim of the GLP is to provide a comprehensive understanding and conceptual model of individual offenders' practical identities, goals with respect to these identities, pathway to offending (direct or indirect), goals with respect to offending, risk factors, internal and external capabilities and constraints, and the interrelationships between these factors that will direct intervention and function as a guide for implementation. The GLP should also take into account relevant environments and specify the internal (e.g., competencies, beliefs) and external (e.g., opportunities, social environment) conditions required to achieve primary goods and to manage risk. The plan also explicitly includes dynamic risk factors and ways to target them, offense pathway and attendant intervention needs, and follow-up intervention and supervision needs with respect to both risk management and the acquisition and maintenance of good lives (Yates, 2007; Yates & Ward, 2008).

The basic steps in this process are described below. It is noted that this GLP, while constructed by the practitioner based on assessment, is developed in a collaborative manner with the offender in the form of mutual goal setting, particularly with respect to intervention targets and the development of a plan. It is suggested that such collaboration will increase engagement with intervention and can be revisited with individuals periodically to evaluate their progress and to ensure the relevance of the plan.

### Detection of Offending-Related Phenomena

The *first phase* in the GLP conceptualization process concerns the detection of the clinical and broader physical, social, psychological, and environmental phenomena implicated in individuals' sexual offending. In other words, what kind of problems and issues do they present with and what criminogenic needs or dynamic risk factors are evident? To accomplish this assessment, we recommend utilization of empirically validated assessment instruments that cover the range of desistance, risk, and psychological factors, which will assist in both determining the appropriate type and intensity level of intervention and the criminogenic needs to be addressed in any specialized treatment program (Beech et al., 2009; Craig at al., 2008; Marshall, Marshall, et al., 2006). Laub and Sampson's (2003) *Life History Calendar* (see Figure 6.2 in Chapter 6) may be a useful way of collecting information on the critical features of an offender's life course. The *Life History Calendar* will also be useful in making a determination of the point(s) at which natural desistance begins. The *Life History Calendar* should be periodically updated. Grasmick et al.'s (1993) measure of self-control will provide data on self-regulation capacity. Dynamic risk factors (criminogenic needs) empirically related to recidivism include such factors as negative social influences, antisocial lifestyle, intimacy deficits, problems with general self-regulation (e.g., problem solving, impulsivity, emotion regulation), cognitive distortions, sexual self-regulation deficits (e.g., deviant sexual interest, problematic hypersexuality), and lack of cooperation with supervision (Hanson, Harris, Scott, & Helmus, 2007; Hanson & Morton-Bourgon, 2005; Ward & Beech, 2004). Criminogenic and noncriminogenic factors associated with responsivity issues and that influence engagement with treatment, such as attachment problems and problems with self-esteem, motivation, learning styles, cognitive abilities, language, personality, and culture (Andrews & Bonta, 2007; Marshall, Marshall, et al., 2006; Serin & Kennedy, 1997), are also assessed. It is also important to inquire into an offender's employment status and skills, his access to social supports, his ability to engage and maintain social and intimate relationships, whether he has strong community links, and who cares about him. The degree to which these factors are present will vary from case to case, and thus each requires comprehensive assessment and inclusion in GLP formulation and intervention planning. Finally, any additional clinical phenomena, such as mental disorder, personality disorder, psychological functioning, and the like are also assessed and included in the GLP.

An important element of this first phase of GLM-D assessment is to seek the presence of data indicating the offender is experiencing a turning point in his criminal career. The existence of a turning point indicates dissonance or conflict between an individual's criminal behavior and some aspect of his or her practical identity. Furthermore, the nature of a crisis point ought to reflect factors such as the age and gender of the offender. It is probable that a young female with a child will be more receptive to desistance opportunities than a young single male (McNeill et al., 2005). This is because of the conflict between her valued identity as a mother based on the primary good of relatedness and its expression in caregiving actions and her identity as a criminal. Arguably, it is conflict between endorsed practical identities and aspects of offending behavior that constitute turning-point situations. For a male offender, conflict might occur between his valued identity as a worker and the mastery experiences this gives him and a threatened loss of liberty and income due to his sexual offending. A significant consequence of being convicted of sexual crimes may well be unemployment and social stigmatization, and subsequent difficulty in providing for his family financially.

In conclusion, this part of the assessment process is designed to simply catalogue the various difficulties and problems evident within a person's life and is essentially descriptive in nature and relatively superficial. In subsequent phases there is an attempt to ascertain what specific practical identities are most important and what particular flaws are evident in an offender's offense-related GLP.

### *Practical Identities: Identification of Offense-Related Primary Goods*

In the *second phase* of the GLP assessment process, the function of offending (i.e., what the individual expected to achieve via offending) is established through the identification of primary goods that are directly or indirectly linked to a person's sexually abusive actions. In addition, the identification of the *overarching good* or value around which the other goods are oriented should also be ascertained. The overarching good informs therapists about what is most important in a person's life and hints at his fundamental commitments. It is strongly constitutive of his practical identity and is a useful way of illuminating how the person sees himself and the world. For example, for one offender, the pursuit of mastery might be his major good (e.g., linked to his employment), while for another it could be the experience of emotional intimacy (e.g., linked to being in a relationship, being a husband). The search for the most heavily weighted goods occurs via an analysis of the themes evident in offending as well as the person's lifestyle around the time of his offending. As stated earlier, such primary goods are "wrapped around" practical identities that glue together or integrate abstract values (primary goods), their expression in concrete practices, and their component actions. Individuals may weight more than one primary good highly, which would be incorporated into the GLP.

The primary method for obtaining information concerning sex offender's primary goods and their associated practical identities is via a structured assessment interview. We have provided detail on the nature of a GLM assessment in a recent monograph and will only make a few general comments here (see Yates, Kingston, & Ward, 2009). Although there are no self-report questionnaires available at present for coding goods, we suggest using a number of structured interview guides and rating scales (e.g., *The Goods Coding Protocol,* Yates et al., 2009).

The *Life Story Interview* (McAdams, 1995; Maruna, 2001), modified as suggested in Chapter 12, is a rich source of data for both past practical identities and hoped-for or feared future ones (we will comment on a coding protocol and a goods table later). Also at this step, if appropriate, offending behavior is evaluated using the nine-phase self-regulation model in order to determine what the individual seeks to achieve via offending, their offense-related goals and strategies, their dynamic risk factors, and the link between these and good lives goals (see Yates, Kingston, & Ward, 2009). The self-regulation model is a theoretically derived, empirically supported analysis of the offense-and-relapse process and describes the cognitive, emotional, behavioral, social, and contextual elements of offending (Ward & Hudson, 2000). Taken together, this provides for a comprehensive understanding of offense dynamics and self-regulation capacity, and forms the foundation of any treatment if this is needed. Thus, at this step, the aim is to identify an offender's core values and commitments, to ascertain their relationship to offending and more broadly to their role within the individual's life, and to link these to self-regulation and risk factors.

By this stage in the assessment process the practitioner should have a strong sense of the reasons why the person committed an offense, his level of risk, the flaws in his GLP at the time of his offending, whether or not the link between his pursuit of primary goods is directly or indirectly connected to offending, offense pathway, offense-related goals and strategies, self-regulation styles and capacities, dynamic risk factors, and any other clinical phenomena requiring intervention. We propose that offenders following the *direct* route to sexual offending are likely to have entrenched offense-supportive beliefs and approach goals, to have marked deficits in their psychosocial functioning, and to follow an approach pathway to offending. They are also likely to be assessed as higher risk to reoffend (Yates & Kingston, 2005, 2006; Yates, 2003), reflecting a lengthy history of sexual offending. By way of contrast, individuals following the indirect route are more likely to be assessed as moderate or lower risk, to have more circumscribed psychological problems (Purvis, 2005; Ward & Gannon, 2006), and to follow an avoidant pathway to offending (Yates & Kingston, 2005, 2006; Yates, Kingston, & Ward, 2009; Yates, 2003).

In order to simplify the process of identifying the nature of an offender's GLP, clinical phenomena implicated in offending, self-regulation capacity, GLP flaws, and dynamic risk factors, we have developed rating scales for each good and also adapted a table derived from research on sexual offenders' goals and good lives conceptions (Purvis, 2005; Yates et al., 2009). These instruments have been found to be extremely helpful in providing an overview of relevant issues and to integrate data derived from coding GLM goods in order to construct a GLP.

The assessment of the 10 primary human goods contained in the GLM (see Chapter 13 and Figure 15.1) is conducted using a semistructured interview and GLM coding protocols (Yates, Kingston, & Ward, 2009). Coding primary human goods begins with evaluating the overall importance of the particular good to the individual. We specify the most common indicators for each good in the GLM coding protocols but allow for the inclusion of unique individual factors. Using coding sheets, the practitioner indicates those primary human goods the individual indicates that he values overall in his life, their relevance for offending, and the various means used by the individual to seek them.

| SCOPE of GOODS SOUGHT | PROBLEMS IN CAPACITY | | MEANS | ASSOCIATED DYNAMIC RISK FACTORS | RELATIONSHIP to OFFENDING Direct/Indirect |
|---|---|---|---|---|---|
| | Internal Obstacles | External Obstacles | | | |
| Life | | | | | |
| Knowledge | | | | | |
| Excellence in Play and Work | | | | | |
| Agency | | | | | |
| Inner Peace | | | | | |
| Relatedness | | | | | |
| Community | | | | | |
| Spirituality | | | | | |
| Happiness | | | | | |
| Creativity | | | | | |

**COHERENCE/CONFLICT:**
**Major source of conflict:**

**OFFENSE PATHWAY:**

**LIFE PLAN**
**(Implicit or Explicit):**

**GOODS NOT SOUGHT:**

**GOODS WITH NO MEANS/AVENUES:**

**FIGURE 15.1.** GLM coding sheet. From Yates, Kingston, and Ward (2009). Copyright 2009 by Pacific Psychological Assessment Corporation. Reprinted by permission.

The GLM coding sheet contains columns reflecting the problems described previously with respect to the implementation of the GLP (i.e., scope, means, capacities, and conflict/coherence), direct/indirect pathways, and a variable number of rows depending on the number of primary goods discerned in an offender's life at the time of his offense. In the first column of the table, "scope of goods sought," the evaluator documents all the major goods and indicates those that are evident in an individual's offending behavior and in his lifestyle during the months leading up to and at the time of offending, based on information gathered from assessment. If possible, it is important that the primary goods most endorsed or heavily weighted by the offender be identified, as these goods will be the subject of intensive therapeutic attention. Primary goods that are missing (i.e., that are not evident or were not stated by the offender) are listed at the bottom of the table and are labeled as such. In the second column, "problems in capacity," the *internal* (e.g., skill deficits) and *external* (e.g., lack of supports) obstacles that are responsible for failure to achieve the primary human goods in a socially acceptable and personally satisfying manner are documented. Examples of internal obstacles include distrust of adults, deviant sexual preferences, impulsivity, intimacy deficits, poor conflict resolution skills, poor self-regulation skills, attachment issues, and so on. External obstacles include stigmatization, interpersonal rejection, poor social supports, lack of employment opportunities, bullying, employer expectations, antisocial peer groups, and so on. In the third column, "means," the evaluator describes the strategies used by the offender to seek each good that is sought or evident. In the fourth column, criminogenic needs or dynamic risk factors associated with goods acquisition are noted. In the final column, "relationship to offending," the evaluator notes, for each primary good, whether the good is *directly* or *indirectly* related to offending. This entails establishing whether goals reflecting the content of a primary good are actively sought by an offender when planning and committing an offense (e.g., intimacy, retribution, emotional relief), or whether goals are indirectly involved (e.g., overworking in service of mastery goals resulting in stress, substance abuse and subsequent sexual offending). Finally, at the bottom of the table, the evaluator records the presence of specific goal conflicts within an offender's GLP or conception, along with the source of the conflict. For example, conflict between the way the goods of relatedness and agency are sought could indicate that an individual is overly controlling or, by contrast, unduly submissive.

In brief, the aim of this point of the assessment process is to identify and describe offenders' practical identities (and associated goods) that were associated with their offending-related actions and lifestyle at the time of offending. Thus the focus is a *backward-looking* one, intended to retrospectively explain what values were guiding an individual's sexually abusive actions and what forms of living and identities these values were reflected in.

### *Selection of Practical Identities: Looking to the Future*

In the *third phase* of the GLP formulation process, the selection of the overarching good(s) or value(s) around which the other goods are oriented is identified and made a focus of the subsequent GLP. The aim at this phase is to begin the transition from viewing the goods in an explanatory way with respect to their functions in the offense process to one of lifestyle planning. That is, rather than being simply backward-looking, there is now an emphasis on looking toward a possible future life for the offender, that is, the focus is *forward-looking*. Having understood that a person's major commitments relate to certain values such as relationships or service to the community, the aim is to use these for intervention planning. This involves specifying the component skills associated with a primary good and the conditions required to allow the skills to be instituted in everyday life. In other words, the task at this phase of the development of a GLP is to begin thinking about how a primary good could be fashioned into a practical identity. As discussed in Chapter 14, because human beings are in part self-constituting beings what is required at this point is the determination of practical identities that specify secondary goods and their related roles in some detail. An example of this process involves learning the constituent skills of achieving intimacy in a caring relationship and adopting the practical identity of a lover. The constituent skills of being a lover/romantic partner include listening, expressing one's needs, and spending time with one's partner. However, in order to achieve the goods comprising intimacy, offenders will also need to possess certain other capacities and opportunities, such as the ability to regulate emotions and the opportunity to spend time and engage in activities that will generate intimacy. Thus, the focus at the third phase is to establish the general components of each primary good and the internal and external resources needed to secure the good, and to incorporate these factors into a viable practical identity or, possibly, identities.

It is especially important when working with offenders to create new ways of achieving valued goods, and thus establishing new practical identities, to exploit any "turning points" that may exist. Moreover, the use of motivational interviewing techniques might prove helpful in creating turning points, or, at the very least, amplifying any doubts offender may have about their criminal actions and their place in their lives (McMurran, 2002). From a desistance perspective, social capital such as education, relationship, and work possibilities are likely to be inherently motivating for offenders and also woven into the fabric of everyday life. This important point reminds practitioners not to look for generic solutions to offenders' arrays of problems but rather to seek to anchor their GLP's within local communities, ones that are hopefully accepting of them, and ideally, that contain allies and friends (see Chapters 4, 5, 6, 9, and 10).

### *Social Ecologies and Practical Identities: Taking Context into Account*

In the *fourth phase*, a greater level of detail is added and the selection of secondary goods or values that specify how the primary goods are translated into practical identities and ways of living is completed. In this phase, identification of the contexts or environments in which the person is likely to be living while in the community or postrelease is conducted. This ecological aspect of the GLM-D is strongly supported by its etiological assumptions concerning the relationship between human beings and the contexts in which they live their lives. The fourth phase also ensures that the intervention plan and expected outcomes are personally relevant to individuals and the contexts in which they live, including the opportunities and limitations that will be present, thus ensuring that the GLP is relevant, realistic, and achievable.

Thus, having determined the primary good, the constituent skills needed to secure the good, and its relationship to a practical identity (wrapped around the primary good), detailed planning is undertaken in order to specify the specific contexts and requirements relevant for an offender. For example, this step involves determining such information as the types of relationships possible, the kind of work that is available, or the particular range of leisure activities that could be undertaken. This information is also integrated with data concerning dynamic risk factors. At this point, the developing GLP will include specific interventions for targeting criminogenic needs and for skill development. For example, specifying what kind of personal relationships would be appropriate, beneficial, and satisfying to the offender are identified, and strategies and interventions to assist the individual to achieve these goals are elucidated.

It is noted that it is not possible to engage in the detailed intervention planning required at the fourth step until an analysis of the overarching goods (most heavily weighted goods) and the internal and external conditions that make them possible has been undertaken in the previous steps. Primary goods are abstract but essentially constitute the heart of a person's practical identity. It is necessary to have a firm grasp of what primary goods are most important to a person before flesh can be put onto the bones of a possible new life (and new reshaped identity). However, although conceptually distinct, in practice, the third and fourth steps are closely linked. Maruna (2001) and Giordano et al. (2002) stress that the transformation of self-narratives for successful desistance is particularly germane at this phase of the intervention planning process.

### Formulation of a Detailed GLP

In the *fifth phase*, the therapist constructs a detailed GLP for the offender based on the above considerations and information. Thus taking into account the kind of life that would be fulfilling and meaningful to the individual (i.e., primary goods, practical identities, secondary goods, and their relationship to possible environments), the practitioner notes the capabilities or competencies the individual requires in order to have a reasonable chance of putting the plan into action. This GLP fully integrates intervention targets and risk management plans in a comprehensive manner. To recall, dynamic risk factors can be conceptualized as flaws in offenders' (typically implicit) offense- related GLP, more specifically in terms of problems with scope, means, coherence, or capacity (internal and external).

An exploration of a sexual offender's good lives conception can assist practitioners to formulate an intervention plan that provides the opportunity for individuals to achieve greater satisfaction and well-being, alongside planning for risk management. If the offender is able to understand how the GLP will directly benefit him in terms of goods and their associated identities that he values, he will be more likely to engage with, and invest in, intervention. Increased engagement with practitioners can lead to reduced dropout rates, which is particularly important given that offenders who do not complete treatment reoffend at higher rates than those who do (Hanson & Bussière, 1998; Hanson et al., 2002).

## Intervention

To reiterate our earlier point, the GLM-D is a *rehabilitation* theory and not a *therapy* model. It functions to provide practitioners with guidance concerning the overall purposes of intervention, how specific programs should be constructed and implemented, and what kind of relationships ought to be cultivated with the offender. As a strength-based perspective, the GLM-D is committed to using cognitive and behavioral techniques to establish competencies that will aid an individual to put into action, and maintain, a GLP that he has endorsed and helped to formulate. Thus, skill acquisition is always in the service of building social and psychological resources and never solely focused on risk or problem reduction. The practice relationship ought to be collaborative and founded on mutual respect. Furthermore, because the purpose of intervention is to strengthen, repair, or create the capacity for agency in ways that balance offenders' and members of the community's interests, it follows that any GLP will address risk concerns. Given the desistance and ecological orientation of the GLM-D, reentry and reintegration are at the forefront of correctional practitioners' minds from the beginning of the assessment process. The GLP developed for an individual will be individually tailored, will be cohesive and holistic in nature, will seek to provide a conduit between aspects of his past and future, and will also integrate the various primary goods. All the various goods ought to be built into a GLP although it is to be expected that people will vary with respect to the good (and practical identities) they weight most heavily. All the primary goods are required as they are thought to be necessary to establish and maintain the necessary well-being and freedom conditions for agency to be possible within a community of fellow human beings, who have similar needs and their own aspirations.

Once a GLP has been constructed, the nature and degree of offenders' offense-related and more general problems will be evident. Armed with this understanding of an individual's values and their relationship to his offending, and furthermore, his aspirations for his future life, it should be relatively easy to work out the right combination of desistance and program interventions. The division of sex offenders into three types of desistance/therapy groups described earlier is only intended to perform a heuristic function and to assist practitioners to think clearly and systematically about how best to proceed. The decision to identify three possible groups was done for illustrative purposes only—in fact there may be more than three. The crucial point we wanted to make is that sex offenders vary with respect to the combination of desistance and standard therapeutic input they require. However, we will use the three-group classification in the rest of this chapter for ease of discussion.

In the first group, offenders who require little in the way of therapeutic assistance are likely to already possess reasonable amounts of psychological and social capital. Practitioners would do best to utilize community agencies and people who are keen to support the offender. Some family meetings and sessions may be helpful to reestablish communication between members of the family and friends, and to share the offender's GLP and work though its implications.

Individuals in the second group with respect to the balance between desistance and traditional sex offender therapy may need some help to be able to take advantage of employment or other opportunities to reenter the community. Offenders within this group may have some functional deficits, for example, impoverished intimacy skills or difficulties with problem solving. However, such deficits are thought to be receptive to relatively modest amounts of intervention and are probably due to the social and psychological consequences of being convicted and sentenced for a sexual offense.

The final group of sex offenders are likely to have varying combinations of profound social alienation and psychological dysfunction. For example, they may have entrenched deviant sexual preferences, exhibit high levels of impulsivity, experience difficulties in identifying and managing emotional states, and hold beliefs about themselves and others that make it harder for them to accept responsibility and to reenter and be ultimately reaccepted into the community (Beech et al., 2009; Marshall, Marshall, et al. 2006; Yates, 2003; Yates, Kingston, & Ward, 2009).

Before describing GLM-D interventions in greater detail by way of three case studies we will briefly discus the relationship between risk level and allocation into desistance/therapy groups. It seems reasonable to assume that the greater the number and severity of dynamic risk factors (e.g., intimacy deficits, deviant sexual preferences, self-regulation deficits) present, the more likely an individual will require intensive specialized sex offender treatment rather than just social and employment interventions (Craig et al., 2008). If this is the case, then the three desistance/therapy groups described earlier should neatly map onto levels of risk, perhaps low to high. However, it is not clear that this follows at all mainly because risk has contextual and dynamic aspects as well as structural ones (Craig et al., 2008). What we mean by this is that if one analyzes risk in terms of the flaws related to an individual's GLP, then while some problems can be unpacked in terms of psychological deficits (e.g., intimacy deficits, deviant sexual preferences), others directly refer to more contextual factors such as poor supervisory relationships, unemployment, or associating with antisocial peers. Therefore, if aspects of the environment are changed in a positive direction, it would seem logical to expect aspects of risk would be similarly affected and an individual's risk level lowered. Once the ecological nature of the self is emphasized the assumption that high-risk individuals ought to undergo psychological (i.e., CBT) therapy is less compelling. It may well be the case that even high risk individuals could benefit more from desistance-type interventions such as establishing new relationships or obtaining employment than individual therapeutic work on their deviant characteristics. In our view, ultimately the decision about the balance of desistance and treatment components in a sex offender's GLP depends on the match between his psychological and social capital. If a person has strong social supports, meaningful job opportunities, a caring partner, and importantly, a commitment to a new practical identity, level of risk might not be so relevant when it comes to considering options for intervention. What is important is that it should be clear in principle and true in practice that a GLP builds and sustains internal and external resources (psychological and social capital in desistance terms) and by doing this, changes or reduces dynamic risk. It is a question of how best to achieve this.

We would now like to demonstrate how a GLM-D approach to working with sex offenders could be undertaken by discussing three case studies. The case studies represent composites of real clients rather than being based on a single individual. Although they are fairly straightforward and possibly overly easy examples of practice situations they serve their purpose of demonstrating how interventions guided by the GLM-D could work. We will follow the various phases outlined earlier and also keep in mind the desirable balance between desistance versus therapy components when reviewing each case.

## Case Study 1: Peter the Tennis Coach

### *Brief Description*

Peter is a 33-year-old, single male who was convicted of sexually molesting two teenage girls while giving them tennis lessons. He caressed their breasts and thighs during coaching session. He received a short jail sentence and has just been referred to a sex offender treatment service for assessment and possible delivery of treatment. Peter is a trained tennis coach and by all accounts is extremely good at his job. He prides himself on his ability to engage with his students and views himself as a born teacher with a strong vocation. Peter has no previous criminal convictions, is well liked in the community, and has many friends. He is intelligent, articulate, and willing to talk openly about his offenses. Peter appears remorseful and desperate to make amends for what he has done and is clearly devastated by the loss of his tennis coaching career. He stated that he "feels like I have been cut adrift, with no clear direction. . . . I feel empty."

### *Detection of Offending-Related Phenomena*

A comprehensive psychological and special assessment reveals that Peter is at low risk for further sexual offending and does not appear to have any significant psychological problems. He does have some mild degree of social anxiety but it is not clinically significant and is generally well managed. There is no evidence of deviant sexual interests. His offending pathway seems to be an approach one, and Peter stated that he was seeking physical affection when abusing the girls.

### *Practical Identities: Identification of Offense-Related Primary Goods*

Peter's practical identities revolve around his ability to be a good tennis coach and a caring person. The relevant primary goods appear to be mastery, service to the community, and relatedness. His GLP lacks sufficient *scope* because of his inattention to his own sexual and relationship needs. In addition, he tends to neglect the good of autonomy and often puts other peoples' problems and interests above his own. These problems point to some mild capacity problems with respect to assertiveness and communication. There are no other apparent flaws in his GLP. It seems apparent that there is a significant degree of dissonance in Peter and that he is acutely aware that his sexual offenses have threatened a valued aspect of his life, and ultimately who he is. This is a significant turning point in his life.

### *Selection of Practical Identities: Looking to the Future*

It is apparent that Peter is a gifted teacher and has a strong sense of duty to the community. The prospect of not being able to teach tennis again to young people is a real loss and has caused him to ruminate endlessly about his future and sense of self. From a practice perspective it would be ideal to help Peter establish a new practical identity based on the primary goods of teaching and community service while also broadening his pursuit of the other primary goods. In particular, attending to his mild social anxiety and helping him to establish relationship with adult females seems to be an important step in Peter's desistance journey.

### *Social Ecologies and Practical Identities: Taking Context into Account*

Peter cannot go back to tennis coaching because of the possibility that young people may be present at some time or another in the coaching situation. Despite the fact he is objectively at low risk, it is simply not a practical option. However, Peter's teaching gifts generalize to other areas: he is adept at teaching other subjects such as yoga, stress management, and reading. Assessment indicated that Peter has many supporters in his local community and an educational institution has agreed to admit him to a course on teaching literacy skills. Furthermore, a community agency that works with ex-offenders and immigrants has offered him part-time work once he has completed the course. An advantage of attending the educational institution is that Peter will be mixing with adults of his own age, including females, and will thus be exposed to prosocial adult values.

### *Formulation of a Detailed GLP*

Peter's GLP is built around two primary goods and their respective practical identities, mastery and service to the community. Concerning mastery, it was decided that taking into account Peter's love of teaching and his demonstrated ability, he would train as a teacher of literacy at a local education institution. This identity is one that Peter endorsed and it would also meet his need to be of service to his community given that he would be working with men who were struggling and down on their luck. In order to take full advantage of the training opportunity Peter agreed to work on his mild anxiety and assertiveness problems and to develop the confidence and ability to communicate more effectively with adult men and woman. He required relatively little specialized psychological therapy for his sexual offenses and most of the rehabilitation focus was on developing and strengthening his social and vocational relationships and opportunities.

## Case Study 2: Tim the Executive

### *Brief Description*

Tim is a 40-year-old married man who has been separated from his wife since his arrest for raping a fellow worker. He is an accountant by training, but in recent years has held a relatively high-level managerial position in a large retail company. Tim had been experiencing some work pressures and to cope started drinking more than he usually did. He had a tendency to be overly sensitive to criticism and what he considered to be unwarranted interference with his job and life by other people. His wife objected to his increased alcohol intake, and they started to argue more frequently about this as well as other domestic issues. Tim's response to the increased tension at home was to drink more. This caused him to struggle with the demands at work and he was given a formal warning by his boss following a series of errors. Ultimately his wife walked out on him. Tim's drinking gradually worsened to the point that he was demoted at work. After an office outing, Tim followed a fellow female worker whom he thought had insulted him into the parking lot and raped her. He was given a medium-length prison term.

### *Detection of Offending-Related Phenomena*

A comprehensive developmental, social, and psychological assessment revealed that Tim had a number of significant problems that appeared to be causally related to his sexual offending. His risk level was assessed as medium. He had the following criminogenic needs and additional problems: substance abuse (alcohol), emotional regulation problems, held demeaning attitudes toward women, and tended to be socially isolated. Before his recent difficulties at work Tim was held in high regard and his employers thought he would one day be promoted to a regional manager's position, reaching the top of the company. He had a few close male friends but his tendency to overwork meant that he saw them relatively infrequently. In the past he had been a good softball player and enjoyed the camaraderie of playing with a team.

### *Practical Identities: Identification of Offense-Related Primary Goods*

Tim's primary goods appeared to be mastery and autonomy. He resented being "told what to do" and had a low threshold for perceiving threats to his sense of autonomy. Although Tim was extremely competent at his job he was not satisfied with his level of performance or what he thought was a lack of recognition by others. The practical identities evident at the time of his offending were that of an expert business manager and an independent man who could cope with all manner of challenges on his own, a person who did not need others. It was apparent that Tim's life lacked the full range of goods, particularly those of relatedness, health, and leisure. In addition, his ability to control his anger was poor. For all of these primary goods Tim lacked effective ways to achieve them, and tended to use alcohol as a way of releasing tension. Furthermore, there was conflict between his desire to excel at his job and his desire to have a loving relationship. Tim's determination to stand up for himself whenever he thought he was being unfairly treated also led him to appear to be controlling and dominating at times. Although he was clearly unhappy with his life, he seemed ambivalent about change and was not convinced that he needed to.

### *Selection of Practical Identities: Looking to the Future*

Tim had lost his job upon conviction and there was little chance he would ever be able to work as an executive again. His marriage, however, was still intact, and his wife indicated a desire to try and make it work. Taking into account Tim's primary goods of mastery and autonomy and their previous presence in his manager role, it seemed sensible to use a work-related option as a key part in Tim's GLP. His training and skills as an accountant and his desire to work more independently provided a possible way forward. In terms of his identity as an autonomous person, it was decided that accepting his need to be independent was important, while equally important were attempting to build wider social networks and assisting him in developing greater communication skills within his close relationships.

### *Social Ecologies and Practical Identities: Taking Context into Account*

It happened that one of Tim's old softball friends had remained in contact during his imprisonment and was keen to help him get back on his feet. One way of helping Tim establish better community links and also help improve his relatedness experiences was by encouraging him to join his friend's softball team, which he agreed to do. Furthermore, a local church found Tim a voluntary position as a bookkeeper for a local charity, a one-person position where if he was successful could result in a permanent appointment for the church and its satellite agencies. One of the virtues of this position was that it resonated with Tim's desire for mastery and independence while also assisting him to become more sensitive to the needs of others. Members of the church and the softball team could provide Tim with additional support and also give him time to develop his sense of masculinity in an informal and nonthreatening manner.

### *Formulation of a Detailed GLP*

Tim's formal GLP placed the voluntary position and its association with his need for work-related mastery and independence at its center and also gave a prominent role to his involvement with the softball team. It was felt that both of these secondary goods and their associated practical identities directly mapped onto Tim's major goods and concerns, and also addressed a number of his other problems. His adversarial relationships with females and tendency to overreact to perceived threats to his sense of masculinity and autonomy were likely to be gently confronted by his softball teammates. Working as a bookkeeper would introduce him to the broader church community and provide both Tim and his wife with much-needed support. The church also had a strong social orientation and would help Tim become less self-absorbed and more involved in the lives of others. Finally, all of the above, plus some specialized therapy to help with his emotional competency and relationships, should assist him to improve his marriage. Tim was an active participant in the construction and implementation of his GLP and while still struggling to accept full responsibility for his sexual offending, he was fully engaged in his reentry and reintegration process.

## Case Study 3: Sam the Gang Member

### *Brief Description*

Sam is a 42-year-old member of a Native American gang who has a long criminal history and several past periods of imprisonment for assault, rape, and robbery. His most recent sentence was for rape of a young woman and an assault on her boyfriend. He was recently released on parole and is still associating with gang members. His role in the gang is "intelligence officer," essentially the person who plans all the gang's criminal activities and gathers information and resources necessary to carry out the crimes. Sam had attended several RNR-type programs in the past, without much success. He had spent much of the last 25 years in prison or on parole. He was estranged from his family (father, mother, four siblings) and had several children with a partner, from whom he was now separated.

### *Detection of Offending-Related Phenomena*

Sam underwent a comprehensive psychological and social assessment that revealed a significant number of criminogenic needs and more general problems, and also determined that he was at high risk. The specific problems identified were substance abuse, attitudes and beliefs supportive of both sexual and nonsexual offending, high levels of aggression and anger, gang membership (with known criminal activities), alienation from his Native American tribe and culture, and lack of intimacy. Sam was a highly intelligent self-educated individual who read widely about Native American history and culture. He seemed dissatisfied about his current lifestyle but felt that he had few realistic options for change.

### *Practical Identities: Identification of Offense-Related Primary Goods*

Sam's central primary goods were those of knowledge and community. He enjoyed the planning aspect of his role in the gang, and was meticulous in gathering and analyzing information relating to a crime. Furthermore, he read widely on American history and researched his cultural heritage. From Sam's perspective, he was a thinker and planner, something he enjoyed for its own sake although there were also elements of mastery evident as well. In addition, he obtained a sense of belonging through being a member of the gang which he described as a brotherhood, "being part of a community." Identifying as Native American was of particular importance to Sam although he was unable to speak the language of and lacked formal ties with his tribe. Thus Sam's two primary practical identities were being an intellectual, a strategic thinker, and being part of a Native American fellowship. It was evident that Sam was at a turning point as he had started to feel frustrated over the narrowness of his gang role and distressed at the violent nature of his community and their relationships with others and between themselves. The primary flaws in his offense-related GLP were those of conflict between his pleasure in knowing and the narrowness of his role and a lack of formal opportunities to explore his cultural heritage. Furthermore, he still had problems controlling his anger at times and found it difficult to regulate his drug taking (capacity problems).

### *Selection of Practical Identities: Looking to the Future*

When asked about his future aspirations, Sam replied that he had always wanted to attend a university to study Native American culture and history, and also wished that he was in a stable and loving relationship with a woman. It was clear that continued membership in the gang was a significant constraint in advancing his endorsed primary goods of community, knowledge, and relatedness. Sam was desperate to turn his life around and was sick of being in and out of prison and of having relationships undercut by fear and lack of commitment.

### *Social Ecologies and Practical Identities: Taking Context into Account*

The dean of arts at the local university was willing to enroll Sam in a preparatory university course and if he was successful allow him to enroll full time. A condition of this enrollment was that he did not wear his gang patch on campus, did not attend classes intoxicated or high, and did not behave in a threatening or violent manner. Furthermore, Sam was introduced to a Native American support group which contained a number of mature students like himself. Around this time he decided to leave the gang and after some initial problems was allowed to do so. Another possibility was that he would renew contact with his tribe through a fellow student at the university.

### *Formulation of a Detailed GLP*

Sam's GLP explicitly linked the goods of knowledge, community, and relatedness to his practical identities (secondary goods and contexts) of being a university student and member of the university and other local Native American support and cultural groups. He learned how to manage his anger and his alcohol and drug use, and to apply more adaptive norms and beliefs when dealing with people during therapy he received from a correctional psychologist. This work built upon his past participation in RNR violence programs but because they were recruited in the service of goals he was committed to, were more eagerly utilized by Sam. It was anticipated that he would cultivate social and even romantic relationships with the nongang people he mixed with in the various support groups he attended, possibly taking up the numerous opportunities to join in recreational and sporting activities. The whole range of primary goods was built into Sam's GLP with an emphasis being on the two primary practical identities of a Native American history and culture student and being a member of a Native American community and tribe.

## Comments on the Case Studies

A notable feature of the three case studies is that from the viewpoint of the GLM-D there no such thing as psychological therapy without a significant degree of desistance-oriented interventions, even with high-risk individuals. Effective interventions always involve the reintegration of offenders into the community. The various skills they acquire while in therapy help in this process. Social, intimacy, self-regulation, problem-solving, sexual regulation, and emotional management skills work by enhancing individuals' agency capacity and therefore allowing them to build lives that align with their needs and core commitments. As we saw in the case of Sam, arguably most of the decisive rehabilitation work was done outside the therapy room and in the community with the assistance of friends, community agencies, and educational personnel. Essentially this rehabilitation work involved the utilization of social and cultural resources, or social capital. Psychological interventions were useful in all three cases but their role was to facilitate reentry and reintegration processes rather than such processes following on from intensive therapy, as is the case in traditional sex offender therapy. In our view, it is typically assumed that major changes occur to people when they are participating in programs in prisons or within correctional agencies, and that social support and employment opportunities that occur after therapy simply reinforce or entrench these gains. This is an extremely important point and gets to the center of what desistance theory and research can offer: psychological interventions work because they help individuals to formulate and implement their GLP in their local environments. In our view, arguing that program-induced change is the critical event and subsequent reentry and reintegration follows from this fact is the tail wagging the dog. Desistance research has consistently shown that important life events such as obtaining a job, getting married, having supportive peers, and receiving training or an education are decisive factors in individuals desisting from crime (see Chapters 4, 5, 6, 9, and 10). Furthermore, while the outcome literature in the general and sex offending domains indicates that RNR intervention programs can be effective, it does not satisfactorily explain why this is the case or how such changes occur (see Chapter 8). We propose that such changes occur because individuals have sufficient psychological and social capital to put their GLP into action. The successful implementation of a GLP requires reflective endorsement by an offender, the possession of the necessary competencies, and the availability of social opportunities.

The three case examples touch upon a number of other issues that we will briefly comment on. First, they demonstrate how it is possible to develop a coherent, concrete GLP that reduces risk factors by establishing offender competencies and opportunities for a better life. Second, the case studies indicate how such plans can motivate offenders because they are rooted in practical identities, and their embedded primary goods, that are truly valued and give life meaning. Finally, the case studies reveal the importance of respecting offenders' agency and actively working with them to develop a GLP. Such respect is more likely to result in a strong alliance with offenders and can add additional value to intervention efforts in terms of increased efficacy (see Leibrich, 1994; Marshall et al., 2003; McMurran, 2002; McNeill, 2006). The literature on the importance of the therapeutic alliance and common factors in therapy speaks to the importance of "common factors" and therapist factors, all likely to be enhanced with the use of the GLM-D. All of the above factors find support in the desistance literature and point to a need to work with sex offenders in ways that are less focused on psychopathology and more concerned with social facilitation and the establishment of capabilities required to help them resume their place within the community.

## Desistance without Treatment: Capitalizing on Natural Desistance

The three case studies above all involve the delivery of therapeutic elements alongside the experience of desistance interventions. This is because most of the work correctional practitioners undertake has prominent treatment aspects. We have questioned the assumption, apparent in some clinicians, that the most effective way to reduce recidivism rates is by delivering empirically supported interventions in "doses" that match offenders' level of risk. In all of the case studies, interventions that were intended to increase offenders' social capital such as vocational training, family work, community liaison, and so on play crucial roles in the reentry and reintegration process. All well and good, we stand by these assertions and observations.

However, the research literature indicates that there are many situations where the natural desistance process proceeds relatively smoothly without any input from psychologists or social workers, or participation in treatment programs on the behalf of offenders (see Chapters 4, 5, and 6). In these situation what role, if any, should correctional practitioners have? We will briefly consider two examples of natural desistance and make suggestions about how practitioners might strengthen or promote such processes.

The first example is where an offender has been given employment in a trade or occupation that he finds worthwhile and satisfying (Sampson & Laub, 1993). Being employed offers a number of opportunities that individually or collectively can increase an offender's well-being and diminish his chances of recidivism. Access to constructive peer relationships can affirm the value of prosocial norms and also help the offender meet his needs for relatedness, mastery, and a sense of community or fellowship. Furthermore, a regular (lawfully acquired) income can help him to look after his family and also to purchase material and leisure goods that are inherently enjoyable. Psychological help with managing the inevitable conflict between colleagues or in assisting employers and workmates to understand the offender's occasional behavioral difficulties could prove useful. In all probability offenders in these situations would deal with their difficulties reasonably effectively but some further skills-based work could make these hiccups less stressful, and also reinforce their feeling of efficacy and self-worth. Knowing the age, gender, and possible criminal trajectory of individuals could also usefully inform the type and aims of the practitioners' actions and thus make them more precise and ecologically valid (Laub & Sampson, 2003).

A second example is connected to desistance research indicating that a strong romantic relationship such as marriage can cause an offender to reflect on his priorities and to reevaluate his aspirations and goals for the future in ways that excludes crime. Marriage appears to provide needed structure in an offender's life. Due to the fact that a newly married individual often changes address and even leaves neighborhoods, it is less likely that he would be in contact with antisocial peers. From the standpoint of the GLM-D, we would also add that establishing a strong marriage should meet an offender's intimacy and sexual needs and thus reduce the intensity of these particular criminogenic needs (Craig et al., 2008; Hanson & Morton-Bourgon, 2007). Just as ordinary couples can benefit from advice on communication skills and intimacy enhancement, we suggest that offenders and their partners might as well. Whether through community education, marriage guidance groups, or more specialized targeted sessions, it is probable that interventions of these types will accelerate or facilitate the desistance process.

In both the natural desistance examples described above, offenders were already benefiting from a number of social and vocational resources encountered within their local communities. We propose that in these kinds of scenarios, although not strictly necessary, the further refinement of psychological and social competencies could strengthen the process of reentry and reintegration.

## Conclusions

In this chapter we have discussed the application of the GLM-D to sexual offending assessment and treatment. Our aim was to provide an overview of the key features of such an approach rather than to describe it in detail. In our view, the GLM-D has the theoretical resources, range, depth, and flexibility to provide guidance for practitioners working both within and outside sex offender treatment programs. It can easily accommodate GLPs that are centered upon employment training or the creation of social relationships and community support structures. And its utility in clinical settings is without doubt and has been the thrust of most research and clinical attention in recent years. The GLM-D can span the range of treatment, reentry, and reintegration initiatives because of a primary emphasis on agency and its role in supporting the pursuit of good lives. People look to lead meaningful lives that are structured around their practical identities and contain the necessary well-being and freedom components to make this possible. Desistance and traditional sex offender interventions in their own ways both help in the process of making good, and are both essential pieces of the rehabilitation puzzle.

# VII

# WHERE TO FROM HERE?

## Chapter 16

# Dignity, Punishment, and Human Rights

## *The Ethics of Desistance*

Offender rehabilitation or reintegration is an evaluative and capacity-building process because of its emphasis on both practitioners' and offenders' practical reasoning (Ward & Maruna, 2007; Ward & Nee, 2009). *Practical reasoning* is a form of rationality that involves evaluating goals and the values that underlie them, and formulating an action plan to achieve these goals in an efficient manner (Ward & Nee, 2009). One way of conceptualizing correctional intervention programs is as systematic attempts to provide offenders with the requisite internal and external resources to implement plans likely to result in better lives. The *evaluative* component of rehabilitation is evident in its concern to reduce risk of further reoffending by reorienting individuals' value judgments from those associated with criminal actions to those that are personally meaningful and socially acceptable. The *capacity-building* process involves applying psychological and social interventions to help offenders acquire capabilities and opportunities to secure socially endorsed outcomes that they value. This component of rehabilitation is based upon the facts of human functioning and the technology of skill acquisition.

---

Portions of this chapter appeared in Ward (2009). Reprinted by permission of the *European Journal of Probation*.

Once it is acknowledged that interventions with all offenders are underpinned by values as well as scientific knowledge, it is not possible to quarantine ethical questions from discussions of best practice. It is apparent that in the psychological literature on offender rehabilitation the level of ethical debate has frequently been superficial and oriented around procedural matters such as duty to warn, conflicting roles, and risk prediction and management (e.g., Bush, Connell, & Denny, 2006; Haag, 2006). There has been little analysis of such important topics as offenders' moral status, the relationship between punishment and rehabilitation, or the degree to which offenders retain their basic human rights (Ward & Birgden, 2007; Ward & Salmon, 2009). This neglect cannot be dismissed as essentially benign in terms of its effects on assessment and program delivery. Rather, it is a critical oversight that threatens the ethical integrity of correctional practice and any empirically supported interventions that are based on unexamined and arguably unacceptable assumptions about what is ethically permissible in the realm of practice. Too often policymakers and practitioners have unthinkingly accepted a crude utilitarian ethical theory that assumes that the only justifiable outcome of punishment and interventions with offenders is reduced risk to the community. Offenders are regarded primarily as threats rather than as moral agents in their own right. But as fellow members of the moral community who are reasonably held accountable for their actions, they have certain entitlements as well as obligations—entitlements that mean offenders' core interests and inherent dignity ought to be taken seriously when the state and its various agencies make decisions that will have an impact on their freedom and well-being.

Desistance research aims to describe the processes and structural factors that stop individuals from reoffending and subsequently sustain the state of nonoffending. Theories of desistance set out to explain why desistance processes and factors work the way they do and to specify the mechanisms that are responsible for individuals' desistance from crime. However, once the science of desistance has converged upon its causes and provided policymakers and researchers with intervention targets, ethical problems start to emerge. Actually, science has its own normative issues, but in this chapter we would like to put them to one side and reflect critically on the ethical issues related to the practice implications of desistance research. In our view there are four major ethical concerns associated with correctional practice in general. First, there is the foundational question concerning what we want the correctional system to accomplish. Is it to "correct" something? To achieve justice, restore balance, provide reparations, send a (deterrent) message that violations of rules are not tolerated, protect society, prevent a convict from reoffending, or provide a convict with a better life than he had before he offended (J. Nageotte, personal communication, November 21, 2009)? Second, there is the question of what ethical concepts and principles ought to underpin correctional practice. Third, given that criminal acts are by definition illegal and are almost always ethically unacceptable because of the unjustified harm intentionally inflicted on innocent parties by persons who are held accountable, what is the relationship between punishment and treatment (Kleinig, 2008)? Fourth, what specific ethical concerns and matters are associated with desistance-oriented interventions?

Our aim in this chapter is to provide an expanded ethical canvas from which to approach correctional practice with sex offenders. The cornerstone of this broader ethical perspective will be the concept of human dignity and its protection by human rights norms and theories. We also explore the relationship between responses to crime and offender rehabilitation based on an enriched theory of punishment that is sensitive to offenders' moral equality and their attendant rights. Finally, we discuss how the specific ethical issues raised by desistance approaches to practice with sex offenders can be accommodated within the above ethical framework.

## Human Dignity and Vulnerable Agency

The concept of human dignity is an ancient moral idea concerned with the presumed intrinsic value and universal moral equality of human beings. Because of their inherent dignity human beings are assumed to possess equal moral status and therefore are expected to receive equal consideration in matters that directly affect their core interests. The equal moral standing of each person within a moral community means that every person is entitled to make specific claims against other members of the moral community, and in turn is expected to acknowledge his or her own obligations to others' respective legitimate claims. In essence, the concept of dignity denotes the moral *worth* or value of all human beings, although the meaning of this term has changed considerably since its origins several thousand years ago (Sulmasy, 2007).

The key role of the concept of human dignity in regulating human relationships and coordinating competing interests is evident in most major moral theories and various human rights treaties such as the Universal Declaration of Human Rights (UDHR; United Nations [UN], 1948/2007). The preamble of the UDHR asserts that "recognition of the inherent dignity and of the equal and inalienable rights of all members of the human family is the foundation of freedom, justice and peace in the world" (Nickel, 2007, p. 191). The UDHR was followed by the European Convention on Human Rights (1953; Smit & Snacken, 2009) and two international covenants in 1966 (the International Covenant on Civil and Political Rights and the International Covenant on Economic, Social, and Cultural Rights) that provided more detail on the various articles outlined in the original UN declaration (Freeman, 2002). There are also references to human dignity in the various articles of the UDHR and in the other treaties, as well as in the many books and commentaries on these important human rights documents. It is apparent that from the standpoint of the authors of the UDHR, human dignity is a core moral idea rather than primarily a legal concept, and therefore theoretically grounds or justifies laws and political norms that are designed to protect fundamental human needs and interests (Churchill, 2006).

While it is commonly accepted that *dignity* refers to human worth, the term has been conceptualized in various ways by modern theorists (Beyleveld & Brownsword, 2001; Malpas & Lickiss, 2007). More specifically, dignity has been defined in terms of the minimal living conditions required for an acceptable level of existence (Nussbaum, 2006). For example, a lifestyle characterized by inadequate drinking water, lack of nutritious food, and a polluted environment, and a deficit of caring relationships is likely to slip beneath the minimal threshold of a dignified human life. Another attempt to define dignity states that a person has dignity when he or she is free to form his or her own intentions and is able to act in accordance with them without interference (Driver, 2006). By way of contrast, some theorists have proposed that individuals have dignity if they live their lives in accordance with the norms of their community and its practices and traditions (Beyleveld & Brownsword, 2001). Such a viewpoint is more constraining than that allowed by a conception of dignity based on autonomy. For example, certain actions or lifestyles may be evaluated as undignified and therefore as ethically unacceptable if they are believed to violate cherished community sexual or social norms (Beyleveld & Brownsword, 2001). A final conception of dignity evident in the literature is based upon the idea that dignity depends on being a flourishing member of a kind. According to this standpoint, individuals have dignity if they are fulfilling themselves as *human* beings and their unique abilities are fully developed (Miller, 2007; Nussbaum, 2006).

The above conceptions of dignity represent only a few of the ways this important concept has been defined. In a seminal analysis Beyleveld and Brownsword (2001) set out to unify the multiple meanings of dignity by making a distinction between dignity as *empowerment* and dignity as *constraint*. The notion of dignity as empowerment stresses the importance of uncoerced choice and freedom of movement for human beings as they go about their lives. The emphasis placed on empowerment points to the value of self-governance and the capacity and opportunity of individuals actively and freely to pursue their self-selected goals without interference from others. The second aspect of dignity acknowledges its links with constraints on the way people are treated and also on how they behave. According to this viewpoint, people retain their dignity only if they follow the norms of their community and do not act in ways that cast shame on themselves or others.

Relying on the analysis by Beyleveld and Brownsword (2001), we would argue that the dignity of human beings is located in their capacity to formulate and pursue their interests in the world without unjustified interference by other people. However, individuals' own judgments are not the only determinants of what constitutes a dignified life, as sometime people can act in ways that are freely chosen that diminish their status as human beings. An example in the correctional domain might be an offender who agrees to harsh and humiliating interventions because he does not believe he is worthy of better treatment. A notable implication of a concept of dignity based on empowerment and constraint is that it points to the vulnerabilities of human beings stemming from their nature as embodied, social animals. In order to be able to act in pursuit of personally selected goals basic needs have to be met as well and educational opportunities and social scaffolding provided. In other words, human beings require certain primary goods and opportunities to be able to act in ways worthy of their intrinsic value. Because of their critical role in helping people lead a life of dignity and ensuring they have the necessary capabilities to function according to their inherent dignified nature, these resources are viewed as *entitlements* and therefore are protected by fundamental moral and legal rights (human rights—see below).

In conclusion, individuals' inherent dignity grounds their authority to claim basic entitlements to resources and also to noninterference from others in pursuit of justified goals. Alternatively, and crucially, because all people possess equal dignity, each has a corresponding obligation to respond appropriately to other people's legitimate claims and wishes. It is important to emphasize that because respect for all individuals ultimately stems from their inherent dignity, this dignity cannot justifiably be *taken* from them through the actions of the state or by other people. Darwell's (2006) distinction between *recognition respect* and *appraisal respect* nicely captures the inviolate nature of dignity. Recognition respect is based upon the assumed moral equality and standing within a moral community of all individuals. All people have an equal voice in matters that affect their core interests, and there is agreement that accountability goes hand in hand with entitlements to certain levels of treatment and functioning. On the other hand, the level of appraisal respect accorded persons ought to reflect their actions toward others and the degree to which they are evaluated as morally praiseworthy or blameworthy at any particular time. The key point is that recognition respect modulates the way appraisal respect is translated into ethical responses to unacceptable actions. For example, punishments ought to be implemented in a manner that fully acknowledges an offender's inherent dignity, and should never be delivered in a demeaning or humiliating way.

## Human Rights

The above discussion of human dignity has demonstrated its foundational role in locating the intrinsic value or worth of human beings in their capacity for action and in achieving a certain level of well-being. A significant insight arising from our analysis is that the concept of dignity is necessarily connected to peoples' relationship to others within their community, and arguably to the wider human race. The dependence of dignity on interconnectedness emerges because a capacity for action and an ability to achieve acceptable levels of well-being only make sense, and are only possible, within a social network. A second implication is that ethical issues arise when there are conflicting interests. A major function of ethical norms is to establish practices that effectively coordinate the diverse, and often competing, interests of individual agents (Driver, 2006). The implication for correctional practitioners is that all offenders are entitled to be treated in ways that reflect this inherent dignity, or, to put it in Darwell's (2006) language, the fact that offenders have behaved unethically and merit punishment does not mean they forfeit their status as moral equals. In other words, any response to crime or interventions that occur while individuals are within the criminal justice system ought to be delivered in ways that ensure recognition respect is evident. One of the strengths of a desistance intervention framework is that it is oriented toward a communitarian ethical framework where the core interests of all members of the community are considered to be of equal relevance when making important social and political decisions. What is lacking in such work is the development of an ethical theory that can justify such an approach. We propose that the first component of such an ethical framework is the concept of dignity.

### *What Are Human Rights?*

While establishing the crucial role of dignity in ethical thought is an important first step in developing an enriched ethical framework for correctional practitioners, it is not sufficient. What is needed is the specification of norms that are designed to protect the empowerment and well-being requirements that comprise dignity. In our model (derived from Ward & Birgden, 2007) human dignity emerges from the capacity of individuals to fashion their own goals and to formulate ways of living that are based around these goals. Human rights are an important set of norms that were designed with this purpose in mind and can usefully be regarded as protective capsules. The relationship between values and human rights is well articulated by Freeden (1991), who argues that

> a human right is a conceptual device, expressed in linguistic form, that assigns priority to certain human or social attributes regarded as essential to the adequate functioning of a human being; that is intended to serve as a protective capsule for those attributes; and that appeal for deliberate action to ensure such protection. (p. 7)

Freeden's definition points to the fact that human rights are intended to function as *protective capsules*, to provide a defensive zone around individuals so that they can get on with the business of leading good and meaningful lives, that is, lives that are chosen by them and that involve the unfolding of personal projects embodying their particular commitments. Summarizing their key properties, Nickel (2007) asserts that human rights:

- Are universal and extend to all peoples of the world.
- Are moral norms that provide strong reasons for granting individual significant benefits.
- Exert normative force through both national and international institutions.
- Are evident in both specific lists of rights and at the level of abstract values.
- Set minimum standards of living rather than depicting an ideal world.

The possession of human rights by individuals will not necessarily guarantee that they will achieve rich and satisfying lives; arguably they are necessary but not sufficient conditions for a good life. Rather, the ability to claim certain fundamental entitlements for core goods from others and to have these entitlements accepted is likely to result in the acquisition of the basic capabilities required to shape a life that is valued and one's own. In other words, the possession of the attributes protected by human rights gives people a fair shot at a good life rather than leaving them at the mercy of the natural (e.g., inherited characteristics and talents) and unnatural (e.g., birth circumstances, opportunities) lotteries. Human rights both reflect and confer moral status and remind governments, agencies, and other people that they must consider rights holders' essential interests when pursuing outcomes that are likely to harm or benefit those individuals.

How are human rights defined? In essence, a human right is a *claim right* legitimately possessed by persons because they are human beings (Griffin, 2008; Morsink, 2009; Orend, 2002). A claim right reflects the duties another person or agency has to the claimant to provide specific goods such as essential materials for survival or to allow the claimant to engage in certain actions (i.e., noninterference in the rights holder's affairs). Following on from this analysis a claim right has five key elements: a *rights holder,* the assertion of a *claim,* an *object* of the claim (e.g., education), the *recipient* of the claim (i.e., duty-bearer), and the *grounds* for the claim. Human rights have a metaphysical basis in the nature of human beings and therefore conceptually exclude secondary characteristics such as social class, professional group, culture, racial group, gender, or sexual orientation. In other words, individuals hold human rights simply because they are members of the human race and as such are considered to be entitled to a life characterized by a certain level of dignity. As stated earlier, a dignified life is one characterized by personal choice and a certain level of well-being. In order to achieve such a life it is necessary that certain *well-being* and *freedom* goods are available to the person (Gewirth, 1996; Griffin, 2008; Miller, 2007).

It is possible to trace the origins of human rights from Middle Eastern legal codes to their modern manifestation in natural rights-inspired declarations such as the French Declaration of the Rights of Man and the Citizen (Donnelly, 2003). Eventually the Enlightenment versions culminated in the publication of the Universal Declaration of Human Rights in 1948 with its focus more on human dignity than natural law (United Nations, 1948/2007). The UDHR consists of a preamble expressing the inherent dignity of human beings and 30 articles specifying rights to objects such as freedom from torture, security of the person, a fair trial and due process, right to own property, freedom from discrimination, freedom to marry, the right to work, and religious freedom (United Nations, 1948/2007). One difficulty with the UDHR is that it is simply a list of relatively specific claims for access to goods or noninterference from others (negative rights). The Canadian philosopher Orend (2002) has usefully conceptually collapsed the articles of the UDHR into five clusters, each cluster associated with a particular human rights object. The five types of goods determined by Orend are personal freedom, material subsistence, personal security, elemental equality, and social recognition.

### *Justification of Human Rights*

The question of how to justify human rights remains. In our view, the most powerful theoretical defenses of human rights are universal in nature and go beyond legalistic conceptions rooted in power politics. Instead, the aim is to identify aspects of human functioning that are considered to be particularly important and to present an argument for anchoring human rights and their value in these features. A number of theorists have presented justifications of human rights based on needs or agency/personhood concepts, arguing that such ideas reliably extend the reach of human rights to all persons within a society and those living in different countries. Griffin (2008) proposes that human rights can be grounded in three core features of persons: (1) autonomy, or the ability to make important decisions for oneself; (2) possession of a set of minimal resources and capabilities, such as education and health; and (3) liberty, where other people do not prevent someone against their will from applying their conception of a worthwhile life (p. 33). Relatedly, Gewirth (1981, 1996) asserts that human rights function to protect the fundamental conditions necessary for people to operate as moral agents, that is, as individuals capable of formulating their own personal projects and realizing them in their lives. According to Gewirth, individuals have rights to whatever is necessary to achieve the purposes of their actions because without such guarantees they may not be able to effectively act at all (i.e., will be unable to achieve valued outcomes). A third important rights theorist, Miller (2007) argues that human rights are justified by their ability to facilitate the satisfaction of peoples' intrinsic human needs. Miller defines intrinsic needs as "those items or conditions it is necessary for a person to have if she is to avoid being harmed" (p. 179).

All three theorists claim that what holds for individuals with respect to their rights also extends to all other people and that in any community the rights and obligations of every person need to be respected and incorporated into social and political decisions (Ward & Birgden, 2007; Ward & Langlands, 2009). According to the above theorists, human rights impose both positive and negative duties on states and other people, which they are ethically obligated to meet within certain practical constraints (e.g., that they have the resources and/or abilities to meet the claim). Furthermore, when there are conflicting interests and demands arising from individuals' human rights claims, it is necessary to evaluate each claim with respect to its importance and to arrive at a solution that seeks to achieve a balance between the entitlements of all individuals concerned. Sometimes, it may not be possible to satisfy all just entitlements and the respective duties may be prioritized according to their degree of need or urgency. The crucial point is that it is ethically obligatory to engage in a process that acknowledges the inherent dignity and associated rights of all members of the moral community and not to arbitrarily dismiss or seek to strip away an individual's basic entitlements. Theorists such as Griffin, Miller, and Gewirth argue that human rights are designed to protect the essential interests of all human beings: needs, capacities, and experiences that if instantiated respect their dignity as persons and if violated result in diminished and broken lives. The breaching of human rights occurs when individuals are treated primarily as the means to other peoples' goals rather than as valued agents themselves. An example of this is when individuals from a certain ethnic group are denied basic health services because of the expense to the state and yet are exploited as sources of cheap labor. A correctional example could be when sex offenders are detained indefinitely in special hospitals because they are considered a high risk for future offending (Vess, 2009).

In summary, human rights create a space within which individuals can lead at least minimally worthwhile lives that allow them to maintain a basic sense of human dignity. Human rights are a relatively narrow set of rights and are only intended to protect the internal and external conditions necessary for a *minimally* worthwhile life. We agree with human rights theorists who assert that the core requirements of personhood and agency constitute these basic conditions and therefore such conditions ought to be provided and defended by the state, relevant agencies, and all citizens. We will consider the correctional practice implications of human rights later in this chapter. At this point we would respond to individuals who argue that offenders have forfeited their human rights by replying that if such rights are inherent to human beings, they cannot legitimately be taken away. And if the purpose of human rights is to ensure that the inherent dignity of all human beings is maintained, then it follows that offenders' entitlements to agency and well-being should be safeguarded to the fullest degree possible (Lippke, 2002). Any restrictions upon their liberty and conditions of living need to be carefully argued for and not simply be assumed to be ethically acceptable. Furthermore, punishment practices ought to be implemented in accordance with the dignity and rights of offenders and not delivered in a manner that is demeaning and dehumanizing (Lazarus, 2004; Lippke, 2002).

## Punishment and Rehabilitation

We have suggested that the concept of human dignity is the ethical foundation for human rights protocols and theories. A dignified human life is one that allows a person to make fundamental choices concerning his or her life goals and also addresses core well-being needs. Human rights theories provide the justification for specific treaties and other normative mechanisms that are designed to protect the core conditions required for a dignified life. Because offenders are human beings, it follows that they hold human rights and therefore ought to be treated in accordance with the basic values and the specific norms evident in human rights protocols. It now remains to examine the ethical implications of punishment and its relationship to offender rehabilitation. In the following section we argue that an ethically justified theory of punishment is some kind of restorative or communicative theory, such as that developed by Duff (2001). One of the major reasons this theory is ethically justifiable is that it advocates treating offenders with respect and also acknowledges their right to be reconciled with the community following completion of a sentence. Punishment requires ethical justification, as it is commonly accepted that harming another person without sound reasons is wrong.

We do not have space in this chapter to critically examine the other two main theories of punishment, consequential and nonconsequential theories (for a comprehensive analysis, see Ward & Salmon, 2009). Briefly, consequential theories of punishment are based on an evaluation of the total amount of happiness or good obtained through punishment practices, while nonconsequential theories tend to focus on the intrinsic rightness of inflicting proportionate harm on someone who has harmed others (Boonin, 2008; Golash, 2005). A problem with the former is that it can involve treating offenders as simply means to advance the community's ends (e.g., reduced risk), while the latter may ignore legitimate well-being needs of offenders. Both theories run the risk of failing to acknowledge the inherent dignity of offenders and the fact that they are moral agents who are embedded within communities to whom they are accountable but also against which they have legitimate claims to primary goods such as the possibility of social reentry. Because of their emphasis on the role of the community in punishment, and also on the equal moral status of all members of a community, communicative approaches are a natural fit with desistance-oriented intervention practices.

### What Is Punishment?

Essentially, state-inflicted punishment in the criminal justice system involves the intentional imposition of harm on an individual who has unjustifiably harmed a fellow citizen (Bennett, 2008; Duff, 2001). More specifically, punishment in the criminal justice system has five necessary elements (Boonin, 2008): punishment practices are *authorized* by the state, *intentional, reprobative* (they express disapproval or censure), *retributive* (they follow a wrongful act committed by the offender), and *harmful* (they result in suffering, a burden, or deprivation to the offender).

There are three major reasons why correctional practitioners are unable to avoid addressing the ethical challenges posed by the institution of punishment. First, it is possible that psychologists, social workers, therapists, and program staff may work within institutions that are unduly harsh and abusive. Second, assumptions concerning the justification of punishment are likely to be reflected in the specific penal policies and practices embedded in the criminal justice system, and shape professional tasks and roles. For example, the emphasis on risk assessment and management currently evident in the correctional systems throughout the Western world is conceptually dependent upon a consequential ethical theory (Ward & Salmon, 2009). Third, punishment and rehabilitation practices are distinct but overlapping normative frameworks (Ward & Salmon, 2009). Punishment is a response to crime based on ethical values, while rehabilitation aims to facilitate social reentry, and is based on prudential (well-being) values. However, some aspects of what have been called treatment may in fact be punishment given their intended effects (Glaser, 2003; Levenson & D'Amora, 2005). For example, cognitive restructuring in sex offender intervention programs is partly designed to cause offenders to feel remorse and take responsibility, arguably an aspect of punishment. The point is that unless practitioners are able to justify punishment, then such interventions are unethical and ought to be avoided.

These examples indicate that the justification of punishment is of relevance and ethical concern for all practitioners. It is not possible to insulate the role of program deliverers from the ethical issues associated with punishment. Therefore, correctional practitioners ought to endorse punishment practices external and internal to their practice by reference to an acceptable punishment theory. In our view, any such theory ought to be responsive to the inherent dignity and associated human rights of offenders. We now briefly describe a communicative theory of punishment which we argue meets these requirements.

### Communicative Theory of Punishment

Communicative justifications of punishment have their basis in a liberal communitarian view of political and moral public institutions (Duff, 2001). According to Duff (2001), communicative theories of punishment have a *relationship focus* and as such insist that the rights of all stakeholders in the criminal justice system, including offenders, are taken into account when constructing theories of punishment. Because all individuals are presumed to have equal moral status, offenders are viewed as fellow members of a normative community (i.e., offenders are viewed as "one of us") and therefore are bound and protected by the community's public values of autonomy, freedom, privacy, and pluralism. Duff argues that these values are those of a liberal democracy, where all human beings are considered to possess inherent dignity and therefore have equal moral standing within the community. A major assumption of communicative perspectives is that punishment practices ought to be *inclusive* of offenders rather than involving some type of social exclusion or quarantining. Duff asserts that while individuals who have committed public wrongs ought to be held accountable, because of their moral status they should be treated with respect in the process of administering punishment. Therefore, he proposes that any punishment inflicted upon offenders should seek to *persuade* rather than to coerce them to take responsibility for their crimes. Furthermore, because offenders are viewed as fellow members of the moral community, it is accepted that the primary aim of punishment is to *communicate* to them the wrongness of their actions. The aim of this process of communication is to give wrongdoers an opportunity to redeem themselves and ultimately to be reconciled to the community. Duff argues that hard treatment such as imprisonment is obligatory within the criminal justice system because it draws offenders' attention to the seriousness of the wrongs committed and appropriately expresses social disapproval. Crimes are regarded as violations of community norms that the offender as a fellow moral agent is assumed to endorse as well. There are three aims integral to the institution of punishment from the standpoint of Duff's communicative theory: secular repentance, reform, and reconciliation through the imposition of sanctions. The communitarian orientation of this theoretical position is nicely captured in his statement that punishment is "a burden imposed on an offender for his crime, through which, it is hoped, he will come to repent his crime, to begin to reform himself, and thus reconcile himself with those he has wronged" (Duff, 2001, p. 106).

### Intervention

As a theory of punishment, Duff's communicative theory has the virtue of being inclusive rather than exclusive in its ethical reach. The interests of all relevant stakeholders affected by crime are taken into account in the implementation of punishment. The offender is regarded as an equal moral agent and treated with the respect and dignity this status entails. A significant feature of communicative theories of punishment is that crime is conceptualized as a community responsibility rather than simply an individual one. While offenders are held accountable to the community, their core interests are not neglected. Relatedly, victims are not ethically required to forgive offenders but do owe them a meaningful opportunity to be reintegrated within the community once they have served their sentences or fulfilled other legal requirements. Thus, the community is obligated to actively help offenders in the process of integration through resources such as education, work training, accommodation, and access to social networks.

From a practice viewpoint, *secular repentance* takes the moral agency of offenders seriously and emphasizes the importance of their acknowledging the unjustified harm they have inflicted on members of the community. The *reform* strand of the communicative theory of punishment refers to the desirability of offenders becoming motivated to change themselves and their behavior for ethical as well as prudential reasons. The realization that they have unjustifiably caused other people to suffer, it is hoped, will lead to a firm resolution to do what is necessary to become law-abiding citizens. Finally, the *reconciliation* strand of the communicative theory of punishment expresses both offenders' and the community's desire for reconciliation following repentance and efforts at reform. There are two aspects to the process of reconciliation that are practically relevant: offenders' obligation to apologize and make appropriate reparations to victims and possibly other people affected by their crimes, and the community's obligation to help the offender reintegrate back into the community following the completion of a sentence.

## Practice Implications

Four key implications arise from the preceding discussion. First, a rehabilitation approach that focuses entirely on risk management elements may violate the inherent dignity and rights of offenders. Second, the two core aspects of a dignified life have direct relevance for practice and the type of programs that are ethically acceptable. Third, punishment practices that fail to acknowledge the inherent dignity and entitlements of offenders are ethically unacceptable and ought to be rejected by practitioners. Fourth, strength-based approaches are ethically more justified because of their commitment to offenders' entitlements and autonomy, alongside the interest of the community.

First, intervention programs for offenders that focus primarily on risk reduction are ethically problematic because they are rooted almost entirely in the interests of the community and typically ignore the legitimate interests of offenders. Risk management initiatives such as civil commitment and community notification for sex offenders aim to protect the community from possible future sexual offenses. Offenders, who after a systematic assessment are deemed to be high risk in many U.S. jurisdictions, are committed to high-security, special hospitals indefinitely (Vess, 2009). Sex offenders who are released from prison are often subject to severe geographical restrictions and also can have their identities and residential location made publicly available. A danger of such initiatives is that offenders experience stigmatization and find it extremely difficult to resume or start a normal life within the community. An ethically more acceptable model would be to offer offenders social supports and the available resources to live personally meaningful and better lives. In desistance terms, better lives will involve establishing social bonds with other people, and being engaged in the lifeblood of the community by way of work and leisure activities, rather than being effectively quarantined. The importance of respecting the agency of offenders is evident in an emphasis on allowing individuals to make their own choices about what life plans they formulate and pursue. Of course, following a human rights ethical platform, such plans are expected to acknowledge the core interests of other members of the community. The fact that Western criminal justice systems often refuse to do this does not make it ethically acceptable or suggest practitioners should simply accommodate to such practices. The main problem with risk management strategies such as those outlined above is that they leave offenders living marginal lives devoid of dignity and undermine their chances of reconciliation and redemption. The key decisions concerning permissible treatment plans and postrelease options are determined by risk assessments and little room is left for the offenders to plan their own lives. The ethical problem is that it is simply assumed that what matters to offenders is not relevant or of particular importance. Instead, the aim is to engineer arrangements that are thought most likely to keep the rest of the community safe from predation. The irony is that while this is a legitimate goal, isolating offenders and overriding their agency may not be the best way to achieve secure and safe communities. Such initiatives may simply create additional risk and by loosening the social ties between offenders and people that care about them impede the process of desistance (Ward & Maruna, 2007).

Second, the two strands of the concept of dignity evident in our analysis have direct relevance for correctional programming and practice with sex offenders. Individual empowerment is basically concerned with the need to address agency and autonomy requirements in order to ensure that offenders can actively participate in a life shaped by their own values and goals. The constraint strand of dignity sets out conditions within which such a life ought to be lived. First, the prudential aspect dictates that individuals need to have their basic needs for relationships, health, education, and nourishment met because without such goods their capacity to function in an autonomous (free) way would be severely compromised. Second, because dignity is inherent in all individuals, offenders are ethically unjustified in seeking to implement a life plan that harms other people. Therefore, intervention programs should strengthen offenders' abilities to function as moral agents and thus aim to equip them with coping skills such as self-regulation abilities, problem-solving skills, and emotional competencies. All of these abilities are core targets of current correctional programs. In addition, well-being-oriented programs include social skills training, anger management, leisure, substance abuse interventions, and sexual health programs. Again, all of these types of interventions are currently offered to offenders. What our analysis indicates is that the concept of dignity and its attendant concerns of empowerment and constraints are arguably the ethical foundation of correctional practices. An advantage of making this dependence more explicit is that such programs will become more integrated and also reduce the chances of the interests of both offenders and members of the community getting overlooked. As we will discuss later, an advantage of desistance-oriented interventions is that because the aim is to capitalize on offenders' personal aspirations and social networks, empowerment and constraint issues are always in the forefront of clinicians' minds.

Third, correctional practitioners ought to be aware of the punishment practices occurring within the institutions where they work and also those contained within their own practice. If punishment is underpinned by an unacceptable ethical theory, one that violates the inherent dignity and associated rights of offenders, then practitioners have an ethical obligation to address such concerns. When therapists or social workers are unreflectively engaged in punishment within an intervention program, they ought to immediately think about its ethical acceptability. An example of an unacceptable practice is when group workers consider it their responsibility to take an overly hard line with offenders and consistently challenge and harshly confront them. Intervention practices like these are clearly punishment but without a legitimate justification, and are often erroneously promoted as therapeutic practices. Such abusive behavior is neither acceptable therapy nor ethically justified punishment and should not to be engaged in. Sometimes a reason for overly harsh and untherapeutic behavior is that practitioners are so preoccupied with attempting to reduce offenders' level of risk that they fail to appreciate their rights and entitlements as well, entitlements grounded in their inherent dignity and their status as moral equals.

Finally, an ethical advantage of strength-based rehabilitation theories such as the GLM is that they seek to equip offenders with the resources to pursue their own visions of better lives while also reducing risk for reoffending. Programs derived from rehabilitation theories like the GLM are able to achieve this because of an emphasis on individual agency and also the interconnectedness of all people. Therefore, any intervention plan that is guided by the assumptions of the GLM will be sensitive to risk factors while taking offenders' personal goals and aspirations seriously. The provision of the internal and external conditions required to implement offenders' plans of living will be undertaken in a way that also ensures individual and contextual risk elements are targeted. Because the GLM is an ecological model, it is always a question of balancing the core, and sometimes competing, interests of all individuals rather than privileging the interests of the community at the expense of offenders. To do this is to effectively ignore the moral equality of offenders and therefore deny them recognition respect. A notable feature of strength-based programs is that they locate responsibility for crime prevention and management with the community as well as with the individual offender.

## Ethics

As we have been arguing, an acceptable ethical framework for practice with offenders needs to be based on an acknowledgment that all human beings have inherent dignity based on their capacity to engage in personal projects that are self-determined. By "self-determined" we mean projects that spring from individuals' reflections on their deep commitments and aspirations. The implications for practice are that any ethically justified treatment or intervention program ought to respect offenders' agency and acknowledge the entitlements and obligations that reflect this emphasis. Moreover, because people are socially embedded and rely on others to help them to further their own interests (indeed, often other peoples' interests are also our own!), it follows that interventions should be broadly focused and take offender relationships to the wider community into account. There is a natural resonance between human rights, communicative approaches to punishment, and desistance-oriented practice with offenders. Treatment programs centered on risk management concerns will most probably struggle to find sufficient room to address offenders' needs for social relationships, meaningful work, and community involvement. In our view contemporary treatment programs for sex offenders tend to be heavily weighted toward risk reduction and subsequently ignore offenders' needs and entitlements. Ethical practice relies on mutual respect and recognition of each person's legitimate claims and duties. While being convicted of a sex offense inevitably results in justified severe restrictions on liberty and access to social goods, it should not mean complete forfeiture of rights or neglect of offenders' status as moral agents.

Despite the ethical advantages of desistance-oriented intervention initiatives (see Chapters 1, 13, 14, and 15), there are also risks. A possible source of ethical conflict emerges from the communitarian focus of desistance-related practice (or at least a tendency toward such an emphasis). The danger we allude to is that the good of the community is automatically valued over and above the well-being and freedom rights of individuals. Furthermore, as stated above, the ethical thrust of a communitarian perspective is to seek a balance that supports and sustains the goods of the community, in terms of such things as safety, trust, and the authority of ethical norms. The tensions between the various stakeholders' interests and those of the offender are unavoidable and care ought to be taken to ensure that in any given context offenders' human rights are not violated, although some degree of curtailment may be justified. To respect the dignity of offenders, victims, and members of the community, core entitlements and duties ought to be carefully balanced and safeguards installed to ensure that the minimal requirements for a dignified and worthwhile life are met.

Miller (2007) has argued that human rights, because they protect the threshold between a minimally worthwhile life and one characterized by suffering and a lack of dignity, trump what he calls citizen rights (i.e., community-based norms). Thus while human rights do not exhaust issues of justice such as what comprises a reasonable sentence or how best to deal with the legitimate grievances of victims, they do override citizen and communitarian rights when there is direct conflict. In other words, human rights ground citizen rights and the correctional practices related to these rights, although in most instances the two sets of moral concepts overlap and are quite consistent. Human rights function as an ethical anchor that is able to justify correctional practices that do not violate core rights values.

## Conclusions

Ethical thinking ought to be regarded as integral to the role of a correctional practitioner and not simply viewed as an additional, slightly peripheral, consideration wrapped around the core business of assessment and program delivery. We have argued that the concepts of human dignity and human rights are the ethical cornerstones of correctional practice and penetrate deeply into every facet of our work. Furthermore, it is the responsibility of individuals involved in the delivery of correctional programs to be aware of the punishment assumptions supporting practice and to reflect upon the adequacy of any justification given. We have supported a communicative theory of punishment, largely because of its assertion that all the major actors involved in the criminal justice system are mutually accountable and have intrinsic value. The value of dignity demands that each person is treated with respect and is also responsive to others in a mutually sustaining manner. If as practitioners go about their various professional tasks they keep in mind the intrinsic value of offenders and victims, it is less likely they will act in ways that deny the inherent dignity of either.

Desistance-oriented rehabilitation programs aim to ensure that offenders have realistic opportunities to establish meaningful personal and social links within the community. From this perspective, treatment seeks to provide the psychological and social resources to enable offenders to have a chance at lives that reflect their particular values but that at the same time are responsive to the legitimate concerns of other people. Intervention programs for sex offenders that privilege the needs and concerns of the community at the expense of offenders, and those that ignore offenders' potential for harming others, are equally ethically unacceptable. Desistance research and theory can provide practitioners with the knowledge to design treatment plans for sex offenders that are ecologically valid and that look beyond the narrow confines of correctional and security concerns. The scope of such programs will be wide and underpinned by ethical ideas that justify their inclusive nature. Offenders are people like us and therefore deserve a chance to live the kinds of lives that we collectively aspire to rather than be consigned to ones we all dread.

## Chapter 17

# Moral Strangers or One of Us?

## *Concluding Thoughts*

Every intellectual journey starts from a beginning rooted in a secure and familiar place, then moves toward new and sometimes unexpected territory. We may stride off into the unknown with self-assurance that the terrain ahead will be pretty much like that we have left behind, confident of our ability to deal with problems and moments of doubt. Such self-belief is founded upon a conviction that our resources have time and time again proved equal to any challenges encountered along the way. For correctional researchers and practitioners the guiding star is arguably the scientific method. The knowledge and skills developed over the last 30 years or so in the pursuit of empirically guided interventions are viewed as precious resources and a source of comfort and certainty. It is assumed that as long as we hold such things close everything will work out in the end; our communities will be safe and bad people will become good citizens or forever remain safely contained in prisons or special hospitals. It is also maintained that correctional programs should be founded on hard facts leavened with compassion for the victims and a bottom-line concern for the welfare of offenders. However, our society tends to construe people who commit crimes essentially as bearers of risk to be managed, objects to be manipulated so the rest of the community can sleep more easily. The default view seems to be that once you cross the line and commit an offense, you have voluntarily relinquished your claim to the goodwill of others and no longer retain any fundamental moral rights.

It is our contention that this picture is misleading and dangerously so. We have made sex offenders into moral strangers (outlaws). In 1983 Laws and Osborn noted that, if we looked too closely at sex offenders, we would find a lot of ourselves there. This position was echoed by Maruna in 2001 when he said that it is necessary to create bogeymen to whom we can readily assign blame for misdeeds and not have to examine our own propensities for bad behavior. Rather than moral strangers, offenders are people like us who have made bad choices and acted upon them in ways that unacceptably harm others. Because they share our inherent value when we hold them to account, which we must, it should be in a way that is respectful of their status and that seeks to draw them back into the communities from which they came. Or for many, into communities that are better equipped to truly include them and provide resources so they can fashion "good" lives. Thus, the real starting point should not be scientific certitude and our CBT or RNR programs. Risk assessment resources are not sufficient to effectively deal with crime and its aftermath.

In our view, the crucial piece missing from the above image of scientific and humane practice is an ethical one. We need to ask ourselves, Who are our fellow travellers and what paths forward ought to be regarded as too dangerous to follow because of their physical, psychological, and, importantly, ethical risks? The trouble with putting all our faith in the science of correctional practice is that it is far too easy to forget that science is always in the service of values. Science constitutes a powerful way of finding out how the world and its inhabitants work and then utilizes that knowledge to benefit people and to remove threats as best it can. At the center of such explorations are a set of values, a sense of why such activities are worth pursuing. Earlier in this book we argued that the rehabilitation of offenders is a normative and capacity-building process, and therefore, from a practice perspective, both science and ethical judgment are equally important. In our view, the only legitimate place to start a journey that involves the infliction of significant harm upon others is one where all human beings are regarded as equal in dignity and moral standing.

Unfortunately, when it comes to offenders, perhaps particularly sex offenders, this seems to be too difficult a step for society to take. Throughout the 19th and 20th centuries, and now in the 21st, we see continuous evidence of "moral panic." People fear that society is disintegrating, that no one is really safe, that danger surrounds us. In the present moral climate in North America, people fear that the crime rate is rising (although it is decreasing), that crimes are fuelled by drugs and alcohol (some are but most are not), that nudity and coarse language are prevalent in all forms of entertainment (but not all), that literature is too frank in exposition of human problems (too little would be more like it), that schools teach dangerous, "liberal" ideas (but not enough of them), and that criminal predators roam the streets (dead wrong). If all this is "true," it is assumed that someone must be responsible and be held accountable. "Responsibility" is largely a media and political creature. Low-frequency sensational crimes are given huge coverage in print and visual media, fuelling a demand for necessary retribution. Politicians pound their desks (and chests) and grimly intone that "something must be done."

But what exactly does this claim of responsibility amount to? Criminological literature clearly shows that only a small percentage of offenders, perhaps as few as 5–6%, cause the bulk of the problems (Wolfgang et al., 1972). Similar findings have been replicated time and again in the trajectory analyses. Sex offenders would likely be included here because of the observed low base rate. Furthermore, trajectory analyses (Bushway et al., 2003; see Figure 3.2) reveal that there are many different patterns of offending and that life-course-persistent offenders are one of the very smallest groups. This is consistent with Moffitt's (1993) observations on young persons quitting crime in their early 20s. Do sex offenders desist? There is absolutely no reason to suppose that they do not, that their behavior should not follow the same course that we see in ordinary criminal offenders (see Lussier et al., 2010). There is evidence of desistance features in the work of Hanson (2002; see Figures 7.1 and 7.2) and Blanchard and Barbaree (2005; see Figure 7.3) but it is interpreted for the wrong reasons. From this point of view, desistance across the lifespan is seen as a moderator of risk, not as evidence of giving up crime, even though it amounts to the same thing.

Thus, it seems that most offenders do not go on to live lives of deviancy and predation, and that we should be careful when responding to such individuals that we do not overreact to their crimes. A cornerstone of ethically justifiable sentencing is the concept of proportionality: offenders should receive sanctions that are approximately equal in harm to those they inflicted on their victims. In our view, this means that punishment ought to be responsive to the rights of offenders to renter the community when they have completed their sentences. Rehabilitation initiatives should look to provide the social and psychological capital to enable offenders to fashion meaningful and law-abiding lives within the community. This may necessitate giving individuals opportunities to participate in treatment programs or it could involve supporting natural desistance processes. Often it will entail a combination of the two intervention strategies.

As Travis (2005) has noted, the community does not set a place at the table for the returning offender. Chapter 9 outlines the virtually insurmountable barriers thrown up against the reentering offender. Apart from the easily met conditions of parole or probation, there are what Travis calls "invisible punishments," all the things that are not in the parole orders—restrictions on jobs, housing, companions, and so on. There is almost nothing on the books that permits overcoming these restrictions. The Second Chance Act is too weak to be of any substantial value. Reentry courts are a great idea but have not yet filtered down to courts seeing ordinary criminals, let alone sex offenders.

What are the tools-to-take-home messages of this book? First, we are committed to the idea of only subjecting offenders to interventions that are empirically supported and that are underpinned by sound theory. It is our contention that there is still much to be done in the arena of correctional practice and that desistance theory and research can offer those working with sex offenders a plethora of good ideas and practices. The GLM-D is a natural ally of desistance theory because of the overlapping nature of the two perspectives' theoretical assumptions and their common stress on the importance of both agency and social resources.

Second, offenders *are* people like us, and if we start relating to them in ways that reflect this attitude correctional outcomes may well improve and reoffending rates drop. The desistance research is clear that offenders respond well to practitioners who show an interest in them and believe in their capacity to turn their lives around (McNeill et al., 2005). And what is more, treating offenders with respect and decency rather than as sources of contamination to be quarantined (not cured) is likely to make us better people and lessen the risk that we might acquire some of the vices we despise in those who commit crimes.

Third, we have argued that crime occurs because people lack the psychological and social capital to construct and put into action GLPs that are personally meaningful and socially acceptable. The causes for such flawed GLPs are primarily social and psychological. Normally as children develop they learn from adults around them how to effectively meet their needs in supportive environments. As adults themselves, they then have the capabilities to resolve personal crises and challenging problems in adaptive ways. However, children unlucky in the natural and social lotteries may find themselves consistently handicapped in their attempts to satisfy their desires. The absence of adequate scaffolding and subsequent capability development makes it so much harder to live lives that are law-abiding and socially responsible. The fault lies both within the person and within the society; there are issues of justice as well as issues of individual accountability. A strength of desistance viewpoints and the GLM-D is that they have multiple points of accountability and action: sometimes the fault lines reside in the environments in which individuals exist and at other times the cause of crime is primarily a matter of personal choice. The point is that ethical and effective rehabilitation initiatives need to be able to pursue actions across a range of targets, from individuals to social structure and processes. A problem with risk management practice models is that they tend to be overly focused on individual offenders and lack sufficient theoretical and ethical resources to enlarge their vision to the broader social and cultural vista. In other words, if we want to help individuals to cease offending and stay on the straight road it is necessary to have a just, caring, and mutually accountable society.

## A Final Note

Offenders deserve the chance for better lives, not merely the promise of less harmful ones. This is only possible in a society that, while punishing unlawful acts, actively assists errant individuals to find their way back to us, people like them.

# References

American Psychiatric Association. (2000). *Diagnostic and statistical manual of mental disorders* (4th ed., text rev.). Washington, DC: Author.

Amodeo, M., Kurtz, N., & Cutter, H. S. G. (1992). Abstinence, reasons for not drinking, and life satisfaction. *International Journal of the Addictions, 27,* 707–716.

Andrews, D. A. (1995). The psychology of criminal conduct and effective treatment. In J. McGuire (Ed.), *What works: Reducing re-offending: Guidelines from research and practice* (pp. 35–62). Chichester, UK: Wiley.

Andrews, D. A., & Bonta, J. (2007). *The psychology of criminal conduct* (4th ed.). Cincinnati, OH: Anderson.

Andrews, D. A., Zinger, I., Hoge, R. D., Bonta, J., Gendreau, P., & Cullen, F. T. (1990). Does correctional treatment work?: A psychologically informed meta-analysis. *Criminology, 28,* 369–404.

Anstiss, B. (2003). Just how effective is correctional treatment at reducing reoffending? *New Zealand Journal of Psychology, 32,* 84–91.

Archer, M. S. (2000). *Being human: The problem of agency.* Cambridge, UK: Cambridge University Press,

Armstrong, T. (2005). Evaluating the competing assumptions of Gottfredson and Hirschi's (1990) *A General Theory of Crime* and psychological explanations of aggression. *Western Criminology Review, 6,* 12–21.

Arneklev, B. J., Ellis, L., & Medlicott, S. (2006). Testing the general theory of crime: Comparing the effects of "imprudent behavior" and an attitudinal indicator of "low self-control." *Western Criminology Review, 7,* 41–55.

Arnhart, L. (1998). *Darwinian natural right: The biological ethics of human nature.* Albany: State University of New York Press.

Aronson, A., Wilson, T. D., & Akert, R. D. E. (2009). *Social psychology-7th ed.* New York: Prentice-Hall.

Aspinwall, L. G., & Staudinger, U. M. (Eds.). (2003). *A psychology of human strengths: Fundamental questions and future directions for a positive psychology.* Washington, DC: American Psychological Association.

Audi, R. (2006). *Practical reasoning and ethical decision.* Oxford, UK: Routledge.

Aylwin, A. S., & Studer, L. H. (2008, August). *There are no secrets in long term treatment efficacy: A Western Canadian experience.* Paper presented at the conference of the

International Association for Treatment of Sexual Offenders, Cape Town, South Africa.

Barbaree, H. E. (2006, September). Current modes of treatment evaluation are sub-optimal. In J. Marques, H. Barbaree, A. Beech, & R. Packard, *Treatment of sex offenders: Where do we go from here?* Plenary presentation at the conference of the Association for the Treatment of Sexual Abusers, Chicago.

Barbaree, H. E., & Blanchard, R. (2008). Sexual deviance over the lifespan: Reductions in deviant sexual behavior in the aging sex offender. In D. R. Laws & W. T. O'Donohue (Eds.), *Sexual deviance: Theory, assessment, and treatment* (2nd ed., pp. 37–60). New York: Guilford Press.

Barbaree, H. E., Langton, C. M., Blanchard, R., & Cantor, J. M. (2009). Aging versus stable enduring traits as explanatory constructs in sex offender recidivism: Partitioning actuarial prediction into conceptually meaningful components. *Criminal Justice and Behavior, 36,* 443–465.

Beech, A. R., Craig, L. A., & Browne, K. D. (Eds.). (2009). *Assessment and treatment of sex offenders.* Chichester, UK: Wiley-Blackwell.

Beier, K. M., Ahlers, C., Goecker, D., Neutze, J., Mundt, I. A., Hupp, E., et al. (2009). Can pedophiles be reached for primary prevention of child sexual abuse?: First results of the Berlin *Prevention Project Dunkelfeld* (PPD). *Journal of Forensic Psychiatry and Psychology, 20,* 851–867.

Beirne, P. (1987). Adolphe Quételet and the origins of positivist criminology. *American Journal of Sociology, 92,* 1140–1169.

Bennett, C. (2008). *The apology ritual: A philosophical theory of punishment.* Cambridge, UK: Cambridge University Press.

Beyleveld, D., & Brownsword, R. (2001). *Human dignity in bioethics and law.* New York: Oxford University Press.

Birgden, A. (2008). Offender rehabilitation: A normative framework for forensic psychologists. *Psychiatry, Psychology and Law, 15*(3), 1–19.

Blanchard, R., & Barbaree, H. E. (2005). The strength of sexual arousal as a function of the age of the sex offender: Comparisons among pedophiles, hebephiles and teleiophiles. *Sexual Abuse: A Journal of Research and Treatment, 17,* 441–456.

Blud, L. (2007, April). *Young men, alcohol, and violence: A poisonous relationship.* Paper presented at the 2nd Unhooked Thinking Conference, Bath, UK.

Blumstein, A., & Nakamura, K. (2009). Processes of redemption should be built into the use of criminal-history records for background checking. In N. A. Frost, J. D. Freilich, & T. R. Clear (Eds.), *Contemporary issues in criminal justice policy: Policy proposals from the American Society of Criminology conference* (pp. 37–52). Belmont, CA: Cengage/Wadsworth.

Boer, D. P., Hart, S. D., Kropp, P. R., & Webster, C. D. (1997). *Manual for the Sexual Violence Risk—20: Professional guidelines for assessing risk of sexual violence.* Burnaby, BC: Mental Health, Law, and Policy Institute, Simon Fraser University.

Boonin, D. (2008). *The problem of punishment.* New York: Cambridge University Press.

Bottoms, A., Shapland, J., Costello, A., Holmes, D., & Muir, G. (2004). Towards desistance: Theoretical underpinnings for an empirical study. *Howard Journal of Criminal Justice, 43,* 368–389.

Bouffard, L. A., & Laub, J. H. (2004). Jail or the army: Does military service facilitate desistance from crime? In S. Maruna & R. Immarigeon (Eds.), *After crime and punishment: Pathways to offender reintegration* (pp. 129–151). Collompton, Devon, UK: Willan.

Bradley, K., Oliver, R. B., Richardson, N., & Slayter, E. (2001). *No place like home: Housing and the ex-prisoner.* Boston: Community Resources for Justice.

Brame, R., Bushway, S. D., & Paternoster, R. (2003). Examining the prevalence of criminal desistance. *Criminology, 41,* 423–448.

Brody, S. (1976). *The effectiveness of sentencing* (Home Office Research Study No. 35). London: HMSO.

Brookes, M. (2008, June). *Working with personality disordered offenders in a therapeutic community setting at HMP Grendon.* Paper presented at the British Psychological Society, Division of Forensic Psychology Conference, Edinburgh, UK.

Bureau of Justice Statistics. (1996). *Correctional populations in the United States, 1994.* Washington, DC: Office of Justice Programs, U.S. Department of Justice.

Bureau of Justice Statistics. (2000). *Probation and parole in the United States, 2000.* Washington, DC: Office of Justice Programs, U.S. Department of Justice.

Bureau of Justice Statistics. (2009). *Key crime and justice facts at a glance.* Washington, DC: Office of Justice Programs, U.S. Department of Justice.

Burnett, R. (2002). *The dynamics of recidivism.* Oxford, UK: University of Oxford Centre for Criminological Research.

Burnett, R. (2004). To reoffend or not to reoffend?: The ambivalence of convicted property offenders. In S. Maruna & R. Immarigeon (Eds.), *After crime and punishment: Pathways to offender reintegration* (pp. 152–180). Collompton, Devon, UK: Willan.

Burnett, R., & Maruna, S. (2006). The kindness of prisoners: Strengths-based resettlement in theory and action. *Criminology and Criminal Justice, 6,* 83–106.

Bush, S. S., Connell, M. A., & Denny, R. L. (2006). *Ethical practice in forensic psychology: A systematic model for decision making.* Washington, DC: American Psychological Association.

Bushway, D., Stoll, M. A., & Weiman, D. F. (Eds.). (2007). *Barriers to reentry?: The labor market for released prisoners in post-industrial America.* New York: Russell Sage Foundation.

Bushway, S. D., Piquero, A., Mazerolle, P., Broidy, L., & Cauffman, E. (2001). An empirical framework for studying desistance as a process. *Criminology, 39,* 491–515.

Bushway, S. D., Thornberry, T. P., & Krohn, M. D. (2003). Desistance as a developmental process: A comparison of static and dynamic approaches. *Journal of Quantitative Criminology, 19,* 129–153.

California Department of Corrections and Rehabilitation. (2009). California Men's Colony (CMC). Available from *www.cdcr.ca.gov/visitors/facilities/CMC.html.*

Chajewski, M., & Mercado, C. C. (2009). An evaluation of sex offender residency restriction functioning in town, country, and city-wide jurisdictions. *Criminal Justice Policy Review, 20,* 44–61.

Chasen-Taber, L., & Tabachnick, J. (1999). Evaluation of a child sexual abuse program. *Sexual Abuse: A Journal of Research and Treatment, 11,* 279–292.

Chui, W. H., & Nellis, M. (Eds.). (2003). *Moving probation forward: Evidence, arguments and practice.* Harlow, Essex, UK: Pearson Education.

Churchill, R. P. (2006). *Human rights and global diversity.* Upper Saddle River, NJ: Pearson Prentice Hall.

Clark, A. (2007). Soft selves and ecological control. In D. Spurrett, D. Ross, H. Kincaid, & L. Stephens (Eds.), *Distributed cognition and the will* (pp. 101–122). Cambridge, MA: MIT Press.

Clark, A. (2008). *Supersizing the mind: Embodiment, action, and cognitive extension.* New York: Oxford University Press.

Clear, T. R. (2009). *Imprisoning communities: How mass incarceration makes disadvantaged neighborhoods worse.* New York: Oxford University Press.

Collaborative Outcome Data Committee. (2007). *Sexual offender treatment outcome research: CODC guidelines for evaluation.* Public Safety Canada Department of Corrections. Available from *www.publicsafety.gc.ca/res/cor/rep/codc-en.asp.*

Control theory (sociology). (2010, March 28). In *Wikipedia, The Free Encyclopedia.* Retrieved April 12, 2010, from *en.TorontoWikipedia.org/w/index.php?title=Control theory(sociology)&oldid=352433119.*

*Correctional Psychologist.* (2009). In brief: The U.S. prison system. *41*(2), 19.

Craig, L. A., Browne, K. D., & Beech, A. R. (2008). *Assessing risk in sex offenders: A practitioners guide.* Chichester, UK: Wiley.

Craun, S. W., & Theriot, M. T. (2009). Misperceptions of sex offender perpetration: Considering the impact of sex offender registration. *Journal of Interpersonal Violence, 24,* 2057–2072.

Crombie, I. K., & Davis, H. T. (2009). *What is meta-analysis?: Evidence-based medicine* (2nd ed.). Available from *www.whatisseries.co.uk/whatis.*

Crosner, S. H. (2007–2008). Parolees and the erosion of the Fourth Amendment: A constitutional analysis of California Penal Code Section 3067 and the suspicionless search regime it authorizes. *Loyola of Los Angeles Law Review, 41,* 413–444.

Cullen, F. T., Myer, A. J., & Latessa, E. J. (2009). Eight lessons from *Moneyball*: The high cost of ignoring evidence-based corrections. *Victims and Offenders, 4,* 197–213.

Cummins, R. A. (1996). The domains of life satisfaction: An attempt to order chaos. *Social Indicators Research, 38,* 303–328.

Darwell, S. (2006). *The second-person standpoint: Morality, respect, and accountability.* Cambridge, MA: Harvard University Press.

Deci, E. L., & Ryan, R. M. (2000). The "what" and "why" of goal pursuits: Human needs and the self-determination of behavior. *Psychological Inquiry, 11,* 227–268.

Delson, N., Kokish, R., & Abbott, B. (2008). *Position paper on sex offender residency restriction.* San Jose: California Coalition on Sexual Offending.

Denny, D. (2005). *Risk and society.* London, UK: Sage.

Donnelly, J. (2003). *Universal human rights in theory and practice—2nd ed.* London: Cornell University Press.

Doren, D. M. (2006). What do we know about the effect of aging on recidivism risk for sexual offenders? *Sexual Abuse: A Journal of Research and Treatment, 18,* 137–157.

Dowden, C., & Andrews, D. A. (1999). What works in young offender treatment: A meta-analysis. *Forum on Corrections Research, 11,* 21–24.

Dowden, C., & Andrews, D. A. (2000). Effective correctional treatment and violent reoffending. *Canadian Journal of Criminology, 42,* 449–467.

Driver, J. (2006). *Ethics: The fundamentals.* Oxford, UK: Blackwell.

Duff, R. A. (2001). *Punishment, communication, and community.* New York: Oxford University Press.

Duguid, S. (2000). *Can prisons work?: The prisoner and object, and subject in modern corrections.* Toronto, ON: University of Toronto Press.

Duwe, G., Donnay, W., & Tewksbury, R. (2008). Does residential proximity matter?: A geographic analysis of sex offense recidivism. *Criminal Justice and Behavior, 35,* 484–504.

Eldridge, H., & Findlater, F. (2009). A community residential treatment approach for sexual abusers: A description of the Lucy Faithfull Foundation's Wolvercote Clinic and Related Projects. In A. R. Beech, L. Craig, & K. Browne (Eds.), *Assessment and treatment of sex offenders* (pp. 349–366). Chichester, UK: Wiley.

Emmons, R. A. (1999). *The psychology of ultimate concerns.* New York: Guilford Press.

Emmons, R. A. (2003). Personal goals, life meaning, and virtue: Wellsprings of a positive life. In C. L. M. Keyes & J. Haidt (Eds.), *Flourishing: Positive psychology and the life well-lived* (pp. 105–128). Washington, DC: American Psychological Association.

*Encarta World English Dictionary.* (1999). New York: St. Martin's Press.

Fader, J. (2009, November). The Second Chance Act: An interview with Jeremy Travis. *DCS Newsletter,* American Criminological Society, pp. 1, 3.

Farrall, S. (2002) *Rethinking what works with offenders: Probation, social context and desistance from crime.* Cullompton, Devon, UK: Willan.

Farrington, D. P. (2007). Advancing knowledge about desistance. *Journal of Contemporary Criminal Justice, 23,* 125–134.

Fazel, S., Sjöstedt, G., Långström, N., & Grann, M. (2006). Risk factors for criminal recidivism in older sexual offenders. *Sexual Abuse: A Journal of Research and Treatment, 18*, 159–167.

Fortney, T., Levenson, J., Brannon, Y., & Baker, J. N. (2007). Myths and facts about sexual offenders: Implications for treatment and public policy. *Sexual Offender Treatment, 1*, 1–22.

Freeden, M. (1991). *Rights*. Minneapolis: University of Minnesota Press.

Freeman, M. (2002). *Human rights*. Cambridge, UK: Polity Press.

Freund, K., Sedlacek, F., & Knob, K. (1965). A simple transducer for mechanical plethysmography of the male genital. *Journal of the Experimental Analysis of Behavior, 8*, 169–170.

Furby, L., Weinrott, M. R., & Blackshaw, L. (1989). Sex offender recidivism: A review. *Psychological Bulletin, 105*, 3–30.

Gannon, T. A., & Polaschek, D. L. L. (2006). Cognitive distortions in child molesters: A re-examination of key theories and research. *Clinical Psychology Review, 26*, 1000–1019.

Gewirth, A. (1981). *Reason and morality*. Chicago: University of Chicago Press.

Gewirth, A. (1996). *The community of rights*. Chicago: University of Chicago Press.

Gibbs, R. W. (2006). *Embodiment and cognitive science*. New York: Cambridge University Press.

Giordano, P. C., Cernokovich, S. A., & Rudolph, J. L. (2002). Gender, crime and desistance: Toward a theory of cognitive transformation. *American Journal of Sociology, 107*, 990–1064.

Giordano, P. C., Longmore, M. A., Schroeder, R. D., & Seffrin, P. M. (2008). A life-course perspective on spirituality and desistance from crime. *Criminology, 46*, 99–132.

Giordano, P. C., Schroeder, R. D., & Cernkovich, S. A. (2007). Emotions and crime over the life course: A neo-Meadian perspective on criminal continuity and change. *American Journal of Sociology, 112*, 1603–1661.

Glaser, B. (2003). Therapeutic jurisprudence: An ethical paradigm for therapists in sex offender treatment programs. *Western Criminology Review, 4*, 143–154.

Glueck, S., & Glueck, E. (1950). *Unraveling juvenile delinquency*. New York: Commonwealth Fund.

Glueck, S., & Glueck, E. (1968). *Delinquents and nondelinquents in perspective*. Cambridge, MA: Harvard University Press.

Golash, D. (2005). *The case against punishment: Retribution, crime prevention, and the law*. New York: New York University Press.

Goring, C. (1913). *The English convict*. Montclair, NJ: Patterson Smith.

Gorman, K., Gregory, M., Hayles, M., & Parton, N. (Eds.). (2006). *Constructive work with offenders*. London: Jessica Kingsley.

Gottfredson, M. R., & Hirschi, T. (1990). *A general theory of crime*. Stanford, CA: Stanford University Press.

Grasmick, H. G., Tittle, C. R., Bursik, R. J., & Arneklev, B. J. (1993). Testing the core empirical implications of Gottfredson and Hirschi's general theory of crime. *Journal of Research in Crime and Delinquency, 30*, 5–29.

Griffin, J. (2008). *On human rights*. Oxford, UK: Oxford University Press.

Haag, A. D. (2006). Ethical dilemmas faced by correctional psychologists in Canada. *Criminal Justice and Behavior, 33*, 93–109.

Hanson, R. K. (2002). Recidivism and age: Follow-up data from 4,673 sexual offenders. *Journal of Interpersonal Violence, 17*, 1046–1062.

Hanson, R. K. (2006). Does Static-99 predict recidivism among older sexual offenders? *Sexual Abuse: A Journal of Research and Treatment, 18*, 343–355.

Hanson, R. K., Bourgon, G., Helmus, L., & Hodgson, S. (2009). The principles of effective correctional treatment also apply to sexual offenders: A meta-analysis. *Criminal Justice and Behavior, 36*, 865–891.

Hanson, R. K., & Bussiére, M. T. (1998). Predicting relapse: A meta-analysis of sexual offender recidivism studies. *Journal of Consulting and Clinical Psychology, 66*, 348–362.

Hanson, R. K., Gordon, A., Harris, A. J. R., Marques, J. K., Murphy, W., Quinsey, V. L., et al. (2002). First report of the Collaborative Outcome Data Project on the effectiveness of psychological treatment for sex offenders. *Sexual Abuse: A Journal of Research and Treatment, 14*, 169–197.

Hanson, R. K., Harris, A. J. R., Scott, T., & Helmus, L. (2007). *Assessing the risk of sexual offenders on community supervision: The dynamic supervision project* (User Report No. 2007-05). Ottawa, ON: Public Safety Canada.

Hanson, R. K., & Morton-Bourgon, K. E. (2005). The characteristics of persistent sexual offenders: A meta-analysis of recidivism studies. *Journal of Consulting and Clinical Psychology, 73*, 1154–1163.

Hanson, R. K., & Morton-Bourgon, K. E. (2007). *The accuracy of recidivism risk assessments for sexual offenders: A meta-analysis.* Ottawa, ON: Public Safety Canada. Available from *www.ps-sp.gc.ca/res/cor/rep/_fl/crp2007–01–en.pdf.*

Hanson, R. K., Steffy, R. A., & Gautier, R. (1993). Long-term recidivism of child molesters. *Journal of Consulting and Clinical Psychology, 61*, 646–652.

Hanson, R. K., & Thornton, D. (1999). *Static-99: Improving actuarial risk assessment for sex offenders* (User Report No. 1999-02). Ottawa, ON: Department of the Solicitor General of Canada.

Harris, G. T., & Rice, M. E. (2007). Adjusting actuarial violence risk assessment based on aging or the passage of time. *Criminal Justice and Behavior, 34*, 297–313.

Harris, M. K. (2005). In search of common ground: The importance of theoretical orientations in criminology and criminal justice. *Criminology and Public Policy, 4*, 311–328.

Hart, S. D., Kropp, P. R., Laws, D. R., Klaver, J., Logan, C., & Watt, K. A. (2003). *The Risk for Sexual Violence Protocol (RSVP): Structured professional guidelines for assessing risk of sexual violence.* Burnaby, BC: The Mental Health, Law, and Policy Institute, Simon Fraser University.

Izzo, R. L., & Ross, R. R. (1990). Meta-analysis of rehabilitation programmes for juvenile delinquents. *Criminal Justice and Behavior, 17*, 134–142.

Johnson, M. (2007). *The meaning of the body: Aesthetics of human understanding.* Chicago: University of Chicago Press.

Johnstone, G. (2002). *Restorative justice: Ideas, values, debates.* Cullompton, Devon, UK: Willan.

Katz, J. (1988). *Seductions of crime: Moral and sensual attractions in doing evil.* New York: Basic Books.

Kazemian, L. (2007). Desistance from crime: Theoretical, empirical, methodological, and policy considerations. *Journal of Contemporary Criminal Justice, 23*, 5–27.

Kekes, J. (1989). *Moral tradition and individuality.* Princeton, NJ: Princeton University Press.

Kleinig, J. (2008). *Ethics and criminal justice: An introduction.* Cambridge, UK: Cambridge University Press.

Korsgaard, C. M. (1996). *The sources of normativity.* Cambridge, UK: Cambridge University Press.

Korsgaard, C. M. (2009). *Self-constitution: Agency, identity, and integrity.* New York: Oxford University Press.

Langevin, R., & Paitich, D. (2002). *Clarke Sex History Questionnaire for Males—Revised (SHQ-R).* Toronto: Multi-Health Systems.

Langlands, R., Ward, T., & Gilchrist, E. (2009). Applying the Good Lives Model to male perpetrators of domestic violence. In P. Lehmann & C. Simmons (Eds.), *Strengths based batterer intervention: A new paradigm in ending domestic violence* (pp. 217–235). New York: Springer.

Laub, J. H., & Sampson, R. J. (2001). Understanding desistance from crime. In M. H. Tonry & N. Norris (Eds.), *Crime and justice: An annual review of research* (pp. 1–78). Chicago: University of Chicago Press.

Laub, J. H., & Sampson, R. J. (2003). *Shared beginnings, divergent lives: Delinquent boys to age 70.* Cambridge, MA: Harvard University Press.

Laws, D. R. (1989). *Relapse prevention with sex offenders.* New York: Guilford Press.

Laws, D. R. (2003). Sexual offending is a public health problem: Are we doing enough? In T. Ward, D. R. Laws, & S. M. Hudson (Eds.), *Sexual deviance: Issues and controversies* (pp. 297–316). Thousand Oaks, CA: Sage.

Laws, D. R. (2008). The public health approach. A way forward? In D. R. Laws & W. T. O'Donohue (Eds.), *Sexual deviance: Theory, assessment, and treatment* (2nd ed., pp. 611–628). New York: Guilford Press.

Laws, D. R. (2009, April). *The recovery of the asylum: Observations on the mismanagement of sex offenders.* Keynote address presented at the Tools to Take Home conference, Birmingham, UK.

Laws, D. R., & Marshall, W. L. (1990). A conditioning theory of the etiology and maintenance of deviant sexual preferences and behavior. In W. L. Marshall, D. R. Laws, & H. E. Barbaree (Eds.), *Handbook of sexual assault* (pp. 209–229). New York: Plenum Press.

Laws, D. R., & O'Donohue, W. T. (Eds.). (2008). *Sexual deviance: Theory, assessment, and treatment* (2nd ed.). New York: Guilford Press.

Laws, D. R., & Osborn, C. A. (1983). How to build and operate a behavioral laboratory to evaluate and treat sexual deviance. In J. G. Greer & I. Stuart (Eds.), *The sexual aggressor* (pp. 293–335). New York: Van Nostrand Reinhold.

Lazarus, L. (2004). *Contrasting prisoners' rights: A comparative examination of England and Germany.* New York: Oxford University Press.

Levenson, J., & D'Amora, D. (2005). An ethical paradigm for sex offender treatment: Response to Glaser. *Western Criminology Review, 6,* 145–153.

Lewis, S. (2005). Rehabilitation: Headline or footnote in the new penal policy? *Probation Journal, 52*(2), 119–136.

Liebling, A., & Maruna, S. (2005). *The effects of imprisonment.* Cullompton, Devon, UK: Willan.

Leibrich, J. (1994). What do offenders say about going straight? *Federal Probation, 58,* 41–46.

Linley, P. A., & Joseph, S. (2004). Applied positive psychology: A new perspective for professional practice. In P. A. Linley & S. Joseph (Eds.), *Positive psychology in practice* (pp. 3–12). New York: Wiley.

Lippke, R. L. (2002). Toward a theory of prisoners' rights. *Ratio Juris, 15,* 122–145.

Lipsey, M. W. (1992). Juvenile delinquency treatment: A meta-analytic inquiry into the variability of effects. In T. Cook, D. Cooper, H. Corday, H. Hartman, L. Hedges, R. Light, et al. (Eds.), *Meta-analysis for explanation: A casebook* (pp. 83–127). New York: Russell Sage Foundation.

Lipsey, M. W. (1995). What do we learn from 400 research studies on the effectiveness of treatment with juvenile delinquency? In J. McGuire (Ed.), *What works?: Reducing reoffending* (pp. 63–78). Chichester, UK: Wiley.

Lipsey, M. W., Chapman, G. L., & Landenberger, N. A. (2001). Cognitive behavioral programs for offenders. *Annals of the American Academy of Political and Social Sciences, 578,* 144–157.

Lipton, D. S., Martinson, R., & Wilks, J. (1975). *The effectiveness of correctional treatment: A survey of treatment evaluation studies.* New York: Praeger.

Lösel, F. (1995). Increasing consensus in the evaluation of offender rehabilitation: Lessons from research synthesis. *Psychology, Crime and Law, 2,* 19–39.

Lösel, F., & Schmucker, M. (2005). The effectiveness of treatment for sexual offenders: A comprehensive meta-analysis. *Journal of Experimental Criminology, 1,* 117–146.

Lucken, K., & Ponte, L. M. (2008). A just measure of forgiveness: Reforming occupational licensing regulations for ex-offenders using BJOQ analysis. *Law and Policy, 30,* 46–72.

Lussier, P., Proulx, J., & LeBlanc, M. (2005). Criminal propensity, deviant sexual interests and criminal activity of sexual aggressors against women: A comparison of models. *Criminology, 43,* 247–279.

Lussier, P., Tzoumakis, S., Cale, J., & Amirault, J. (2010). Criminal trajectories of adult sex offenders and the age effect : Examining the dynamic aspect of offending in adulthood. *International Criminal Justice Review, 20,* 147–168.

Lynch, J. P. (2006). Prisoner reentry: Beyond program evaluation. *Criminology and Public Policy, 5,* 401–412.

Malpas, J., & Lickiss, N. (Eds.). (2007). *Perspectives on human dignity: A conversation.* Dordrecht, The Netherlands: Springer.

Mandatory sentencing. (2010, March 28). In *Wikipedia, The Free Encyclopedia.* Retrieved April 12, 2010, from *en.Wikipedia.org/w/index.php?Title=Mandatory sentencing&oldid=355127982.*

Mann, R. E., Webster, S. D., Schofield, C., & Marshall, W. L. (2004). Approach versus avoidance goals in relapse prevention with sexual offenders. *Sexual Abuse: A Journal of Research and Treatment, 16,* 65–76.

Manza, J., & Uggen, C. (2006). *Locked out: Felon disenfranchisement and American democracy.* New York: Oxford University Press.

Marlatt, G. A., & Gordon, J. R. (Eds.). (1985). *Relapse prevention: Maintenance strategies in the treatment of addictive behaviors.* New York: Guilford Press.

Marranci, G. (2007, June 26). Faith, ideology, and fear: The case of current and former Muslim prisoners. *IQRA Annual Lecture: House of Lords.* HMSO.

Marshall, W. L., Anderson, D., & Fernandez, Y. (1999). *Cognitive behavioural treatment of sexual offenders.* Chichester, UK: Wiley.

Marshall, W. L., & Barbaree, H. E. (1990). An integrated theory of the etiology of sexual offending. In W. L. Marshall, D. R. Laws, & H. E. Barbaree (Eds.), *Handbook of sexual assault* (pp. 257–275). New York: Plenum Press.

Marshall, W. L., Fernandez, Y., Hudson, S. M., & Ward, T. (Eds.). (1998). *Sourcebook of treatment programs for sexual offenders.* New York: Plenum Press.

Marshall, W. L., Fernandez, Y. M., Marshall, L. E., & Serran, G. A. (Eds.). (2006). *Sexual offender treatment: Controversial issues.* Chichester, UK: Wiley.

Marshall, W. L., Fernandez, Y. M., Serran, G. A., Mulloy, R., Thornton, D., Mann, R. E., et al. (2003). Process variables in the treatment of sexual offenders. *Aggression and Violent Behavior: A Review Journal, 8,* 205–234.

Marshall, W. L., Marshall, L. E., Serran, G. A., & Fernandez, Y. M. (2006). *Treating sexual offenders: An integrated approach.* New York: Routledge.

Martinson, R. (1974). What works?: Questions and answers about prison reform. *The Public Interest, 10,* 22–54.

Martinson, R. (1979). New findings, new views: A note of caution regarding the sentencing system. *Hofstra Law Review, 7,* 243–258.

Maruna, S. (2001). *Making good: How ex-convicts reform and rebuild their lives.* Washington, DC: American Psychological Association.

Maruna, S., & Farrall, S. (2004). Desistance from crime: A theoretical reformulation. *Kolner Zeitschrift fur Soziologie und Sozialpsychologie, 43,* 171–194.

Maruna, S., & LeBel, T. (2003). Welcome home?: Examining the "reentry court" concept from a strengths-based perspective. *Western Criminology Review, 4,* 91–107.

Maruna, S., LeBel, T., Mitchell, N., & Naples, M. (2004). Pygmalion in the reintegration process: Resistance from crime through the looking glass. *Psychology, Crime and Law, 10,* 271–281.

Maruna, S., LeBel, T., Naples, M., & Mitchell, N. (2009). Looking-glass identity transformation: Pygmalion and Golem in the rehabilitation process. In B. Veysey, J. Christian, & D. J. Martinez (Eds.), *How offenders transform their lives* (pp. 30–55). Cullompton, Devon, UK: Willan.

Maruna, S., & Roy, K. (2007). Amputation or reconstruction?: Notes on the concept of "knifing off" and desistance from crime. *Journal of Contemporary Criminal Justice, 23,* 104–124.

McAdams, D. P. (1995). *The Life Story Interview.* Unpublished manuscript, School of Education and Social Policy, Northwestern University, Evanston, IL.

McAlinden, A.-M. (2005). The use of "shame" with sexual offenders. *British Journal of Criminology, 45,* 373–394.

McClintock, F. H., & Avison, H. H. (1968). *Crime in England and Wales.* London: Heinemann.

McGrath, R. J., Cumming, G. F., & Burchard, B. L. (2009). *The safer society 2009 North American survey: Current practices and emerging trends in sexual abuser management.* Presented at the 28th Annual Research and Treatment Conference of the Association for the Treatment of Sexual Abusers, Dallas, Texas.

McGuire, J., & Priestly, P. (1995). Reviewing what works: Past, present and future. In J. McGuire (Ed.), *What works: Reducing re-offending—Guidelines from research and practice* (pp. 3–34). Chichester, UK: Wiley.

McMahon, P. M., & Puett, R. C. (1999). Child sexual abuse as a public health issue: Recommendations of an expert panel. *Sexual Abuse: A Journal of Research and Treatment, 11,* 257–266.

McMurran, M. (2002). *Motivating offenders to change.* Chichester, UK: Wiley.

McMurran, M., & Ward, T. (2004). Motivating offenders to change in therapy: An organizing framework. *Legal and Criminological Psychology, 9,* 295–311.

McNeill, F. (2004). Desistance, rehabilitation and correctionalism: Developments and prospects in Scotland. *Howard Journal, 43,* 420–436.

McNeill, F. (2006). A desistance paradigm for offender management. *Criminology and Criminal Justice, 6,* 39–62.

McNeill, F. (2009). What works and what's just? *European Journal of Probation, 1,* 21–40.

McNeill, F., Batchelor, S., Burnett, R., & Knox, J. (2005). 21st century social work. In *Reducing re-offending: Key practice skills.* Edinburgh: Scottish Executive.

Miller, D. (2007). *National responsibility and global justice.* Oxford, UK: Oxford University Press.

Modell, J. (1994). Book review of *Crime in the Making: Pathways and Turning Points Through Life. American Journal of Sociology, 99,* 1389–1391.

Moffitt, T. E. (1993). Adolescence-limited and life-course persistent antisocial behavior: A developmental taxonomy. *Psychological Review, 100,* 674–701.

Moffitt, T. E., Caspi, A., Harrington, H., & Milne, B. J. (2002). Males on the life-course persistent and adolescence-limited antisocial pathways: Follow-up at age 26 years. *Development and Psychopathology, 14,* 179–207.

Morsink, J. (2009). *Inherent human rights: Philosophical roots of the universal declaration.* Philadelphia: University of Pennsylvania Press.

Murphy, M. C. (2001). *Natural law and practical rationality.* New York: Cambridge University Press.

Nagin, D. S., & Land, K. C. (1993). Age, criminal careers, and population heterogeneity:

Specification and estimation of a nonparametric, mixed Poisson model. *Criminology, 31*, 327–362.

Nagin, D. S., & Tremblay, R. E. (2005). Developmental trajectory groups: Fact or a useful statistical fiction? *Criminology, 43*, 873–904.

Neison, F. G. P. (1857). *Contributions to vital statistics.* London: Simpkin, Marshall.

Nickel, J. W. (2007). *Making sense of human rights* (2nd ed). Oxford, UK: Blackwell.

Nussbaum, M. (2006). *Frontiers of justice: Disability, nationality, species-membership.* Cambridge, MA: Belknap Press of Harvard University Press.

Nussbaum, M. C. (2000). *Women and human development: The capabilities approach.* New York: Cambridge University Press.

O'Hear, M. M. (2007). The Second Chance Act and the future of the reentry movement. *Federal Sentencing Reporter, 20*(75), Marquette Law School Legal Studies Paper No. 07-15. Milwaukee: Marquette University Law School.

Orend, B. (2002). *Human rights: Concept and context.* Peterborough, ON: Broadview Press.

Paitich, D., Langevin, R., Freeman, R., Mann, K., & Handy, L. (1977). The Clarke SHQ: A clinical sex history questionnaire for males. *Archives of Sexual Behavior, 6*, 421–436.

Petersilia, J. (2003). *When prisoners come home: Parole and prisoner reentry.* New York: Oxford University Press.

Porporino, F. (2008). *Bringing sense and sensitivity to corrections: From programs to "fix" offenders to services to support desistance.* A research brief submitted to the National Institute of Corrections, USA.

Pratt, T. C., & Cullen, F. T. (2000). The empirical status of Gottfredson and Hirschi's general theory of crime: A meta-analysis. *Criminology, 38*, 931–964.

Prentky, R. A., Lee, A. F. S., Knight, R. A., & Cerce, D. (1997). Recidivism rates among child molesters and rapists: A methodological analysis. *Law and Human Behavior, 21*, 635–659.

Presser, L. (2004). Violent offenders, moral selves: Constructing identities and accounts in the research interview. *Social Problems, 51*, 82–101.

Purvis, M. (2005). *Good lives plans and sexual offending: A preliminary study.* Unpublished doctoral dissertation, University of Melbourne, Australia.

Quételet, A. (1831/1984). *Research on the propensity for crime at different ages* (S. F. Sylvester, Trans.). Cincinnati, OH: Anderson.

Raynor, P., & Robinson, G. (2006). Against the tide: Non-treatment paradigms for the twenty-first century. In P. Raynor & G. Robinson (Eds.), *Rehabilitation, crime, and justice* (pp. 134–158). Basingstoke, UK: Palgrave Macmillan.

Raynor, P., & Robinson, G. (2009). *Rehabilitation, crime and justice.* Basingstoke, UK: Palgrave MacMillan.

Re-Entry Policy Council. (2005). *Executive summary. Report of the Re-Entry Policy Council.* New York: Council of State Governments.

Ripple, L., Alexander, E., & Polemis, B. W. (1964). *Motivation, capacity and opportunity: Studies in casework theory and practice.* Chicago: School of Social Service Administration, University of Chicago.

Robbins, P., & Aydede, M. (Eds.). (2009). *The Cambridge handbook of situated cognition.* New York: Cambridge University Press.

Robertson, C., Beech, A. R., & Freemantle, N. (in press). A meta-analysis of treatment outcome studies: Comparisons of treatment designs and treatment delivery. *Sexual Abuse: A Journal of Research and Treatment.*

Robertson, D. (2008). *Indigenisation and developomental adaptation of the Good Lives Model.* Unpublished manuscript, Youth Horizons, Tauranga, New Zealand.

Robinson, G. (2008). Late-modern rehabilitation: The evolution of a penal strategy. *Punishment and Society, 10*, 429–445.

Rosenthal, R., & DiMatteo, M. R. (2001). Meta-analysis: Recent developments in quantitative methods for literature reviews. *Annual Review of Psychology, 52*, 59–82.

Rothman, D. J. (2002). *Conscience and convenience: The asylum and its alternatives in progressive America.* New York: Aldine de Gruyter.

Salter, A. C. (1988). *Treating child sex offenders and their victims: A practical guide.* Newbury Park, CA: Sage.

Sampson, R. J., & Laub, J. H. (1993). *Crime in the making: Pathways and turning points through life.* Cambridge, MA: Harvard University Press.

Sampson, R. J., & Laub, J. H. (2005). A life-course view of the development of crime. *Annals of the American Academy of Political and Social Sciences, 602,* 12–45.

Sawyer, S. P., & Pettman, P. J. (2006). Do clients retain treatment concepts?: An assessment of post treatment adjustment of adult sex offenders. *Sexual Offender Treatment, 1,* 1–15.

Second Chance Act (reentry). (2009, April 7). In *Wikipedia, The Free Encyclopedia.* Retrieved April 12, 2010, from *en.Wikipedia.org/w/index.php?Title=SecondChanceAct(reentry)&oldid=282447947.*

Seligman, M. E. P. (2002). Positive psychology, positive prevention, and positive therapy. In C. R. Snyder & S. J. Lopez (Eds.), *Handbook of positive psychology* (pp. 3–9). New York: Oxford University Press.

Seligman, M. E. P., & Csikszentmihalyi, M. (2000). Positive psychology: An introduction. *American Psychologist, 55,* 5–14.

Seligman, M. E. P., & Peterson, C. (2003). Positive clinical psychology. In L. G. Aspinwall & U. M. Staudinger (Eds.), *A psychology of human strengths: Fundamental questions and future directions for a positive psychology* (pp. 305–318). Washington, DC: American Psychological Association.

Serin, R., & Kennedy, S. (1997). *Treatment readiness and responsivity: Contributing to effective correctional programming.* Ottawa, ON: Correctional Service of Canada.

Serin, R. C., & Loyd, C. C. (2009). Examining the process of offender change: The transition to crime desistance. *Psychology, Crime and Law, 15,* 347–364.

Shelby, L. B., & Vaske, J. J. (2008). Understanding meta-analysis: A review of the methodological literature. *Leisure Sciences, 30,* 96–110.

Sherman, L. W. (1993). Defiance, deterrence, and irrelevance: A theory of the criminal sanction. *Journal of Research in Crime and Delinquency, 30,* 445–473.

Siegert, R., Ward, T., Levack, W., & McPherson, K. (2007). A Good Lives Model of clinical and community rehabilitation. *Disability and Rehabilitation, 29,* 1604–1615.

Smit, D. Z., & Snacken, S. (2009). *Principles of European prison law and policy: Penology and human rights.* New York: Oxford University Press.

Spivakovsky, C. (2007–2008). Approaching responsivity: The Victorian Department of Justice and indigenous offenders. *Flinders Journal of Law Reform, 10,* 649–652.

Steiner, F. (2002). *Human ecology: Following nature's lead.* Washington, DC: Island Press.

Sterelny, K. (2003). *Thought in a hostile world: The evolution of human cognition.* Oxford, UK: Blackwell.

Stop It Now! (2000a). *About Stop It Now!* Retrieved from *www.stopitnow.com/about.htm*

Stop It Now! (2000b). *Four year evaluation: Findings reveal success of Stop It Now!* (Report No. 5). Haydenville, MA: Author.

Sulmasy, D. P. (2007). Human dignity and human worth. In J. Malpas & N. Lickiss (Eds.), *Perspectives on human dignity: A conversation* (pp. 9–18). Dordrecht, The Netherlands: Springer.

Swinburne Romine, R., Dwyer, S. M., Mathiowetz, C., & Thomas, M. (2008, August). *Thirty years of sex offender specific treatment: A follow-up study.* Paper presented at the conference of the International Association for the Treatment of Sexual Offenders, Cape Town, South Africa.

Takacs, S. (2008, July). *20 years of sex offender treatment programming: Durability of treatment effects.* Paper presented at the conference of the International Association of Forensic Mental Health Services, Vienna, Austria.

Taxman, F., Young, D., Byrne, J. M., Holsinger, A., & Anspach, D. (2002). *From prison safety to public safety: Innovations in offender reentry*. Unpublished manuscript. University of Maryland, College Park.

Thompson, A. C. (2009). *Releasing prisoners, redeeming communities: Reentry, race, and politics*. New York: New York University Press.

Thornton, D. (2006). Age and sexual recidivism: A variable connection. *Sexual Abuse: A Journal of Research and Treatment, 18*, 123–135.

Tomasello, M. (1999). *The cultural origins of human cognition*. Cambridge, MA: Harvard University Press.

Travis, J. (2005). *But they all come back: Facing the challenges of prisoner reentry*. Washington, DC: Urban Institute Press.

Uggen, C. (2000). Work as a turning point in the life course of criminals: A duration model of age, employment, and recidivism. *American Sociological Review, 67*, 529–546.

Uggen, C., Manza, J., & Behrens, A. (2004). Less than the average citizen: Stigma, role transition and the civic reintegration of convicted felons In S. Maruna & R. Immarigeon (Eds.), *After crime and punishment: Pathways to offender reintegration* (pp. 261–294). Cullompton, Devon, UK: Willan.

Uggen, C., & Staff, J. (2001). Work as a turning point for criminal offenders. *Corrections Management Quarterly, 5*, 1–16.

United Nations. (2007). Universal declaration of human rights. In J. W. Nickel (Ed.), *Making sense of human rights* (pp. 191–197). Oxford, UK: Blackwell. (Original work published 1948)

Vaughan, B. (2007). The internal narrative of desistance. *British Journal of Criminology, 47*, 390–404.

Vess, J. (2009). Fear and loathing in public policy: Ethical issues in laws for sex offenders. *Aggression and Violent Behavior, 14*, 264–272.

Ward, T. (2009). Dignity and human rights in correctional practice. *European Journal of Probation, 1*(2), 110–123.

Ward, T. (2010). Extending the mind into the world: A new theory of cognitive distortions. *Journal of Sexual Aggression, 15*(1), 49–58.

Ward, T., & Beech, A. (2004). The etiology of risk: A preliminary model for sexual offenders. *Sexual Abuse: A Journal of Research and Treatment, 16*, 271–284.

Ward, T., & Beech, A. R. (2008). An integrated theory of sexual offending. In D. R. Laws & W. T. O'Donohue (Eds.), *Sexual deviance: Theory, assessment, and treatment* (2nd ed., pp. 21–36). New York: Guilford Press.

Ward, T., Bickley, J., Webster, S. D., Fisher, D., Beech, A., & Eldridge, H. (2004). *The self-regulation model of the offense and relapse process. Vol. 1. Assessment*. Victoria, BC: Pacific Psychological Assessment Corporation.

Ward, T., & Birgden, A. (2007). Human rights and correctional clinical practice. *Aggression and Violent Behavior, 12*, 628–643.

Ward, T., & Brown, M. (2004). The good lives model and conceptual issues in offender rehabilitation. *Psychology, Crime and Law, 10*, 243–257.

Ward, T., & Gannon, T. (2006). Rehabilitation, etiology, and self-regulation: The Good Lives Model of sexual offender treatment. *Aggression and Violent Behavior, 11*, 77–94.

Ward, T., & Hudson, S. M. (2000). A self-regulation model of relapse prevention. In D. R. Laws, S. M. Hudson, & T. Ward (Eds.), *Remaking relapse prevention with sex offenders: A sourcebook* (pp. 79–101). Thousand Oaks, CA: Sage.

Ward, T., & Langlands, R. (2009). Repairing the rupture: Restorative justice and offender rehabilitation. *Aggression and Violent Behavior, 14*, 205–214.

Ward, T., Louden, K., Hudson, S. M., & Marshall, W. L. (1995). A descriptive model of the offence chain for child molesters. *Journal of Interpersonal Violence, 10*, 452–472.

Ward, T., Mann, R., & Gannon, T. (2007). The Good Lives Model of offender rehabilitation: Clinical implications. *Aggression and Violent Behavior, 12*, 87–107.

Ward, T., & Marshall, B. (2007). Narrative identity and offender rehabilitation. *International Journal of Offender Therapy and Comparative Criminology, 51,* 279–297.

Ward, T., & Maruna, S. (2007). *Rehabilitation: Beyond the risk paradigm.* London: Routledge.

Ward, T., & Nee, C. (2009). Surfaces and depths: Evaluating the theoretical assumptions of the cognitive skills programmes. *Psychology, Crime and Law, 15,* 165–182.

Ward, T., Polaschek, D. L. L., & Beech, A. R. (2006). *Theories of sexual offending.* Chichester, UK: Wiley.

Ward, T., & Salmon, K. (2009). The ethics of punishment: Correctional practice implications. *Aggression and Violent Behavior, 14,* 239–247.

Ward, T., & Stewart, C. A. (2003). The treatment of sex offenders: Risk management and good lives. *Professional Psychology: Research and Practice, 34,* 353–360.

Ward, T., Yates, P., & Long, C. (2006). *The self-regulation model of the offense and relapse process: Vol. 2. Treatment.* Victoria, BC: Pacific Psychological Assessment Corporation.

Warr, M. (1998). Life-course transitions and desistance from crime. *Criminology, 36,* 183–216.

Weaver, B., & McNeill, F. (in press). Travelling hopefully: Desistance research and probation practice. In F. Cowe, J. Deering, & J. Pakes (Eds.), *What else works?: Creative work with offenders and other socially excluded people.* Collompton, Devon, UK: Willan.

Wexler, H. K., Falkin, G. P., & Lipton, D. S. (1990). Outcome evaluation of a prison therapeutic community for substance abuse treatment. *Criminal Justice and Behavior, 17,* 71–92.

White, H. R., Bates, M. E., & Buyske, S. (2001). Adolescence-limited versus persistent delinquency: Extending Moffitt's hypothesis into adulthood. *Journal of Abnormal Psychology, 110,* 600–609.

Whitehead, J. T., & Lab, S. P. (1989). A meta-analysis of juvenile correctional treatment. *Journal of Research in Crime and Delinquency, 26,* 276–295.

Whitehead, P., Ward, T., & Collie, R. (2007). Time for a change: Applying the Good Lives Model of rehabilitation to a high-risk violent offender. *International Journal of Offender Therapy and Comparative Criminology, 51,* 578–598.

Williams, K. M., Cooper, B. S., Howell, T. M., Yuille, J. C., & Paulhus, D. L. (2009). Inferring sexually deviant behavior from corresponding fantasies: The role of personality and pornography consumption. *Criminal Justice and Behavior, 36,* 198–222.

Wilson, J. Q. (1985). *Thinking about crime.* New York: Basic Books.

Wilson, J. Q., & Herrnstein, R. J. (1985). *Crime and human nature.* New York: Simon & Shuster.

Wolfgang, M., Figlio, R., & Sellin, T. (1972). *Delinquency in a birth cohort.* Chicago: University of Chicago Press.

World Health Organization. (2007). *International classification of diseases–10 (ICD-10).* Geneva, Switzerland: United Nations.

Yates, P. M. (2003). Treatment of adult sexual offenders: A therapeutic cognitive-behavioral model of intervention. *Journal of Child Sexual Abuse, 12,* 195–232.

Yates, P. M. (2007). Taking the leap: Abandoning relapse prevention and applying the self-regulation model to the treatment of sexual offenders. In D. Prescott (Ed.), *Applying knowledge to practice: The treatment and supervision of sexual abusers.* Oklahoma City, OK: Wood and Barnes.

Yates, P. M., & Kingston, D. A. (2005). Pathways to sexual offending. In B. K. Schwartz & H. R. Cellini (Eds.), *The sex offender* (Vol. 5, pp. 3:1–15). Kingston, NJ: Civic Research Institute.

Yates, P. M., & Kingston, D. A. (2006). Pathways to sexual offending: Relationship to static and dynamic risk among treated sexual offenders. *Sexual Abuse: A Journal of Research and Treatment, 18,* 259–270.

Yates, P. M., Kingston, D. A., & Ward, T. (2009). *The self-regulation model of the offense and relapse process: Vol. 3. A guide to assessment and treatment planning using the integrated Good Lives/Self-Regulation Model of sexual offending.* Victoria, BC: Pacific Psychological Assessment Corporation.

Yates, P. M., Simons, D., Kingston, D., & Tyler, C. (2009, October). *The Self-Regulation and Good Lives Models of sexual offender treatment: A comprehensive analysis of relationship to risk, treatment progress, and clinical application.* Presented at the 28th Annual Research and Treatment Conference of the Association for the Treatment of Sexual Abusers, Dallas, Texas.

Yates, P., & Ward, T. (2008). Good lives, self-regulation, and risk management: An integrated model of sexual offender assessment and treatment. *Sexual Abuse in Australia and New Zealand, 1,* 2–19.

# Index

*f* following a page number indicates a figure;
*t* following a page number indicates a table.